ROUGH RIDE

ROUGH RIDE

Behind the Wheel with a Pro Cyclist

PAUL KIMMAGE

YELLOW JERSEY PRESS

Published by Yellow Jersey Press 2001

10 9

Copyright © Paul Kimmage 1990

Paul Kimmage has asserted his right under the Copyright, Designs
and Patents Act 1988 to be identified as the author of this work

This book is sold subject to the condition that it shall not,
by way of trade or otherwise, be lent, resold, hired out,
or otherwise circulated without the publisher's prior
consent in any form of binding or cover other than that
in which it is published and without a similar condition
including this condition being imposed on the
subsequent purchaser

First published in Great Britain in 1990 by
Stanley Paul & Co. Ltd.
An imprint of Random House UK

Yellow Jersey Press
Random House UK, 20 Vauxhall Bridge Road,
London SW1V 2SA

Random House Australia (Pty) Limited
20 Alfred Street, Milsons Point, Sydney,
New South Wales 2061, Australia

Random House New Zealand Limited
18 Poland Road, Glenfield,
Auckland 10, New Zealand

Random House (Pty) Limited
Endulini, 5A Jubilee Road, Parktown 2193, South Africa

Random House UK Limited Reg. No. 954009

www.randomhouse.co.uk

A CIP catalogue record for this book
is available from the British Library

ISBN 9780224061704 (from Jan 2007)
ISBN 0224061704

Papers used by Random House are natural,
recyclable products made from wood grown in sustainable forests.
The manufacturing processes conform to the environmental
regulations of the country of origin.

Typeset by MATS, Southend-on-Sea, Essex
Printed and bound in Great Britain by
Cox & Wyman Ltd, Reading, Berkshire

In memory of John Walsh (1982–95)
'Teacher? You said that Joseph and Mary
and the baby Jesus were poor, but . . . what
did they do with the gold from the
three wise men?'

CONTENTS

ACKNOWLEDGEMENTS

Thanks to Sean Kelly and Martin Earley for good times in the *peloton* and support when *Rough Ride* was first published. To David Walsh, Tom Humphries and Gwen Knapp for services to swimming and constant reminders of what great sports writing should be. To editors past and present, Aengus Fanning, Vincent Browne, Marion Paull and Rachel Cugnoni. Thanks to 'Les Amis Français': Gérard and Muriel Torres, Jean and Ginette Beaufils, Marc Mingat and Pascale Budzyn, André Chappuis and Jean-Michel Rouet. Agus do mo cháirde: David and Mary Walsh, Michcál and Bríd O'Braonáin, Pat Nolan and family, Adhamhnán O'Sullivan, Evelyn Bracken, Gary O'Toole, Billy Stickland, Sean Ryan, Dave Hannigan, Dermot Gilleese, Paul Howard, Paul Hyland, Craig Brazil and Matt Quinn. Thanks to Raphael for his constant good humour and to the rest of the Kimmage Mafia: Christy (The Don), Angela, Deborah, Kevin, Aileen and Christy Jr. And finally, thanks to Ann and our children Evelyn, Eoin and Luke . . . I promise I will stop plucking my eyebrows.

Photographic and text permissions
For permission to reproduce copyright photographs, the author and publishers would like to thank the following: AllSport/Vandystadt; Paul Daly; J. P. Filatriau/La Voix du Nord; Inpho; Irish Press; *L'Equipe*; James Meehan; Photosport International; Presse-Sports; Billy Stickland; Muriel Vibert.

'He wishes for the Cloths of Heaven' by W. B. Yeats is reproduced by permission of A. P. Watt on behalf of Michael Yeats.

Had I the heavens' embroidered cloths,
Enwrought with golden and silver light,
The blue and the dim and the dark cloths
Of night and light and the half-light,
I would spread the cloths under your feet:
But I, being poor, have only my dreams;
I have spread my dreams under your feet;
Tread softly because you tread on my dreams.
                              William Butler Yeats

INTRODUCTION
ON THE NINTH DAY . . .

A few weeks ago, after a visit to the publisher in London, I sat down with all sorts of exciting plans for the re-birth of *Rough Ride*. The new edition would be completely re-edited. Its opening chapter would be scripted straight from the Raymond Chandler school of thriller writing ('When in doubt, have a man come through a door with a gun') and begin, not in 1962 with a baby boy and a kindly staff nurse at the Rotunda hospital in Dublin, but twenty-two years later when the boy arrives in Paris in search of fame and fortune. I even had an opening line worked out: 'A man with huge shovel-like hands, greying hair and a tanned, weather-beaten face was waiting at the airport.' OK, so it would take a couple of chapters before the gun was produced, but you get the drift. There would be other changes. *Rough Ride* was a book with too much truth and too little romance and the balance would be redressed second time around. Every chapter would be crafted with the writing that wins literary awards. The sweat would be dried, the rough edges made smooth. *Rough Ride II* would be a profound and important book.

A few days later, I took out my laptop and was tinkering with the text when an old friend, Peter Purfield, faxed me a message he had received on the Internet that afternoon. It read as follows:

Subject: Where's Paul??!!!
Date: Sun. 7 Dec 1997 17:15:45 EST
Organisation: AOL (http://wwwaolcom)
To: purfield@indigo.ie

Mr Purfield,
I am searching for information on Paul Kimmage. Where
is he and why is there no mention anywhere about this
man? I once owned a copy of his (and I hope this is not
taboo) book *Rough Ride* and have lost it. As I am a racing
cyclist in the US and am currently going through a drug
recovery programme, his book is constantly on my mind.
At the time I read it, I didn't realise the impact it would
have on me years later. I guess I have only one question,
maybe two: Where is that damn book? And how do I get
another copy? Most book dealers have no idea. Where is
Paul and how can I find him? I would appreciate any
response and help you could offer.

Shaken by the coincidence and warmed by the interest, it struck
me that maybe the original had not been too bad and I shelved
my plan until I had re-read it. I say *re-read* it, but when I sat
down with the book last week, it was a first – I'd never actually
read the whole thing through before. Eight years have passed
since it was first published, eight years when I have occasionally
plucked it from the bookshelf to scan the photographs before
closing it again very quickly. If I could have my time again, I'd
make sure there were a lot more photographs. I love the one
from the Tour de France in 1987, where I'm riding out of
Orléans with my boyhood idol Stephen Roche, all tanned and
looking cool in my shades. I like the one from the Tour of
Britain in 1983 where I'm heading for Halifax and the race lead
with Sean Yates looking bolloxed as he tries to follow my pace.
And I could study that shot where my face is caked with grime
at the World Championships in Villach every day for the rest of

my life. I enjoy studying the photographs because essentially they are a façade. Don't believe any of that rubbish about pictures painting thousands of words. I could look at these pictures all day because the pain, the anguish isn't there.

My story begins with my father, Christy. Da was a champion cyclist and from the day I first saw him race I wanted to be a champion too. When I was ten he gave me a racing bike and planted in my heart a love for cycling that would blossom in my teenage years. Cycling dominated my youth; when my friends were discovering the joys of dancing and music and girls, I was getting my kicks from the thrill of racing a bike. There was nothing to match it, especially when you did it well, and the genes I inherited from my father made sure of that. At the age of nineteen I was the Irish National Champion. By the time I was twenty-three I was the sixth best amateur in the world. And at the age of twenty-four I became a professional cyclist. It was the happiest day of my life, the fulfilment of a childhood dream. Within six months the dream had started to fade.

It was during my first Tour de France in July 1986 that I faced the dilemma which would scar my professional life. Although I had witnessed abuse of drugs on a number of occasions after joining the professionals, I tried to block out the fact that you could break the rules in this sport and get away with it. For six months I convinced myself that I could still reach the summit without recourse to a syringe, but everything changed during that first Tour de France. For eight days the race was everything I had envisaged in childhood: I was the best-placed rider on the team and performing better than at any other stage in my life. But then, on the ninth day, I was knackered. My batteries went completely flat. With fourteen stages still to race, I had a decision to make. A big decision. The biggest decision of my life. Did I want them re-charged?

It was a cruel moment, and one that many sportsmen face in many other sports. A moment of truth. What was Christy thinking that day when he invited me out on the bike? He never told me it would come to this. Where was my safety net? I didn't want to do drugs! I didn't want to break the rules! But where was my safety net? Where were the investigative reporters who would expose this scandal? What controls were in place to ensure crime didn't pay? On the Tour's ninth day, sport betrayed me. I wasn't prepared to take drugs to further my career in the sport. Why? I don't know. It would be nice to state that it was a matter of principle, but that might be dishonest. Maybe I was scared. Maybe, when it came to the crunch, I just didn't have the balls to take the final step. Not blessed with any great natural talent, for me it was always going to be a case of sink or swim. On the Tour's ninth day, I shelved my ambition and began to drown.

The next four years of my life in the professional *peloton* were all about survival. There were some good times and some bad times and it was undoubtedly during one of the latter that I had the idea of writing a book. The book would be my story. There would be no kissing and telling, no ratting on pals. The Union Cycliste International (UCI), the sport's governing body, would be my target. I would expose their nurturing of the cancer and ignite the drive for change.

Rough Ride was published in May 1990, and although I had anticipated some controversy, I believed that once people read it in its entirety, they would agree that it was fair and inherently good. The first warning that a *fatwah* was in the post, that I was about to become the Salman Rushdie of the cycling world, came a week before the book was published when Peter Crinnion, who had once raced with my Da, phoned me. Crinnion, who was managing Stephen Roche at the time, told me he was concerned about some of the rumours he had been hearing and wanted me to assure him they weren't true. Well, to say that I was mildly peeved that he had already made up his mind was an understatement. I told him to expect the worst. But it was my appearance on *The Late Late Show* a few days later that really stoked the flames.

INTRODUCTION

The Late Late Show, or *Late Late* as it is known, is Ireland's most popular TV chat show. Its presenter Gay Byrne, is Ireland's most respected and professional broadcaster. Byrne is an institution in Ireland and has been presenting the *Late Late* for so long (thirty-six years and counting) that you now read him like a book. When he likes his guests, he will almost cuddle them. When he doesn't . . . well, let's just say they know. Delighted with the opportunity to talk about the book, I was pretty sure I was in for a fair, if not an easy ride. Byrne was a big fan of the sport and had always treated me well during my career. But there was something about his body language that put me on my guard and we were a couple of minutes into the interview when Byrne started to get tough. 'The implications from what you've written', he suggested, 'are that everyone is doing it . . .' I didn't need to be a mind-reader to guess what was coming next. Byrne had built his reputation by asking 'the obvious question' and I had anticipated before going on that he would put it to me. I had also given serious consideration to my answer.

'What about the lads?' he asked. 'What about Stephen [Roche] and Sean [Kelly]?'

'What about them,' I replied. 'This is my story. It has nothing to do with them.'

But that wasn't enough and he came after me again and for the first time I realised I wasn't about to be cuddled. Ireland's favourite broadcaster wasn't pleased. He had a look on his face that I would see many times over the next few weeks. A look that said, 'How dare you cast a shadow on our fairytale?' A look that said, 'How dare you poison our dreams?' He expected me to stand now before the good people of Ireland and reassure them only losers like myself got tangled in the drugs web and that the sport's heroes were clean. Byrne wasn't interested in the story of my betrayal. My dreams didn't count. He wanted me to distil 200 pages and five months of toil into simple clean or dirty. Black or white? Yes or no? Heroes or villains? But the book wasn't about heroes or villains and I wasn't prepared to compromise; not for Byrne, not for anyone. Kelly and Roche would understand.

The interview finished amicably enough and I thought no more about it until a week later at a book signing in Dublin when I was handed a copy of the *Evening Press*. One story dominated the front page on 26 May: 'ROCHE MAY SUE OVER LATE LATE':

Ireland's Tour de France hero is taking legal advice after watching a video of last week's *Late Late Show* where his friend and former cycling colleague, Paul Kimmage, spoke about drug-taking in the sport. Roche, Kelly and Martin Earley will this weekend meet to discuss the matter, when they come together for a cycling event in Canada, according to Roche's Irish manager.

Kimmage, now a journalist, has told how he himself once took drugs, amphetamines – 'to fight the battle with the same arms as everyone else'. Interviewed by Gay Byrne, he revealed a serious problem of drug abuse in the sport and told how he had seen other riders injecting stimulants to improve race performances.

Now, it is understood, Stephen Roche is 'taking advice about legal action'. His manager Peter Crinnion, said that 'questions had been left in the air' on the *Late Late Show* and that 'some of the inferences were fairly serious'. However Kimmage, contacted by the *Evening Press*, insisted that he had 'made it clear' that he was not linking the three top Irish riders to drug-taking. 'This is my story, no one else's,' he said, referring to his soon-to-be published book *Rough Ride*.

And Kimmage today won the backing of Sports Minister Frank Fahey. Mr Fahey praised the Ballymun man's honesty in admitting to drug-taking and said that he hoped it would help focus attention on the problem, and that that in itself was a step forward in combating the drug menace in international sport.

Criticism however came from friends and family of the top Irish riders and from a top cycling official. Sean Kelly's father-in-law, Dan Grant, criticised Kimmage for failing to state categorically if his three colleagues had been involved in drug-taking. 'He should have said yes or no,' said an angry Dan Grant.

A senior cycling official said that Kimmage had done Irish cycling no favours. 'He glossed over the fact that top riders like the three mentioned just wouldn't take any drugs because they are tested so often. Kelly was tested nearly every day in the last Tour de France – he just wouldn't risk it.'

The official admitted that drug-taking did go on, but claimed it was confined to a small group of second-rank professionals. He added that the image of cycling in this country would be tarnished by the affair, because the public could draw the wrong inferences from stories of drugs. 'The big guys just don't risk it and the amateurs wouldn't be bothered. It is just the second-string pros who are struggling to scrape a living who go in for it,' he said.

Frank Quinn, manager of Sean Kelly and Martin Earley said that while he didn't know if legal action was necessary, things were left unsaid on the *Late Late Show*.

'The situation wasn't clarified,' he said. 'Paul Kimmage's story is depressing in a lot of places – he was professional for four years without winning a race.'

When I had finished reading, I was too stunned to be angry: not because the idiot who had written it had totally misrepresented the reason I had used amphetamines, not because the cowardly 'top' official had been allowed to spout his lies from behind a mask. I understood why Kelly's father-in-law was upset and why his manager had attempted to dismiss my story as that of a loser. What I didn't understand was the attitude of Stephen Roche. We were friends. We had always been friends. I had admired him since the age of twelve and had reflected that admiration in the book. I think my position with regard to Roche, Kelly and Martin Early is clear enough, but let me re-state it anyway. Nothing I wrote in this book should be read as an allegation against any of these riders. The reason I will not get into discussions about individuals is that, in what I am saying, it is not individuals who matter – what X or Y may have done – but the sport as a whole and the dangers it faces. Why should Stephen not understand this? Why hadn't he read it before racing off to his solicitor? What was he thinking of? Who was advising him?

Life was pretty tough over the next few weeks. Try as I did to leave the controversy behind me, there was no escape. It dominated my every day. It was a difficult period too for my family, but they never wavered in their support and there was no turning back. In July, my return to the Tour de France for the first time as a journalist loomed. I was dreading it.

A few weeks before the race, during the Criterium de Dauphine in June, Stephen Roche invited a journalist from *L'Equipe* into his bedroom one night, produced a copy of *Rough Ride* and began quoting selected excerpts. Had he opened the book on page one, I would have been delighted but Roche wasn't interested in the real story of the book. He couldn't seem to accept that the book was not about him. When I heard about this performance, I was more enraged than at any other time in my life. Because the book wasn't being published in France, I had relied on Roche to vouch for its integrity to my former team-mates. Instead, it looked as though he was putting the boot in. I couldn't believe it. I just couldn't believe it.

What a turn around! Three years previously, in an interview with the *Irish Independent* on the day after he had won the Tour, he told the journalist Tom O'Riordan: 'You can get a false opinion from the excitement which surrounds victory in the Tour de France but I can tell you that many cyclists who were extremely good amateurs found the going very tough after they turned professional. Paul Kimmage and Martin Earley are two very fine cyclists, but it's very hard to make a breakthrough. I would advise young Irish cyclists to have a talk with Paul. It's not all glory and there is a lot more to it than people realise.'

But a month after *Rough Ride* was published, in a ghosted column in the *Irish Times* ('KIMMAGE'S DRUG EXPOSURE IS UNFAIR'), he had obviously changed his mind. In a classic knee-jerk reaction piece that was both inaccurate and a mass of contradiction he said,

I've read Paul Kimmage's book *Rough Ride* and I don't feel concerned about anything he wrote in it. I think Paul has taken one or two of his bad experiences in cycling and has generalised from that. For example, on the drugs issue, he has generalised from one post-Tour criterium at Château Chinon – but in all his career on the continent, Paul only rode a total of two or three such criteriums.

I believe the impression he has given is unfair because it has left Sean Kelly and myself, as the top Irish riders, carrying the can as far as allegations of drug use are concerned. I can show you a list containing hundreds of drugs, including products in everyday use like codeine and caffeine, which would show up positive at a race control.

I don't think it's anyone's business other than mine whether I've taken amphetamines or anything else. If I denied it, no one would believe me and if I said, 'Yes, I do', everyone's going to say I'm a drug user. In my first year in France I won Paris–Nice, the Tour of Corsica and several other big races and no one who knows me and is in his right mind is going to say I went overnight from being a Dublin fitter to using drugs. I didn't even know such things existed at the time.

You have to realise that top riders like me face drug controls far more often than *domestiques* like Paul Kimmage. There's a 99 per cent chance of me getting tested, and only an outside chance of a rider like Paul getting done. I know that if I took something to get me through one day, I would run the risk of it showing up in tests the following day or the day after. I'm not crazy enough to risk that. I can say that throughout my professional career I have never once tested positive in a drug control.

As far as hormones are concerned, any doctor involved in cycling will tell you that they have been rooted out for a long time now, because they were easily traceable for up to three months. Two years ago, Delgado was tested positive after taking a product used for wiping out the traces of hormones – well, those hormones could be traced now.

All sportsmen know that where there is money, fame and fortune there will also be drugs. Cycling was the first sport to seriously introduce drug controls back in the sixties. When you have 2,500 controls per year, as you do now, and there are one or two positive traces, everyone starts moaning. If you had only a hundred controls and no positive findings, would that mean very much in comparison? If you had the same large number of drug tests in other sports, it's likely that you would have the same number of positives.

I learned things from Paul's book that I never knew. He said he's seen riders taking stuff during races. It may happen, but I've been in professional cycling for ten years and I can put my hand in the fire and say I've never seen it. Paul talks about everyone being 'charged up' on the last stage of the Tour de France along the Champs Elysées. That's completely false. The riders know that the day after the Tour ends they'll have to ride in criteriums in Holland, and they are controlled automatically for drugs, unlike in France.

You can't generalise about drug-taking. There are individuals, as in any sport, who use them. Everyone knows these guys. Sometimes leading riders feel other top riders might take drugs, but as long as they continue to test negative in controls, it's not right to accuse them of it.

The only thing that upset me in Paul's book was when he wrote that I paid to win a criterium in Dublin after my 1987 Tour win. But he didn't tell the whole story. I did pay £1000 to win that race, but only in the sense that I put the money in a pool to be shared out among a seven-man combine – Sean Kelly, Martin Earley, myself and four others – to help us beat the forty-five riders who had come over from Britain to beat Kelly and me. Everyone in the combine helped everyone else and we shared the money.

That column in the *Irish Times* signalled the end of my friendship with Stephen Roche. I returned to the Tour in July, but it was a miserable experience. I hated every minute of it. The word was out that I had ratted on my pals. Thierry Claveyrolat and Jean-Claude Colotti, two of my closest friends at my old team RMO, turned their backs on me. When I pleaded with them to forget what they had heard and to reserve judgement at least until they had read what I'd written, they weren't interested. *Pute* (prostitute) was the expression used.

And that's pretty much how it continued for the rest of the year. For months, whenever conversation turned to the book, my blood pressure would soar and I would foam at the mouth in its defence. And though I like to fool myself that I am more dispassionate about it now, I know nothing has changed. When I began writing for a living my friend David Walsh gave me some good advice: 'Never run from the truth.' *Rough Ride* may not be the best sports book ever written but it's honest.

These last eight years as a sportswriter have changed a lot about the way I view the drugs question and there are a couple of things I wrote in Chapter 23 ('Spitting in the Soup') that I totally disagree with now. (In particular I would retract the diplomatic immunity I offered to the sports champions with regard to the 'law of silence'.) Although it pains me to admit it, *Rough Ride* changed nothing. It was the story of a 'bitter little man'. A 'loser's whinge'. The sport just carried on. Had it been scripted by a champion, that wouldn't have happened. The UCI would have been forced to make changes and some of the lives which were lost in the early 1990s, might have been saved. However, apart from the Epilogue and a slight change to Chapter 1, I have resisted the temptation to tamper with the original. The prose style is still very rough. The fawning references to Stephen Roche remain. When it was published in 1990, *Rough Ride* was a bike rider's story, not a sportswriter's. It still is.

Paul Kimmage, January 1998

1

IT WASN'T SUPPOSED TO END LIKE THIS

Toulouse, July 13, 1989
Stage 12: Toulouse to Montpellier (242 kilometres)

I knew it would be hard this morning. In a race that lasts three weeks there are good days and bad days and survival is all about morale. With weak legs and a good head you can go a long way. With good legs and a weak head you go nowhere. This morning, I rode out of Toulouse on the twelfth stage of the Tour de France with a weak head.

If the start had been a little easier it might have made all the difference. Maybe today I would still be a *coureur cycliste professionel.* But we raced out of Toulouse like there was no tomorrow and I was struggling from the start. The Danish rider Jesper Worre attacked and I cursed him because cursing him was easier than following him. I quickly realised that my legs were not responding to the demands I was making on them. I was dropped. To be left behind at such an early stage was demoralising, but I fought back and managed to regain contact with the *peloton*.

I made my way forward through the bunch, but as I did they accelerated away and I started slipping back again. The bunch strung out into a long line and I realised with despair that I could not match the pace and would soon be dropped again. I pulled over, not wanting to obstruct the riders behind me. And then I heard someone laughing. The Belgian Dirk de Wolf was laughing. I had had a run in with him two days earlier. Was he laughing at me? He couldn't be. Yes, yes he was. He was laughing at me. The bastard was laughing at me. On a good day I would probably have gone over and spat in his face. But this was a bad day and I was feeling sorry for myself. Suddenly my spirit snapped. It had always been my greatest asset. Others had reached the top with talent or class mixed with spirit. I only ever had spirit. Fighting spirit. Never say die, spit in your eye. It was spirit that had brought me from a dreaming childhood in Dublin to the Tour de France. It had cracked before, many times, but I had always managed to repair it. Today was different.

I started thinking, 'I don't need this shit. I can go home and be a journalist and live happily ever after. I don't need this Belgian laughing at me. Fuck him. Fuck the whole lot of them.' And then I stopped pedalling. My mind was confused. I hadn't planned it like this. I was supposed to finish the Tour and be presented with a medal (everyone who finishes the Tour gets a medal). I was going to continue racing until the end of the season and end my career in O'Connell Street in Dublin in the Nissan Classic. I wouldn't win a stage or anything like that, that would be dreaming. I stopped dreaming when I turned professional, which was probably part of my downfall. But as an acknowledgement of my modest career, the organisers would present me with a bouquet of flowers and my home would cheer as I waved them goodbye. Slipping happily into oblivion, I would return to the city the next day as an ordinary man to look for a job, any job. This was how it was supposed to end. This was what I had planned. But as the official cars passed me as I freewheeled down the road, fifty-five kilometres out of Toulouse on the twelfth stage of the Tour de France, Dublin was not on my mind. It was the laughing, that horrible moronic laughing. No, I didn't need that shit. The bike stopped and I got off. I was surrounded by photographers who were probably fed up with taking pictures of Greg LeMond and Laurent

Fignon – a sobbing *domestique* as he abandoned the Tour always made a good shot for the evening paper. The best was yet to come and they knew it.

On abandoning the Tour the rider is not allowed simply to slip discreetly into a team car. No, he must wait for the Voiture Balai, the broom wagon, to arrive. I saw it coming and knew what would happen. I spread my legs, placed my arms on the door and stood to the sound of clicking cameras as the commissar removed the two numbers pinned to my jersey. This was the official court-martialling, the stripping of the stripes. When he had finished, I jumped into the back of the bus and buried my head in my hands and cried, 'It wasn't supposed to end like this.'

The rider who abandons the Tour is like a wounded animal. He feels shame and emptiness. He needs privacy to lick his wounds, to heal the mental sores. I just had to get out of Montpellier tonight. I could not face the company of my team-mates or put up with the frowns of my *directeur sportif* (team manager) for five minutes longer than was necessary. My friend Gerard Torres drove my wife Ann down from Grenoble to take me home and I was so grateful to him for relieving me of my torture. My head was filled with so many emotions and questions, all tangled and jamming the switchboard of my brain. On the journey home, Gerard tried to raise my spirits with talk of the future, of the World Championships at Chambéry in August, of the Nissan Classic in October: 'Do you remember how well you rode last year in Dublin?' But I just nodded and tried not to offend his enthusiasm.

There won't be any World Championship or any Nissan Classic. I know I'm not going to race again. My spirit has snapped and it's an unmendable break. My thoughts are not of the future, they are a prisoner of the past.

2
THE FIRST IRISH POPE

Beasy McArdle, the portly staff nurse at the Rotunda maternity hospital in Dublin, loved babies. She used to walk up and down the wards of screaming new-born, pluck them from their cradles and hug and kiss them as if they were her own. Embracing them with tenderness, she caressed them with her soft west of Ireland accent: 'Oh I could love you.'

On the evening of 7 May 1962 another brand-new baby joined the assembly line and took its place beside its mother. Beasy took a long, hard look at the child. She noticed his large head and decided it was the head of a leader – a Pope: 'I'm sure he will be the first Irish Pope,' she said.

My mother smiled. It had been a difficult pregnancy, full of complications, but she was over the worst and was glad her child was healthy. I tipped the scales at nine pounds two ounces, a hefty lad with a huge head. My mother remembers the head – it nearly killed her. She already had a name for me, Paul. She thought about what Beasy had said: 'Pope Paul' had a nice ring to it. She would mention it to Christy when he came in later.

My father worked on a more conventional assembly line. He welded car bodies at the Volkswagen plant on the Naas road in Dublin. It was monotonous, tiring work and he looked forward each night to clocking off and escaping into the countryside for two hours' training on his bicycle.

My Da was born in Dublin, the youngest of the seven children of James and Mary Kimmage. It's an unusual name, from a suburb of Dublin on the south side, but we can't trace our family tree back very far. We don't know where we come from. Da had three brothers and three sisters and it was his elder brothers Jimmy and Kevin who introduced him to cycling. He liked it and joined the Dublin Wheeler's touring section in 1954.

One day they went to see a race, the Circuit of Bray. Seamus Elliot, the best Irish rider in the country, broke clear of the field with two English riders, Harry Reynolds and Dick Bowes. He soon disposed of them both, to the delight of the huge crowd lining the seafront. My Da was touched by the atmosphere, the colour, by Shay Elliot. He wanted to race. The bug had bitten him.

His first year of competition was in 1956. The new sport was tough, but he had a talent for it and it wasn't long before he was winning. In 1957 he returned to the Circuit of Bray – and won, the first of four wins in that once prestigious classic. In 1958 he was selected to represent Ireland at the World Championships in Rheims, France. On a searing hot day the field was whittled down to forty riders with just two laps left. Da was there, he wanted to finish, to be one of the top forty in the world.

A friend of his, John Flanagan, was taking care of him from the pits area. With two laps to go he handed Christy a feeding bottle with brandy in it. In sheeting rain or arctic cold, a nip of brandy would perhaps have been beneficial, but not on a day when the temperature was in the nineties. Da, dying with the thirst, took a swallow from the bottle. It nearly killed him – he abandoned.

Rheims was the end of a very successful season for him. Back in Ireland another season was just beginning. The 'be social' season. The Wheelers advertised their regular Sunday outings in the shop window of the Rutland bike shop in North

Frederick Street. On the third weekend of September a notice read:

Meal 'alfresco' at Roundwood. Tea at Butler's 6 o'clock.

Butler's tearooms, at the Scalp in County Wicklow, was the traditional rendezvous for all Dublin's cycling clubs when they went south of the Liffey. The hungry pedallers would devour tea, home-made scones and cakes and then settle down to an evening of songs, dancing and plenty of fun. It usually ended about midnight, when the last thrill of the day was a mad descent into the city in the dark.

On that Sunday in September, my Da spent the day touring the Wicklow hills and then headed to Butler's for tea. There, a pleasant young *touriste* caught his eye. Her name was Angela. He liked her.

Angela Davis was the youngest daughter of Francis and Mary Davis of Kilfenora Road, Kimmage. They lived in a two-bedroomed corporation terraced house – not very big for a family with fourteen children. Granda worked nights in dispatch at the *Irish Times*. In the modern era his family would undoubtedly have been smaller, but as he says in his typical Dublin accent, 'In dem days der was no television.' My Ma, the twelfth arrival, left school at fourteen and started work as a trainee tailor at Weartex, near her home. She saved hard, bought her first bicycle on hire purchase and joined the Dublin Wheelers with her sister Pauline. It was on a run with the Wheelers that she met Christy at Butler's. They talked, danced and although Ma claims it was 'love at first sight', the relationship did not take off immediately. The first real date was months later – a visit to the Theatre Royal for a film and a show.

The following year, 1958, my father enjoyed the best form of his career. He won anything worth winning. In June Billy Morton organised a prestigious track meeting to celebrate the opening of a new cycling and running track at Santry stadium in Dublin. Shay Elliot, now a professional (Ireland's first), was flown in from France along with French star Albert Bouvet and the Italian *campionissimo*, Fausto Coppi. In front of a huge crowd, Elliot beat the continental pros and my father won the amateur event.

A day later he flew to the Isle of Man for the Viking Trophy race on a small plane with Coppi, Bouvet and Elliot. The flight gave him a nice opportunity to talk to Elliot about the possibility of racing in France. Shay suggested he try his luck in Paris with a club called ACBB. He had contacts there and would arrange it if my Da was interested. He was interested. Elliot won the pro race on the island, but my Da was denied victory on the line to finish a narrow second in the Viking race. Twenty-three years later my brother Raphael won that same race and brought the Viking Trophy back to our house. My Da wouldn't admit it, but I know it meant a lot to him.

When he came back to Dublin, Da organised himself for Paris. He gathered his savings and remembers a friend, John Connon, giving him £25 (a lot of money in those days) and a bike bag. Paris was huge, mind-boggling compared with Dublin. When he arrived he got hopelessly lost in the underground, the Métro. He was hampered in the crowds by his bike and bag, but eventually found his way to his lodgings, a flat in Montparnasse. The club provided him with a new Helyett bike, but in the two weeks he stayed he never raced. Living out of a suitcase, unable to speak a word of the language, he felt desperately alone. The life of a professional cyclist was not for him. He didn't want it. He returned to Dublin and to this day does not regret his decision.

Twenty-five years later Raphael and I arrived in the same city with the same objective, at the same club. Before we left Dublin we had never fully understood why he only stuck it out for two weeks. We soon did.

When he returned home, he was selected to ride in another world championship, but the week before a bad crash at an evening race in Baldoyle sent him to hospital instead. He didn't race again for two years. The crash and the disappointment of Paris had turned him off the sport, but there was also another reason – marriage. Ma always claims he wasn't so much homesick as lovesick in Paris because as soon as he came home he popped the question and started saving for a house.

The wedding was in August 1961 and they honeymooned in Edinburgh before returning to Dublin to begin married life in a run-down Georgian house in Eccles Street. It was divided into eight rooms on two floors and was home to eight families. There was just one toilet in the building and one cold-water tap provided all eight families with their only running water. My parents' flat was on the ground floor and had a window looking out on the street. It was old and run-down, but it was home and they didn't complain – housing in Dublin was hard to come by in the early 1960s.

The flat was my first home in the world. When I was seven months old, Santa Claus brought me a three-wheeled bicycle and it wasn't long before I was racing around the room on it. Ma laughs about that little bike. She remembers that when she was toilet-training me I would charge around the flat with nothing on. One day I got it wrong and deposited a huge stool on the brightly painted seat of the bike; she can still see it today.

She has other, not so pleasant, memories of the street. Late at night Da and she would be awakened by the sound of a fist banging on the windowpane and a man's voice calling out, 'Joan!' This happened regularly. The voices changed, but the demand was always the same: 'Joan!' They made inquiries and found out that 'Joan' had been the previous occupant of the flat. She was a prostitute. The most frightening incident happened three months after they moved in. It was a typical Dublin evening, raining cats and dogs. My mother was pregnant with me and suffering from a kidney infection. At three in the morning, they were woken by a fierce banging on the door. Granda Kimmage was very ill at the time and my father feared it was one of his family with some bad news. He jumped up to answer the door, but it wasn't his brother or sister. There was a tall, uniformed Garda standing in the hall. He was soaked to the skin and reeked of alcohol. He demanded to see 'Joan'. My father explained that Joan had moved out months ago, but the policeman insisted on entering the flat. He walked into the room, looked at my sick mother, apologised and left.

Da started to race again at the start of 1962. My arrival half-way through the year did not upset his form for, two months after my birth, he became the Irish champion at Markethill in County Armagh. He had come second in 1958 and 1959, so the elusive title victory brought him great pleasure. I was taken regularly to watch my Da racing and I'm told my first words were not so much 'Da Da' as 'Come on Da Da'. My brother Raphael was born two years after me in 1964. Da called him after the famous French professional Raphael Geminiani, much to the disgust of Granny Kimmage, who said Raphael was no name to give a child. Kevin, the third son, was born three years later and Eccles Street started to get crowded. We moved to a new complex of flats in Ballymun five miles north of the Liffey.

The flat was bright and clean, had toilets and running water and a unique central heating system – the floors heated. But my parents didn't like it. On the day we moved in the lifts broke down and Da had to carry a washing machine up eight flights of stairs on his back. Soon after he caught Raphael hanging over the balcony and got a terrible fright. Raphael was given the standard punishment: his bum was reddened. I suppose it's what I remember most about my youth – my father's war cry when we misbehaved or were 'bold', as we say in Ireland. It was always: 'I'll redden your arse for you.' He rarely did, the threat was enough to put the fear of God into us.

We stayed in Ballymun for a year and then moved to a new three-bedroomed semi-detached house in Coolock, two miles to the east. My fourth brother, Christopher, eleven years my junior, was brought up here. The family was complete and Kilmore Avenue remains the family home today. My Da stopped racing in 1972: he was thirty-four years old, and raising sons was very time-consuming. He tried to get me interested in every kind of sport, but I was only ever interested in doing one thing. When I was ten years old he bought me a racing bike.

3

PACKET SOUP AND
FRUIT CAKE

Delving into one's past can be discouraging, even disturbing. Questioning my mother about how she met my father was awkward. Questioning my father about my childhood was as bad. It's as if they have something very precious which they don't want to share with anyone. It's strange. Maybe I'll feel the same if I have children of my own one day.

Ma (Dublin kids always call their mother 'Ma' and their father 'Da') says I was a dependable child. To illustrate this she tells the pound of sugar story. She would often come in from the shops having forgotten to buy a pound of sugar. This was a major headache because it meant putting my clothes on to go out again. Sometimes she just left me in the middle of the floor, surrounded by kitchen chairs, and sprinted to Geraghty's in Dorset Street for the sugar. When she came back I would always be there, not having moved an inch. A dependable child.

My St David's Primary School teacher Michael O'Braoinain tells me that at school I fought injustice. I would never let him get away with anything unjust even if I risked a clip on the ear for my insubordination. My father says that as a child I was a nightmare – but he's lying, for I know I was good. This is not to say I didn't get my arse tanned on several occasions. But generally I was good. And this is what disturbs me. It's almost a disappointment to discover that I wasn't a tyrant child, unsuccessful at school and on my way to a life in prison only to be saved by athletic prowess. No, I was good, boringly good.

I have a few vague memories of Eccles Street: of the old and very mad woman we frequently met on the road, who terrified me; of my father leaving me to go to the hospital late one night; of Mrs Geraghty's sweet shop in Dorset Street, and one or two other trivial things.

My memory banks started to function when I was six and we moved to Ballymun. I loved it there. Much of that concrete jungle was still being built and I found the building sites fascinating. Ma would leave me in charge of Raphael (I was dependable, remember) and I would drag him around the sites, where we would play. Lipton's Supermarket was another favourite haunt. We would hang out at the incinerator, eating the half-burned rotten vegetables that we found lying around. It was all pretty harmless but Ballymun did have its dangers. My father made the flats' underground basement a strict 'no go' area after a paedophile was reported to have interfered with a neighbour's daughter.

Scuttin' was also taboo. This involved swinging out of the back of the delivery lorries to Lipton's, hanging on till the truck slowed down at a set of traffic lights and then jumping off. Scuttin' was very popular and I found it hard to obey my father. It took at least two or three arse-reddenings to convince me that it wasn't worth it.

It was in Ballymun that I rode my first two-wheeler. Da bought it and immediately removed the two stabilisers. He sat me on the saddle in the small car park in front of the flats and then pushed me off. I wobbled once or twice, but basically had no trouble and was delighted with myself. I loved cycling; from the time I was born it had always been part of my life. Whenever possible, Da would take us to the races to watch him. I loved the races. I loved it when Da gave me a crossbar from the finish to the car after the race was over. I felt so proud. I was fascinated by his legs, the way the bulging muscles shone from the oils he spread on them. But most of all I loved it when he won.

We have a photo at home of him winning a race at Ballyboghil in the north of County Dublin. Raphael and I are both standing on the small school fence overlooking the finishing line. Raphael has his two hands raised and it is clear to see the joy on our faces. Needless to say he lost quite a few as well. I could never understand him losing and when I questioned him his reply was always, 'Sure I have to give the other fellows a chance sometimes.' This infuriated me. I honestly believed him.

I often asked him if he was the best. Here he never lied. No, he was not the best. He was good but not the best. Peter Doyle was the best. He used to point out Peter Doyle to me, and on occasions when the great man came to our house he would ask, 'Paul, do you know who this is?' And, finger in my mouth, I would reply shyly, 'Peter Doyle'. To me, my Da was God, but Peter Doyle was also God.

Being at the races wasn't always a pleasure. I remember an evening race in the Phoenix Park. I stood with my mother as she chatted with the other cycling widows waiting impatiently for the finishing sprint. There was a gasp from the crowd as a rider hit a parked car, flew over the top and landed on the grass verge. I remember leaving my mother's side and running to the crowd that surrounded the motionless groaning body. I was too small to see over them, but I bent down on my knees and, looking through the legs, spotted the rider's number. Number 22. I wasn't sure but expected that it was Da. Then I saw the crash hat. The blue leather crash hat that he always wore: 'It's him, that's my Da.' And then sprinting back to Ma, shouting, 'It's him, it's Da!' And for some crazy reason being glad that my Da was the centre of all the attention. The thought that he might be injured never crossed my mind. He was taken to hospital but got off lightly. His crash hat, split up the middle, had saved him from injury. When I rode my first race I had the same blue crash hat on my head. There were other, classier, hats, but I wanted this one. This was my Da's. Da was God.

I rode my first official race at ten, but the unofficial ones started much earlier. When we moved to Coolock I used to race the neighbours' kids round the block. I always won or nearly always. Davy Casey my next-door neighbour sometimes beat me. This cracked me up. I was a desperately bad loser and would burst into tears of rage when I did. School gave me other opportunities to race. I entered Michael O'Braoinain's class when I was nine. Michael took a great shine to me and instilled in me a new confidence in my academic ability. He made me write poetry and regularly praised my offerings. He also instilled in us an appreciation of Gaelic culture, and he was a great man for playing a jig and a reel on the tin whistle. We laugh about that now. I've played squash with him regularly in the past six months – he claims he always knew I'd end up writing for a living.

In an effort to improve our Irish, Michael organised class trips to the Gaeltacht for a month in the summer. We stayed with a family, Mrs O'Donnel's in Carraroe, a small village twenty-six miles west of Galway. Speaking Irish for an hour a day at school was fine but having to do it non-stop for a month was terribly difficult. Most of us took our bikes and I loved taking off for an hour to discover the lovely Connemara roads. But riding on my own soon became boring. I wanted a challenge.

Before I left for Connemara, my Da had just come back from the Tour of Britain (the Milk Race), where he had worked with the Irish team as a masseur. His stories about it fascinated me and I decided to organise a 'Carraroe Milk Race' among my classmates. Because it was a stage race, I decided I needed food. I knew from going through the pockets of my father's racing jerseys that he often took raisins with him, so I bought a packet of dried raisins at a small grocery shop across the road. I had a bit of a job persuading the others to race, but finally they agreed and I won the first stage easily. But it was too easy and I wasn't satisfied.

For the second stage I decided not to speed off at the start, but to stay with them for the first mile and then fake a crash. I chose the spot for falling off, a patch of gravel on a corner, as I was planning the circuit. The race started and I skidded purposefully on the gravel in front of the others, making sure they saw me and then jumped back on the bike, caught them and beat them. Persuading them to ride a third stage was now a real problem. I offered them a big handicap before setting out in pursuit. But I was too generous. I soon realised I wasn't going to catch them. I couldn't face being beaten, so I took a short cut that reduced my deficit. I came out just behind the leader, Pat O'Grady, and I passed him for my third win. But he saw me cheating. There was a big argument, and the fourth stage and the race were cancelled.

I was glad to go home at the end of the trip because I was homesick. A month later my father started working on an old racing frame of his. He bought some new parts for it and started putting it together. I hoped it might be for me, but didn't dare ask. My suspicions were confirmed when he presented me with it a week later. I couldn't believe it, a real racer with gears. He asked me if I wanted to ride in the under-age championships in Phoenix Park that Sunday. I did, so he took me on a training ride.

We left the house and headed for Balgriffin. He instructed me on the rules of a game we were to play. The idea was for me to stay behind him and to count to twenty, then I was to pass him and he would count to twenty, and so on. The second part was that I had to ride as hard as I could while at the front – not that I needed any encouragement. At Balgriffin we turned right and straight down to the seafront, then left to Portmarnock and back in the Malahide road, about ten miles in all. The ride finished with a finishing sprint and my Da just pipped me for first to the road sign – although I knew he was faking. When we got back to the house I was shattered, absolutely wrecked. Da sat me down in a chair and asked me if I still wanted to race. After getting the bike, I didn't think 'no' was the right answer so I said that I did.

'Well, that's fine but you must remember, Paul, that in cycling you will experience more heartbreak than happiness.'

God, Da, how right you were.

I don't remember much about my first race, which is unusual when you consider how vivid the memory of beating my classmates in Carraroe remains. Most of the lads were much older than me and I think I finished second to last.

I started going out on regular Sunday runs that winter. A few clubs would meet outside the General Post Office and it wasn't unusual for a thirty-strong peloton to ride out of the city. Most of the lads were from a club on the south side, Orwell Wheelers, so I joined them. When I was riding home a week or two later I noticed one other lad from the group heading in the same direction. He told me he lived in Glin Drive in Coolock and was in the Obelisk Wheelers. Martin Earley was a month younger than me and had only just started cycling. We soon became best friends.

Although I was only eleven, I started taking cycling very seriously. As soon as I came in from school, I'd meet up with Martin and we'd head off for an hour's training. I won two races in my first full year, both times beating Martin in a sprint finish. In the years that followed, the rivalry between us became too great for our friendship and from the age of fifteen until we both turned professional we became bitter rivals.

Looking back on the early years I can't help laughing at the sacrifices I made for my new sport in my quest to reach the top. But this had its advantages. It protected me from that dangerous adolescent period when teenagers are tempted by all sorts of outside influences such as smoking, drinking, drugs and women. Cycling shielded me from all of this. I lived for the school bell on Friday nights. Every second weekend, the Orwell organised youth hostelling weekends to hostels in Wicklow, Meath or Louth. As soon as the bell rang, I'd dash home and pack a sleeping bag, food and spare clothes for the weekend into the carrier of the bike and then speed into town to meet the lads.

PACKET SOUP AND FRUIT CAKE

It was through youth hostelling with the Orwell that I first met Stephen Roche. One of my best friends in the club, Paul (Smidler) Smith, asked me to go hostelling with him one weekend. I rode across to Paul's house in Dundrum, and when I arrived he decided he would ask his neighbour, 'Rochee', if he wanted to come along. 'Rochee' was totally unprepared when we knocked on his door; but he said he would join us at the hostel, Baltyboys near Blessington in County Wicklow, next morning.

Smidler and I cycled off in the pitch dark of the night to Baltyboys and, sure enough, Rochee turned up at the hostel next morning with all his gear, having left Dundrum at first light. They decided (being youngest, I always followed) that we should go to Aghavannagh, which meant a long haul over two mountains; Glenmalure and Aghavannagh. On the slopes of Glenmalure, in a small dry ditch at the side of the road, we bivouacked. Tinned fruit salad, my Ma's best fruit cake and a can of Coke. We munched away in the spitting rain, and laughed and joked about how lucky we were. Then it was back on the bikes and the climb to the Shay Elliot monument, where some film-makers were shooting a clip for *The Thirty-Nine Steps*. The evening meal at the hostel was real 'gourmet' stuff: packet soup, beans, smash and sausages, tinned rice and fruit cake.

Oh, how I loved those weekends. They were completely carefree and wonderful. I'd arrive home, totally knackered, to my Ma's hot apple tart and a mountain of homework. Stephen and I still talk with great affection of those weekends, planning each time to do it once more for old time's sake, but knowing that something will come up to prevent it happening. Could it ever be the same? Probably not, and maybe it is this which prevents us doing it again. But remembering is a joy in itself. When I compare the professional life with its glamour, its corruption and its suffering with those innocent times, I scratch my head and wonder why I bothered.

I stayed on at school until my final exams for the Leaving Certificate. When I left, a friend of my Da's, Peter Brambell, gave me a job binding blocks at a cement-block-making plant five miles from our house. It was great to be earning a few bob, and I enjoyed the work and the new freedom. But my Ma wasn't having me binding blocks for the rest of my life, and she made me apply for every job that appeared in the newspapers. When I wrote my address on the application forms, she always made sure that I wrote Artane instead of Coolock because Artane was much more fashionable. I had an interview for a plumbing apprenticeship at Dublin Airport and was offered the job. I started work immediately.

When I entered the airport in September 1979, I was seventeen and still cycling mad. As a junior, I was perhaps one of the ten best in the country but was a long way off being in the top three. Martin Earley was easily the best junior. This infuriated me and incited me to train even harder. For the 1980 season, my last as a junior, we formed a club of our own, Tara Road Club. Raphael and Gary Thompson were my team-mates, Da was team manager. He oversaw our training and planned team tactics. He was merciless in his approach. In return for his time he demanded full dedication. Bed at 9.30, hard training, tidy appearance and, above all, honesty. He never accepted excuses and he loved attacking, aggressive riding. We were a phenomenal success. From March to July we won every single race we entered. Sometimes myself, sometimes Raphael, sometimes Thompson – but always a Tara man. But the bubble burst at the junior championships in Lurgan. The whole field rode against us – and, to rub salt in the wound, Martin Earley was champion. In our three years as juniors, he was twice champion while I had just one silver for second. The dice seemed always to roll for him and fall off the table for me. I despised him.

4

THE NEARLY MAN

In 1981 I was nineteen and raced my first season as a senior rider. Adapting to the longer races was difficult initially; I was often the victim of my own enthusiasm, attacking too early and exploding before the end. But it didn't take long to adapt and, once I did, I never doubted I would reach the top in Irish cycling. Most of the young guys I had started with had given up, victims of love, alcohol and pop music. I had been in love, tried alcohol and was a great music fan. Love had left me frustrated and unhappy, alcohol happy but unconscious. I liked music because it was the only thing that didn't interfere with cycling, and I was a regular visitor to the record shops. In 1981 Stephen Roche made his professional debut with Peugeot in France. Ireland now had two professionals, Kelly and Roche. Their exploits inspired me and I wanted to be a pro. But all that was further down the road. First, I had to prove I was good enough, which took five years.

In June I represented my country for the first time in the Manx International on the Isle of Man, a 100-mile baptism of fire around the TT course. Pulling on the green jersey should have been a proud moment – it wasn't. The jerseys were faded and torn. They had been used six months previously in the Tour of Ireland and hadn't been washed properly. The washer had forgotten to remove race food from the pockets and I had to pick rotten Mars bars and other stinking remnants out of them. So much for the honour of representing your country.

Martin Earley made his international debut in the same race. We were both in the front group approaching Snaefell mountain for the last time and going really well. But I was stronger on the seven-mile climb and finished tenth, very pleased with myself.

The Irish championships were held a week later in Waterford. One of my Da's greatest fears when riding a championship was to miss the winning breakaway through tactical error. At Waterford I decided that whatever happened I wasn't going to miss the boat. I attacked early in a big group and, on the last lap, went clear with two others, Brendan Madden and Mick Nulty. They were both stronger than I was, but neither was a good finisher. In the finishing sprint, slightly uphill, sheer will to win was the difference between us and I beat them easily. I was Irish champion at nineteen, the youngest ever to win the title. I was thrilled.

Stephen Roche was in Waterford that day. He was home on a break from the Continent and he turned up in a lovely white Peugeot with his name on both doors. He had made a sensational pro debut, winning the Tour of Corsica and Paris–Nice – an instant star. He brought a girl to Waterford. She was French, blonde and wore an outrageous mini-skirt. Her name was Lydia, and seeing her with Stephen that day made professional cycling seem very enticing.

Winning in Waterford was very important to me: I was Irish champion and no one could ever take that away. I loved the title. In the pubs in the off-season I would often bump into someone who would ask if I was into sport.

'Cycling, hmmm that's interesting and have you won anything?'

And I would reply with false modesty, 'Well, actually, I'm the current national champion.'

The glamour of being champion didn't last. Later that month I was picked in an Irish team for the Tour of Scotland.

THE NEARLY MAN

There was a Czech team riding who were huge brutes of men. Milan Jurco was the most impressive; I had never seen so much muscle on one man or anyone quite as ugly. The Czechs taught me a new game – the art of riding in crosswinds. In Ireland the hedges are so high that crosswinds are rarely a factor in deciding race tactics, so we were inexperienced. The Czechs toyed with us all week, and I can remember going to bed one night dreading having to get up for another hammering the next day. I remember the second to last stage in particular. It lashed down with rain all day and I arrived in a group hours down and totally miserable. At the finish we rode straight to the dressing room. The Englishman, Mark Bell from Liverpool, was getting changed. He had just beaten two Czechs to win the stage, a fine performance. Someone asked if he wanted to turn pro. He laughed and in his best scouse accent replied, 'No way! It looks great on the telly, seeing them pulling faces on the climbs, throwing themselves all over the place, but it's not like that in real life. It's pain. No fuckin' way.'

I knew that Mark Bell was right, but it didn't change my mind. I reckoned I was still young and had still a good margin for improvement. I reckoned I would go much better with another two years under my belt. But he did make me think about it.

Stephen came home for the winter and was in great demand all over the country. He had won four stage races in his first season with the professionals and was already a big name. I phoned him and invited him to our house for a chat and some advice about going to France. When he came, he talked of the problems he had faced as an amateur, of the need to be two-faced with the team managers and the French riders because they were always two-faced with you. He told us it was important to 'get them before they get you'. The message struck a chord. He promised to find Raphael and me a place at ACBB at the end of 1983 when we finished our apprenticeships. After the talk, he cleared the spread of cakes and pastries my mother had laid on – it was nice to see he had lost none of his old habits.

1982 started well, then flopped, but was most memorable for meeting Ann. I have always thought it a strange coincidence that I met my wife and my best friend on the same day, at the same time and in the same place. It was in Phoenix Park in Dublin at the end of the week-long Ras Tailteann. I had been noticing Ann since the start of the season. She was a sister of one of the guys who raced, Paul Nolan. I knew Paul was riding the Ras and guessed she might be in the park. I found her in the crowd after the race and we started talking. She had followed the race for the week, taking notes for a journalist from the Irish press, David Walsh. As we talked, David and his wife Mary approached and Ann introduced me. I arranged to meet her later at the post-race dance. We had two more dates during that week and on the following Sunday I won my first race for over two months at Carrick on Suir.

Carrick was one of the rare occasions in 1981 when I beat Raphael. He had a superb year and was heralded by all as the new Kelly. It was hard playing second fiddle to my younger brother; he was the apple of my father's eye, but we were always close and his success did not change this. Meeting Ann was a great consolation. She came into my life at an important time. My poor form frustrated me. The more I tried, the less I succeeded. I was impossible to live with whenever I travelled with an Irish team: moody, grouchy, a real pain. Ann changed me. She lightened me up, brought me out of myself, got me smiling more. It was no coincidence that I started to ride better almost from the first day we met.

For me 1983 was about two races. The Milk Race, a two-week Tour of Britain sponsored by the Milk Marketing Board, had the reputation of being one of the hardest amateur stage races in the world. I was a bit dubious about entering for it as I had never ridden a stage race of more than a week, but decided it was time to test my mettle.

The first stage was a marathon 120-mile trip to Bristol. With about twenty miles to go I went clear in a chasing group with race leader Malcolm Elliot and Tony Doyle and finished sixteenth. It was a good start and I was determined to hang on to my sixteenth place for as long as possible. The morale in the team was excellent. We had been slaughtered by the Irish press before leaving, but the criticism united us and made us try harder. There was no pressure on us, so we had nothing to lose and attacked every day. The good start continued when my mate Phillip Cassidy finished second on the third stage to Welwyn Garden City. He stole some of my thunder and spurred me to attack. On the sixth stage to Leicester I got into an important break that moved me up to sixth overall. Sixth in the Milk Race, I couldn't believe it.

I rang home every night: one call to my parents, another to Ann. They were all very excited and said I was getting rave reviews from the papers. On the ninth stage, a 94-mile mountainous stage from Kirkby to Halifax, I hit the jackpot – race leader. A star at last. But getting the lead was one thing, holding on to it quite another. Our team was young and very inexperienced and I was convinced there was no way we could defend the yellow jersey. I didn't sleep that night and felt a terrible pressure on my shoulders. I had worn a yellow jersey only once before on a Tour of Ulster and had lost it after one day. The Tour of Ulster wasn't a patch on the Milk Race, how could I possibly hope to hang on? I weighed up my options all night. I had a 42-second lead over German rider Ulrich Rottler and 54 seconds on Peugeot professional Sean Yates. The next day was a 100-mile stage to Hull, but this was followed by a rest day. Defending the jersey to Hull would ensure that I kept it for three days. It was a good incentive.

The stage to Hull was flat and proved uneventful. We had a shaky start and let a dangerous break go clear, but regained control half-way through and I rode into Hull with the jersey still in my possession. The rest day was great, it was an extra day to savour the glory. Being race leader was fun but it wasn't enough any more. I wanted to win. I couldn't sleep for thinking about it – the pressure was enormous. There were just three more stages to go; if I held out on two of those the race was mine. The first hilly stage across the Yorkshire Moors to Middlesbrough was the real test. On the first climb, all my team-mates were dropped and I was left alone to defend the yellow shirt. On the savagely steep Farndale Moor, I suffered terribly but broke clear with a sixteen-man group. Rottler, Eaton and Yates were left behind. I was so happy that I didn't bother to go for the stage win and was content to roll in at the back of the group. I had defended the lead on my own. I was convinced I was going to win.

There was just the difficult seventy-mile stage to Harrogate to master. It started with a steep first-category climb, the Stang, but I was flying and crossed the summit in seventh place. The bunch had split in two, and all my team-mates were behind so I was vulnerable. The Americans noticed and started attacking. One by one I brought them back, enjoying the defiance. When they saw they couldn't get rid of me they slowed the pace and my team-mates got back on.

I met my Waterloo after thirteen miles. A mile from the bottom of the second climb, the Fleak, I had a puncture. Eaton noticed my deflating front tyre and ordered his men to attack. My two team-mates Eddie Madden and Mick McKenna waited with me and we changed wheels. I didn't panic because I felt sure we would get back on. But the Americans split the field to shreds on the climb, and neither Madden nor McKenna could stay with me. I picked my way through the stragglers and chased alone down the descent. But I started to take chances, ran off the road at a T-junction and fell off. A puncture and a crash – the bad luck was too much. I got back on the bike, but lost heart; chasing alone was now a pointless exercise. I waited for a group and finished the stage thirteen minutes down. I slid from first to thirty-third overall. The next morning Matt Eaton pulled on my yellow jersey and we strolled to the race finish in

Blackpool. At the race banquet I was presented with a watch as the most unfortunate rider of the race. I gave it to my father, remembering his words: 'In cycling there is more heartbreak than happiness.'

Knowing what I now know, I should not have lost the race. I should have paid money to a team-mate to defend the lead. In the modern era riders do not lose stage races because of punctures and crashes. But I returned to Ireland a hero. Only one other Irishman, Peter Doyle, had ever worn the yellow jersey in the Milk Race. I had equalled God. Not bad.

The Milk Race had made me the top rider in the country, and I confirmed my new status with two good wins on my return home. Two weeks later I rode the Manx International. On the last lap I broke clear on Snaefell mountain with six others. We dashed down the mountain, turned Governor's Bridge and entered the finishing straight. Joey McLaughlin opened the sprint and I came round him, heading for the line like a bullet. I got that feeling, that wonderful, 'I'm going to win the Manx International' feeling. The line was there just in front of me, but then the Swiss Hans Reiss passed me ten feet from the line, edging me out by a hair's breadth. Second. So near and yet so far. Again. The press started calling me 'the nearly man'.

The Tour de L'Avenir was the second memory of 1983. The L'Avenir, starting in Lorient and finishing in Marseille, was a fourteen-day mini Tour de France for pros and amateurs – and my first chance to race against Continental pros. It was very different from my previous races. They rode much closer together; I can remember leaving Lorient on the first stage with brake levers in both buttocks and feeling very uncomfortable. The style of racing was also completely new. With amateurs it was arse-up, head down, and go from the gun. But in the L'Avenir there was no set pattern to the racing, except at the finish, when it was always eyeballs out. From the opening stages survival was the goal.

Before riding the L'Avenir I thought I knew what mountains

were. I didn't. The first mountain stage came after ten days. It was a split, with a morning stage from Bourg-de-Péage to La Chapelle-en-Vercors and in the afternoon a return to Bourg over the same climbs. I had been waiting all week for this day, the day of glory, but I was wiped out. It was so hot and the climbs were so long that I couldn't handle it. On the morning stage I was dropped with John Herety and Paul Sherwen, two British pros riding with French teams La Redoute and Coop-Mercier. Both were noted non-climbers and at the time I felt humiliated to be in their company. I had fancied myself as a Lucien Van Impe. I was deeply discouraged, and for the first time being a professional did not seem such a great thing after all. I reached La Chapelle at least half an hour down. My team-mate John McQuaid finished with me, but Raphael and Gary Thompson, the only other Irish survivors, were further back again. We changed quickly and ate a pretty miserable lunch in a run-down shack of a hotel. Bernard Thevenet, a double Tour de France winner, was at another table. Word had it that he was a native of La Chapelle.

We rested between stages in a cold, stone cottage on damp mattresses. The morale in the team was zero. We just looked at each other with the same thought in all our heads: 'What the hell are we doing here?' I decided that this pro life wasn't for me. I hated it. The afternoon stage was a nightmare. Some Portuguese bastard attacked at the bottom of the first climb and the green jerseys were immediately dropped. Raphael was in a dreadful state and was coughing up blood. Gary Thompson was physically and mentally knackered. They both quickly abandoned. I rode on in a group of five which included a Japanese rider, Takahashi. For a Japanese to get this far in the Tour de L'Avenir was an outstanding achievement. His team manager was leaning out of the car window with a loudhailer in his hand, and screamed encouragement in Japanese every time the road went up, which was regularly. This started getting to me after a while. I was irritated by my poor form and annoyed that I would have to endure the race for another six days. And now, on top of all this, there was this bloody manager making all this noise for a guy who was half an hour down. Had they no shame? The rage became uncontrollable and I turned to the Japanese team manager and shouted at the top of my voice, 'Shut fuckin' up.'

I will never forget the look on his face. He was terrified, horrified; he sat back in his car and did not say another word for the rest of the day. I felt guilty about it the next day, so I went up to him and apologised.

Raphael and Thompson both left for home and I envied them. There were only myself and John 'Kippers' McQuaid left. 'Kippers' would have got great pleasure in returning home the only Irish finisher and I would have heard about it for the rest of my life. I suppose it was this more than anything that made me go on, but I hated it. I dreaded getting up every morning to face another day's racing. And the pros irritated me: always good humoured, always laughing and joking. I had started the race as a morning grouch but by the end I was an all-day grouch. Cyril Guimard, the famous professional *directeur sportif*, also upset me. I was on the massage couch getting a rub and the hotel door was open. Guimard walked in, much to my surprise and delight. I looked at him in wonder. The great Cyril Guimard in *my* room. He approached the massage table, lifted the towel that covered my privates and said 'Baf!', waving his hand in a dismissive way and then walked out. The bastard; I hated him for it.

'Kippers' was eliminated with two stages to go, leaving me the sole Irish survivor. Five of those who had abandoned had flown home but there were no more air tickets and so we had to take the boat. I didn't really care, I just wanted to get away from there. It had been a bad end to a great season. I was saturated with cycling and needed a good rest.

I finished my four-year apprenticeship at Dublin Airport shortly afterwards. It was the policy of the company, Aer

Rianta, to train apprentices and then sack them once the apprenticeship was over. I was out of a job. Where next? My plan had always been to complete my apprenticeship and then go to France to try for a pro contract, but the Tour de L'Avenir had opened my eyes. For four years Raphael and I had told our friends, family and, most importantly, the cycling journalists that we would be going to France in 1984. Could we turn back now? Then there were the Olympics to consider. Los Angeles was fast approaching and, although I was fairly sure of a place, there was no guarantee. France could clinch my selection and offer me the best preparation. So I suppose it was three things, no job, Los Angeles and the fear of being called 'chicken', which led us to the ACBB club in Paris in February 1984. We were following in the footsteps of the greats, Elliot, Roche, Millar and Anderson. We were also following in the not-so-glorious footsteps of our father, who had set out on the same quest twenty-five years earlier.

5

NATIONAL SUCKERS DAY

A big man met us at the airport. He had huge, shovel-like hands, greying hair and tanned skin. We thought he might be Mickey Wiegant, the legendary ACBB manager, or maybe Claude Escalon, the *directeur sportif*, but we weren't sure and hadn't the courage to ask. We sat in the back of his car like two terrified children as he drove us to Boulogne Billancourt, a suburb west of Paris.

On our arrival at the ACBB sports centre, a not quite middle-aged man in a leather jacket approached us. There was something almost sinister about his smile. I took an immediate dislike to him because of it. He introduced himself as Claude Escalon. He gave us two new Peugeot bikes, just like the pros had, and some tracksuits, jerseys and shorts. It was great to be given so much free gear but I wasn't happy with the saddle on the bike. Plucking up some courage I tried to explain to him in pidgin English that I wanted to fit my own. He laughed. We had to use the team issue saddles. Bernard Hinault used the same saddle.

'If they are good enough for Bernard, they are good enough for you.' There was no arguing with that so I agreed to use his saddle.

At four the next morning, we left in a VW van for the south of France. We were not the only foreigners at the club. There were also a New Zealander (Gerry Golder), two Englishmen

(Kenny Knight and Christian Yates, a brother of Sean's), a Canadian and 'les frères Kimmage'. After twelve hours' driving we arrived at our base for the opening races, the Hôtel la Quiétude at Les Issambres on the Côte d'Azur. Mickey Wiegant was at the hotel when we arrived. He was an odd-looking man, impossible to put an age to, just one of those blokes who never seem to get any older. He wore a brown leather jacket and drove a huge Rover. He spoke at 400 miles an hour and we couldn't understand a word he said. He insisted we call him 'Monsieur Wiegant'. We ate when he gave us the order to eat. We spoke when he gave us permission to speak. He made us feel very small.

The team's French riders drove down in their own cars. There was also a Belgian. I remember him because of all the shit he used to take before meals: pills, *ampoules* – he was a right bloody pharmacist. When he'd catch us staring during his pill-popping, he'd say 'vitamins'. The French formed a clan and weren't too friendly towards us. We, the English speakers, formed our own clan. A Norwegian, Dag Otto Lauritzen, arrived a few days later, but he stayed at Wiegant's house and was clearly the old man's favourite. Training started immediately. We set off in a large group and followed the team car, which was driven by Escalon but directed by Wiegant.

They played little games with us. At the top of a hill Wiegant would hold a racing tyre out of the window – the prize for the first rider to the top. On the first training spin, I won two tyres. I found the first races more difficult.

Monsieur Wiegant instructed us that in his team the individual rider's personal honour did not matter. It was the victory of the team that counted. To emphasise this he would buy a huge cream cake and divide it among us equally any time an ACBB rider won. Lauritzen was the star and he won several of the opening races. A fourth place in a race at St Tropez was my best placing of the month-long stay. Raphael was riding better and was narrowly beaten in a race at St Maxime, but there was no cream cake. With Monsieur Wiegant cream cakes were for winning; second was nowhere.

During the month some of the professional riders would come to the hotel to pay homage to their former mentor and guru, Monsieur Wiegant. Bernard Thevenet, Robert Millar, Raphael Geminiani and Stephen Roche all visited and lunched with the old man. Stephen introduced me to his *directeur sportif*, Bernard Thevenet. He had a lovely, warm smile that lit up his face. I liked him.

At the end of February we drove back to Paris to begin the serious races, the amateur classics. Most of the foreigners stayed together in a flat near the team's headquarters but Raphael and I were taken to a small flat on the opposite side of Paris at Vincennes. As we entered the flat, Abel, the giant masseur who had collected us at the airport, led us down to this underground dungeon with a mud floor. I can remember thinking, 'Jesus Christ, how are we going to survive here?', but he was just showing us the shed for the bikes. The flat was five floors up a narrow wooden staircase.

We had no problems in settling in. I did the cooking and Raphael the cleaning. The flat had an old black and white television and a telephone for incoming calls only. The toilet was the hole-in-the-ground type. It doubled as a shower by placing a wooden grille over the hole. This was a great inconvenience at first. To compensate, Raphael took the middle out of one of the wooden kitchen chairs and tried sitting on the wooden frame. It didn't work, and in the end we had to squat. We became such good shots that we could shoot between the gaps in the shower grille after a while. The flat was fine. We liked being independent of the other foreigners and enjoyed the privacy. But it was awkward having to ride across Paris the day before a race to change a tyre or get information about what was going on. Wiegant remained at his house at Les Issambres, coming to Paris for the big races.

Paris–Ezy was the first classic of the season. It started in the darkness of a small foggy village at eight in the morning. I never understood why the classics always started at such a ridiculous hour. An eight o'clock start meant getting up at four. Nutrition was the biggest problem – we had to eat three hours before the race. At four in the morning I would fry minced steak and boil rice. We had no appetite and had to force-feed ourselves. As soon as breakfast-cum-dinner was over we would leave the flat, pick up the bikes from the basement and wait in the marble hallway to be collected. In our racing tights we must have looked a proper sight to the other flat residents coming home from discothèques and nightclubs. Their expressions said it all. Getting up at that hour for a bike race was totally insane, and I never got used to it.

As we waited to start the race, I was approached by a Frenchman who spoke perfect Oxford English. It wasn't our first meeting, as we had talked at a time trial a few years earlier when he had visited Ireland as a guest of the Roche family. I had asked him then about the professional life and he laughed at me, 'You don't want to be a professional, it's a horrible life.' I was shocked that a Frenchman could be so dismissive of what I felt was the greatest profession in the world and thought the guy was a nutcase. Today I admire him for his vision. We are still great friends with Jean Beaufils and his wife Ginette and have not forgotten their kindness to us in a miserable year with ACBB.

Paris–Ezy was run in freezing cold wind and rain. On the finishing circuit, Raphael got into the winning move, but the uphill sprint was too hard for him and he finished fifth. We were absolutely thrilled. Fifth in the first classic of the year, what a great start. But Escalon thought otherwise. There were two other ACBB riders in the break with Raphael and neither had won. One of them, the French rider Thierry Pelosso, had gone to Escalon after the race and said he had lost because of Raphael's 'selfish tactics'. We couldn't understand a word of Escalon's raving and asked Jean Beaufils to interpret. Raphael defended himself but Escalon would have none of it, and made him the scapegoat for the defeat. Raphael's joy soon turned to tears. He was never the same again.

March and April were grim. Living in Paris was awkward for training. We had to ride for forty-five minutes in heavy traffic to find some decent country roads. So if we wanted to do a three-hour ride, we had to spend an hour and a half choking on exhaust fumes. We rode just one race a week with the club, which wasn't nearly enough to develop any kind of good form. Training was no substitute for racing and we didn't ride well. It was easy to get depressed. Some days we didn't bother to train at all; these days we labelled National Suckers Days. It usually rained in the mornings on National Suckers Days. After breakfast we'd sit looking at each other and contemplate going out into the Paris traffic on our bikes: 'No, we'll wait till it clears up.' To pass the time we'd take the Métro and sit drinking coffee on the Champs Elysées and try to figure out exactly where the Tour finished. Afterwards we'd visit the Eiffel Tower and then eat out for lunch. The afternoon was spent walking around the record shops or at an English-version movie on the Champs. The day would finish with dinner at the flat, accompanied by a bottle of cheap *vin de table* and we'd sit back and laugh about how we had been ripped off in tourist- trap Paris. But inside, we were not laughing; inside, we were screaming. ACBB was not working for us.

In April I left Paris for a week. I was picked for the national team for the Sealink International, starting at Skelmersdale near Liverpool. I felt sorry to be leaving Raphael behind. His good humour was a real tonic on the bad days at the flat. He deserved a place on the team more than I did, but Irish selectors were always reluctant to pick the two of us and so I got the nod. It was great to get out of France. My parents came across from Ireland and followed the race for the week. I struggled for the first few days – too many National Suckers Days had left me short of condition. But I started to ride well towards the end, and I returned to Paris with much better morale and form.

The classic Paris–Rouen, was my first race with the club after my week's 'holiday'. The alarm went off at four in the morning and we climbed out of bed wearily. Steak and rice were consumed with the usual enthusiasm and then we gathered our kit and went down to the ground floor. It was a damp, miserable morning so we waited inside the apartment front door, sitting on the cold marble floor. Fifteen minutes, half an hour, an hour. Still no sign of them. We put the bikes back in the shed, walked back upstairs and went to bed. We were sick. Sick of these heartless bastards treating us like scum. Surely we deserved at least a phone call? Furious, I phoned Escalon and demanded why no one had picked us up. He gave me a half-baked excuse about trying to contact us, and to calm me asked if we wanted to ride a race on Tuesday in a place called Ostricourt in northern France.

Ostricourt was a battle between the two strongest teams in the race, ACBB and Wasquehal, a powerful outfit being formed in the north. But the French amateur champion was also riding, and I remember being most impressed with Jean-François Bernard before team tactics got the better of him and he retired. It was a circuit race with a short climb and a kilometre stretch of cobbles on each lap. On the last lap I attacked alone on the climb and time-trialled to the finish for a solo victory. I had almost forgotten how good it felt to win a race. Ostricourt gave me immense satisfaction. Escalon shook my hand with that big smile of his but I remained cool towards him. Sunday was fresh in my mind.

In May, shortly after Ostricourt, I was told of my selection for the Olympic Games at Los Angeles. Raphael, disillusioned and short of form, decided he had had enough. Most of the foreigners who had started the year with us were gone. But there was no shortage of replacements. Australians, Brits, Americans, all were 'warmly' welcomed, tried and then unceremoniously dumped. It was like a factory production line, and it struck me that in discovering a handful of stars the club had destroyed the dreams of hundreds of amateurs whose memories of the club would be bitter and resentful as Raphael was when he returned home. He had a talent, a great talent but never got a break or the encouragement that might have made him a star. The ACBB had destroyed him. How many other great talents had been destroyed in the same way?

Encouraged by my return to form, I decided to stick it out. On the weekend that Raphael returned to Ireland I rode a three-day stage race in the north of France. It was my first stage race with the club. This was because of a French Federation rule that limited each club to one foreign rider per team. The ACBB had up to ten foreigners to choose from and I was never considered good enough, but Ostricourt changed that. Fifth on the first stage, third on the second, I became the race leader with just a seven-kilometre time trial and an afternoon stage to go. Escalon pulled out all the strokes for the time trial. I was given a special carbon-fibre bike and a one-piece racing suit for the short time trial. I was very nervous starting the test. Roche, Millar, Anderson – all had 'honoured' the ACBB in races like this one. This was my chance to join them. I blew it and lost the jersey by four seconds. Four lousy seconds. Escalon was not angry but I knew he was thinking, 'This Irish boy hasn't got it.'

I rode some evening races in Paris shortly after. It was while returning home from one of these that I heard the news. My friend David Walsh, who was working as a freelance journalist in the city for a year, told me that Martin Earley would shortly be signing as a professional with the new Spanish team Fagor for 1985. I was stunned: Earley, my arch rival. The bastard had made it as a professional. I felt more jealous than at any other time in my life.

Martin had also been picked for the Olympic Games. In July we rode a preparation race in Colorado, the Coors Classic, and then flew on to Los Angeles for the Games. I now found I no longer thought of Martin as a rival; he was assured of a pro contract, had escaped up the ladder. We became more friendly towards each other. A few days before the Olympic road race I remember training with him in the Hollywood hills. I told him that if I was given the opportunity I would turn professional for nothing. He said I was mad, but I argued that the ACBB had cost me all my savings and in a pro team I wouldn't have to put up with guys like Escalon. Looking back, I can see just how naïve about the professional game I was. Years later, when I was haggling with my *directeur sportif* Bernard Thevenet over my contract fee, I would often remember that conversation and smile. And there were *directeurs sportifs* far more ruthless than Escalon.

The Olympics were wonderful. I had always been sceptical about them, but I must admit they were one of the highlights of my career. On the big day, I was desperately unlucky – again. I had just bridged a gap to the leading group of twenty riders when a rear wheel-spoke snapped and fell out into the gear mechanism and I skidded to a halt. I didn't see the twenty-man group again. If only . . . if only . . . 'if', that word again, 'the nearly man' once more. I was riding much better than Martin that day and he finished nineteenth, the highest-ever placing by an Irish cyclist at an Olympics. I was twenty-seventh.

I returned to Ireland straight after the Games for the Irish championship in Kelly's home town of Carrick on Suir. My performance at LA had not gone unnoticed in the Irish press, and they made me favourite before the race. I was obsessed with proving that bad luck had robbed me from being top Irishman at the Olympics. I had to win. I attacked from the start and followed every move. With one lap to go, I got clear with Eddie Madden of the Irish Road Club. Eddie was riding strongly and my efforts were starting to tell, making me a bit wary of an attack from him. But incredibly he said to me, 'Don't attack, we'll sprint it out at the finish.' I was surprised, Eddie was a hopeless sprinter – he couldn't have been feeling too good after all. Da drove behind the race carrying spare wheels, with my mother and Ann for company. With two miles to go he drove up alongside and reminded me of the rule forbidding the lifting of both hands from the handlebars in a victory salute. I thought, 'He's sure I will win. But what if I mess it up?' I became suddenly nervous. In the finishing sprint we both kicked at the same time and for a second I doubted but then I drew clear and won easily. Champion again.

I returned to Paris for the end-of-season classics and rode a stage race, the Tour of Seine-et-Marne. I was riding quite well, but in the time trial on the second day, Martin beat me by over two minutes and took the race lead. I made a big effort to win the last stage and thought I had it, but I was swallowed up within spitting distance of the line and finished sixth in a downpour. I remember lifting my head and seeing Martin raise his arms as the race winner; I felt ill. I rode the remaining classics with little motivation or conviction and left Paris with a vague promise from Escalon that I could return the following season. I agreed, but in reality I wasn't sure that I wanted to.

On returning home, the gravity of my situation hit me. Should I go back for another year? Earley had made it, but had taken two years. Why not try once more? Work was impossible to find in Dublin. Raphael was also out of a job and we both signed on for the dole for a few weeks. Then a friend of ours, Michael Collins, found us two places at the government training centre, ANCO in Finglas. Michael, who was cycling mad, seemed very keen that we try again. There was no way Raphael was going back to ACBB, but I couldn't make up my mind – at least they assured you a pro contract if you performed. A phone call from Sean Kelly made up my mind.

He was home for the winter and, besides keeping himself fit, spent his time entertaining the numerous journalists and businessmen who flocked to his door from the Continent in search of a story or a product endorsement. One of them was a man called Guy Mollet, who did PR for a French company, Reydel. Kelly had used Reydel saddles for two seasons and

Mollet was over to negotiate a new deal. Mollet was also the president of CC Wasquehal and he wanted the Irish champion for his team for 1985. He had organised the Ostricourt race which I had won in May. At first I hesitated and told Kelly I would be going back to the ACBB. Kelly said he was coming to Dublin in the afternoon to leave Mollet at the airport, and arranged for us to meet and talk.

Chubby, curly-haired, with nine and a half fingers, Guy Mollet was a shark. He said he was great friends with Kelly's *directeur sportif* Jean de Gribaldy, and assured me a pro contract with him if I produced the goods. He also promised free lodgings, £150 a month to live on and attractive cash bonuses for winning. I did not have to reflect too long. ACBB had cost me £1,000 and I had never received a centime from them in prize money. Mollet was a rogue but he was a likeable rogue. We shook hands and the deal was done.

6
GLORY DAYS

January 1985 was like January 1984, a difficult month. I noticed the change in Ann a week before leaving. She became moody and less gay, and I would often catch her with a tear in her eye, which she would quickly brush away and refuse to talk about. I knew what was upsetting her: soon I would return to France and the long winter we had passed together would be just a memory to sustain her till God knew when. I felt the pain, too, but tried not to show it. Men are not supposed to cry. Our relationship was three years old and we were totally committed to each other, but my obsession with cycling made it impossible for us to plan anything.

Wasquehal would be my last chance. I decided to stay with the club for as long as my savings would support me. Raphael and I left for France at the end of January with about £500 between us, half of what we had taken to ACBB. This time it was make it or bust. A weird twist of fate turned us once more into the hands of Monsieur Wiegant. He had been overthrown at ACBB by a *coup d'état*. Escalon was now in full control of the team. Mollet phoned Wiegant and asked him to look after the Wasquehal riders for the month's pre-season training on the Côte d'Azur, and so, for the second year on the trot, we found ourselves at the Hôtel La Quiétude under the spell of the old sorcerer. He was a bit of a swine, but I respected him and felt almost sorry for him as he pined over his downfall. My form on the Côte was dismal and I didn't get one decent placing. Mollet was getting a little impatient with us, but I promised him I would get better once I was back in the north.

We rode our first northern classic, Amiens–Beaurains, a week after returning from the training camp. With twenty kilometres to go I broke away with three others, and in the finishing sprint was narrowly beaten to the line by my Wasquehal team-mate Jean-François Laffile. Mollet was delighted and kissed and hugged me in gratitude. I was pleased, he was pleased, I liked him.

The competition up north was not quite as tough as in Paris and we raced regularly, which was the big advantage. I won my first big race, the Tour of Cambresis, by out-sprinting a seven-man group in a fierce downpour. Mollet paid us regularly, and as the club won most of the races we always had a share of the prize money, so we made enough to live on. Raphael, too, was riding better. In May he won his first French race in the coastal town of Boulogne – I was second, and the bitter memories of Paris were effaced for us both.

I had good form in May and was probably the club's best rider for the month. Half-way through the month I was third in a Paris–Roubaix-style classic over the worst cobblestones of northern France. The morning after the race I got a phone call from Mollet.

'Bonjour Paul, c'est Guy. You are riding Bordeaux–Paris this weekend.'

(Bordeaux–Paris is 575 kilometres long, and the longest professional race in the world. Because of its savage distance, only a dozen or so professionals started the race. They lined up in Bordeaux before midnight, cycled 250 kilometres to Poitiers, were given twenty minutes for a change of clothes, and then rode the rest of the way with each rider individually paced behind a motorbike.)

'What? You must be joking.'

'No, no, it's no joke. The race organisers contacted Monsieur de Gribaldy and they want one amateur in the race, so I suggested you.'

I was taken aback and unsure how to respond. The race was just five days away. The pros riding would have more than a month's preparation in their legs. I had five days and would be on a hiding to nothing. Mollet and de Gribaldy could hardly criticise me if I refused to ride, but perhaps they would perceive this as a sign of weakness. And this would be a factor against me when I asked them later about a contract. I needed something to throw me into the national limelight; perhaps this was my chance. I agreed.

I trained twice behind a motorbike that week or rather, I had two four-hour sessions behind Guy Mollet's daughter's scooter. On Friday I flew to Bordeaux, with a change of aircraft at Lyon. There I recognised de Gribaldy and two of his riders, Dominique Garde and Eric Guyot, going through the departures hall. I was shy and preferred not to introduce myself. I let them board the aircraft before me. Monsieur de Gribaldy sat in a front row, but Garde and Guyot sat at the back. There was a place vacant beside them so I sat there. It was fun to study them close up. The next day we would be racing back to Paris together, but they hadn't a clue who I was. They read motor-car magazines and half-way through the flight Garde opened a packet of chocolate biscuits which they shared. As they munched, they peered over the top of the seats at de Gribaldy's head and giggled like school kids. I found it all very bewildering, but later, at the dinner table, when I had introduced myself and been accepted into the group, I understood. De Gribaldy surveyed everything we ate. Portions of everything were small, and we were given miserable sweets. Monsieur de Gribaldy frowned at my waistline and said I would ride much better if I lost a couple of kilos. This was news to me. I had always worked on the principle that it was OK to stuff your face as long as you trained hard. But de Gribaldy's method was to train hard and starve. He had extraordinary presence and I didn't dare argue with him.

We went out for a light spin on Saturday morning. After lunch we were ordered to bed from two in the afternoon until eight in the evening. Lunch had been extremely light, but I had brought a bit of my mother's fruit cake. I made sure the door was locked before I cut it. I shared my room with a pro, Guy Galopin, who couldn't believe I had been told just five days earlier I was riding. He took a great liking to my mother's fruit cake.

We left Bordeaux at midnight, riding as a group through the blackness until we came to a small village just before Poitiers. Here, we changed into fresh gear, ate a little (a bit of chicken), used the toilet and then jumped back on the bikes. During the stop-over Guy took out some pills and offered me one. I looked at him suspiciously. He said they were for 'le froid'. My French had improved and I knew that 'froid' meant 'cold'. But it was really warm outside. Why the hell was he giving me tablets for cold when it was thirty degrees? I took the pill and pretended to swallow it as I did not want to offend him, but secretly I threw it in the bin.

Looking back, I realise that Guy *was* trying to help me. He had not in fact offered me anything for 'le froid', but rather something for 'le foie' (the liver). When you ride a bike race that lasts more than seventeen hours, the digestive system gets completely screwed up from eating sweet things. Guy had offered me a tablet to help digestion, but naïvely I had thought he was trying to give me a charge. In my suspicious mind all pills were drugs and I would never take drugs.

I was left behind with about 200 kilometres to go to Paris. Mollet followed in the team car, and each time he was sure that the race commissar was out of sight he instructed my pacer to push me. I freaked out when the pacer put his hand on my back. I told Mollet I was either getting to Paris under my own steam or getting off – a question of honour. I was a sorry sight at the finish and had to be lifted from my bike. Three pros had abandoned and I had beaten one, finishing ninth out of thirteen starters. I had proved my point. This was a test of courage and I passed. But the price was high. That night I hadn't the strength to walk up the stairs to my bedroom – I crawled on my hands and knees. The mental strain of the week was over and I felt I had made a giant step towards my contract.

In July a stage of the Tour de France finished near Wasquehal. I went to the stage start the next day with the intention of talking to Kelly and Roche but instead ended up spending all my time with Martin Earley. He was riding in his first Tour and looked splendid in his Fagor jersey. He looked the real pro, quite unlike the scrawny amateur I had grown up with. I envied him as he rode off on the stage to Rheims. It was the first time in my life that I actually admired him for something.

Later in the month I had my first bad argument with Guy Mollet. I had taken a complete nine days' break from competition but on the tenth day, a Sunday morning, he stormed into the house and demanded that I ride the race later that day. I shouted back at him, replying that the professional contract he had been promising me since Bordeaux–Paris was long overdue. He assured me that he would fulfil his promise, but only on condition that I raced immediately. I raced and he was happy.

At the end of July I rode the Tour of Poland for the Irish national team. It was probably the hardest amateur stage race I ever rode. Conditions were horrible, the hotel food was tasteless – the bare minimum – and it was impossible to buy supplements. The racing was pretty savage and we took a hiding for the first couple of days. On the seventh stage I broke clear twenty kilometres from the finish with a Polish rider who left me with a kilometre to go and won the stage. I was really disappointed with second place, but I learned a month later that the Pole had tested positive in dope control after the stage and I had been awarded the victory. But it wasn't the same. It was a prestigious addition to my list of victories, but I had been robbed of the pleasure of winning. The Pole had raised his hands to the huge crowd, he had milked their applause and kissed the pretty girl with the flowers. No, it wasn't the same.

From Poland I returned to France and raced the Tour of Normandy again with the national squad. Peter Crinnion was our manager. Peter was an ex-pro and had helped Stephen Roche to go to France. I respected him greatly. Before the race he pulled me aside from the others in our team group and told me I could win the Normandy. I looked at him as if he had two heads, but then asked myself: 'Why not?' It was one of the best weeks of my career. I won a stage and finished second in two others and finished fifth overall. I would undoubtedly have finished higher, but in the race's only time trial I had the incredible misfortune to puncture twice in ten kilometres. I was flying.

I returned to Wasquehal and rode a small race that Mollet insisted I ride. A five-man Mafia, a mix of Poles and French who toured France and split all prize money between them, were riding. Near the end of the race I broke clear in a five-man group with two Mafia men. One of them approached me on the last lap and offered me £50 if I did not sprint. Surprised, I thought about it but said, 'No'. He increased the bid to £100. I had become a bit hungry for money, so I agreed – but it bothered me. So I thought about it: 'Mollet would probably give me a bonus if I won, and another win would do my chances of a contract no harm.' I went back to the Mafia man and told him there was no deal. He spat in disgust, and I immediately felt pressure. If I won, I would justify my argument. If I lost, I'd be £100 poorer and the laughing stock of the Mafia. The sprint to the line was a desperately close thing, but I managed to edge him out. Mollet was delighted. He announced to the crowd at the prize ceremony that Kimmage would be riding the World Championships for Ireland one week later in Italy. But he also announced that Kimmage would soon be turning professional. I laughed, very pleased with myself, I liked winning. I had no idea that it was the last race I would ever win.

The World Amateur Championships were in Montello, Italy. Even though it was very hot, I managed to pick up a bad head cold two days before the race. We rode the circuit in training: it had a hard hill, and I liked it and felt optimistic about my chances. Poland and Normandy had given me a new confidence. On race day, I was given a great boost when a note scribbled on a piece of paper was handed to me. It said: 'Compared with all you went through in Bordeaux–Paris this will be nothing. Good luck. Raphael.' The note gave me great heart and I started the race, tense but incredibly determined. I was content to just follow the others for the first half of the race and didn't feel too good.

To please the Irish supporters on the circuit, I attacked on the climb at half-way, but I didn't get very far and instantly regretted my foolishness. The World Championships were a gradual process of elimination. Over 200 had started, but with just one lap to go there were just twenty-six men in front and I was one of them. Just before we entered the finishing straight I noticed that my rear tyre was deflating ever so slowly. There was no question of changing a wheel so close to the finish, so I carried on. I started the sprint early to avoid being boxed in; the tyre was softening but holding. The Polish rider Lech Piasecki passed me like a bomb but as the line approached, no one else arrived and I thought: 'Christ I'm going to get a medal.' But then a Danish rider, Weltz, passed, then a Belgian, another Dane and an Italian, Maurizio Fondriest. I crossed the line and counted. Six. Sixth in the world. The sixth best amateur in the whole fucking world. I was overjoyed. It was the summit of my career.

I watched the pros ride next day. I visited the pits after the race and received congratulations from Roche, Kelly and Earley. Kelly was the last to leave for his hotel. A man of few words, he turned to me just before getting into the team car, and said, 'De Gribaldy will be talking to you.' This was music to my ears and I returned to Wasquehal a happy man. I met 'de Gri' on the eve of the pro-am classic, the Grand Prix d'Isbergues, at the small hotel where his team was staying. He made me wait for half an hour but then sat down beside me at a table in the bar. He looked at me and said I would have to lose some weight and then asked me some details, including my age. I had expected him to produce a contract for me to sign and had already decided I would not sign for less than £600 a month – de Gri was a notoriously bad payer. But he produced no contract and made no promises. He just said we would meet again after the race, which I was riding with the Irish national team. Three-quarters of the way through I was following French pro Jacques Bossis down a narrow gravel-lined descent. There was a sharp right-hand bend at the bottom, which I failed to round and ran off the road. The front wheel dropped into a sharp dip in the ditch, throwing me over the handlebars, and I landed face down at the roadside. I don't remember much, just the pain from my back and left wrist and the sensation that someone had kicked me in the mouth. I spent five days in hospital in Béthune with a fractured vertebra and left wrist. I had expected de Gri to call at the hospital with my contract, but he never came. I left hospital dejected. Raphael packed my things and we went home to Ireland – to wait.

The phone rang six weeks later. It was Mollet. He was sending me a professional contract with a new French team, RMO. I would be paid £700 a month and the contract was for two years. I put the phone down and danced a jig of joy. The struggling was over. All the sacrifices had paid off. I had made it.

7

BRAND-NEW ANORAK

The first team meeting took place at a ski station at Grand Bornand, on the slopes of the Col de Colombier. RMO, a firm specialising in temporary employment, gathered together the eighteen cyclists who would wear their colours in the professional peloton for 1986. It was a mixed bunch of old-timers, established names and new pros, four of whom had been taken on. Two, Jean-Louis Peillon and Bruno Huger, were French. Per Pedersen was Danish and I was Irish. It was hard for Pedersen and me to integrate. He spoke no French, and shyness prevented me from using the bit that I knew. I spoke only when I was spoken to and tried to smile as much as possible. I wanted desperately to be accepted. I felt so awkward, so out of place, just like my first day in school.

In the mornings we would ski cross-country. I had never skied before and spent the whole week slipping on my arse. This helped my integration as I was a source of constant amusement to the suave French, who had learned to ski in childhood. I tried to fall as little as possible, not because I was afraid of getting laughed at but because it was excruciatingly painful. The vertebra I had broken while riding my last amateur race three months earlier had not quite healed. No one knew I had cracked a vertebra, and I wasn't telling them. I had fought all my life for this pro contract and I feared that the revelation of a back problem might discourage my new sponsor from employing me. So I said nothing and secretly skied with a steel corset strapped to my back for support. In the afternoons we were free to do what we pleased. The French lads invited me for football, but fearing for my back I hired a mountain bike and cycled to the top of the Colombier alone. I had never seen such an enormous climb and was so overawed by the view that I wandered off the road, plunged down a sharp incline and went over the bars, landing on the steel corset. I went numb with pain. Picking myself up, I quickly descended the Col and took refuge in a small tearoom in the village.

I was half-way through a *brioche chaude* when one of the French guys came in. I tried to hide, as I was enjoying my solitude and was in no humour for making small talk; but he saw me and sat at my table. He ordered a cake and coffee and we chatted amiably. He liked the ambience in the team and said the absence of real stars would mean we would get on so much better. He paid for both of us, and as he walked out the door I tried to put a name to his face. It was Chappuis – André Chappuis. I immediately took a shine to him.

The evenings were taken up with team talks. Bernard Thevenet our team manager, or *directeur sportif*, gathered us round after dinner and explained the early season programme of racing, ironing out any problems we might have. I never had any. As far as I was concerned, it was all a game of survival. Two years spent as an amateur in France had taught me to keep my mouth closed and my ears open and to pedal as quickly as I could. I decided to adopt the same tactics as a professional, at least until I understood what it was all about.

After the meetings we were free to do as we pleased. The French played cards among themselves, I chatted with Pedersen and, without realising it, two clans were formed. I returned to Dublin on 23 December with a jersey, a bag and a red anorak, all adorned with my sponsors' logo, RMO. I didn't dare ask them for the travelling expenses for the trip. I was afraid they might change their mind about hiring me – I was so naïve. But

BRAND-NEW ANORAK

I was a pro. The bag, the jersey and the red anorak said so. I wore them whenever the occasion presented itself, it was my way of saying: 'Look at me, I'm a pro, I've made it.'

This was my first mistake.

8

SHATTERED DREAMS

January was spent in Ireland, preparing. The broken wrist and vertebra had left me immobile for most of the winter and as a result my physical condition suffered. I trained most weekends with my brothers, Raphael and Kevin, and I was a little concerned as both of them were riding more strongly than I was. I trained twice with Martin Earley and Stephen Roche. Stephen had ridden with five of my team-mates, Gauthier, Claveyrolat, Le Bigaut, Simon and Vermote, the year before on the La Redoute team. He recommended Jean-Louis Gauthier as the most dependable, and praised him as being one of the best *domestiques* he had ever had. I made a mental note of this; for Stephen, a perfectionist who demanded perfection from everyone around him, did not distribute praise for others easily. This Gauthier must really be good.

We talked of other things, of drugs. I was worried about the job I was going into. I had heard so many stories of professional cyclists taking drugs and was frightened that they might all be true. Now that I was a professional I felt I had the right to ask Stephen to enlighten me on the subject. He talked first of our two *soigneurs*. The verb *soigner* means 'to treat' or 'to take care of'. A s*oigneur* takes care of his riders by massaging their legs, listening to their problems, dressing wounds and giving vitamins and minerals. Stephen had worked with Claude Wery and Emile Thiery at La Redoute. He said that Claude was a bit lazy, he preferred Emile and told me he would ask him to take me under his wing. He said that professional cycling was not like amateur cycling – one had to take care of oneself. The racing was so hard and frequent that it was important to keep up the vitamin and mineral level in the body, and to do this vitamin B_6 and B_{12} injections during the season were a necessity. I said nothing and just nodded my head, but inside I was horrified. In my mind a syringe was drugs, and to have to take injections meant having to take drugs. I returned home and talked to my father about my fears. He told me just to do the best that I could without getting caught up in it and I put it out of my mind.

On Tuesday 4 February I made my professional debut at the Etoile de Bessèges stage race in the south of France. I arrived late the night before and was handed a new bike and all my equipment on the morning of the race. I was also handed my wages for January, a cheque for £700. I was shitting bricks before the start. The bike was all wrong, but there was no time to change and I raced the 100 kilometres feeling like an alien. It was strange to be riding alongside Fignon and Zootemelk. The previous five years I had been a star, a top amateur, recognised and admired. Now I was just another one in the bunch. Everything I had ever done now meant nothing and I was starting all over again at the bottom of the ladder. My two worries were crashing and bringing a star off, and getting dropped, and I managed to avoid both.

Later in the evening I bumped into my team-mate Regis Simon while taking a leak in the bathroom. He was bent over the bathroom sink scrubbing the jersey and shorts made filthy by the wet roads earlier in the day. I almost laughed and asked him why he was washing his clothes by hand. 'Why, who else will wash them for me?' was his reply. I had always thought the gear would be washed for us – but no, we had to scrub it and dry it ourselves, so I borrowed his washing powder and set to work. It was the hardest part of the day.

Bessèges, being the first stage race of the year, was not too hard and I managed to finish in the bunch most days. It felt great to be encouraged in the time trial by Thevenet, a double Tour de France winner, whose photograph had adorned my bedroom wall when I was a child. The only real problem was the bitterly cold weather. The team rode well; Per was riding really strongly, and he took the race lead with one day to go. It would have been great publicity for a new team, RMO, to win the first race of the season; but his advance was slim and that night Thevenet was forced to telephone the other *directeurs sportifs* to try to do a deal. The idea was to offer money to a rival team, who did not have a man well placed overall, in return for help to defend a jersey. If the team accepted, then for the following stage RMO would defend the lead alone until they could no longer control it, and then it was time for the others to earn their money. This was no surprise to me, for as an amateur I had ridden stage races and seen leaders in trouble with no team-mates to control things, only for a rival team suddenly to intervene and restore order. I suppose it was just good business sense, for if there was one thing I was learning it was that pro cycling was a business. Before each race we were told how much of a bonus we would receive from the sponsor for winning, and how much of this bonus we could use to negotiate with other riders if we got into a winning position near the end of a race.

All of our rival French teams had men well placed for overall victory and none were interested in doing a deal. The next option was to approach a Belgian or Dutch team, but this was dismissed. The Belgians, and especially the Dutch, were really mercenary bastards. They would do the job, but the price was always very high and for a small race like Bessèges it was not worth it. So the pressure was on us to defend Per's lead alone. I did what I could, but it was bitterly cold and I couldn't feel my legs at all. My drinking bottle froze solid and I abandoned the race when I was dropped, with forty kilometres to go. Per lost the lead but wasn't too disappointed, for it was a great debut for a new pro.

The Tour of the Mediterranean was next. This was limited to eight riders per team and I was surprised when Thevenet announced the selection as I did not think I was worth my place on my Bessèges form. I wasn't; it was just the fact that Pedersen was riding so well. He spoke no French and Thevenet little English, so I was brought along as interpreter. It was during the Med that my problems really started. I was four kilos over-weight and, as a result, suffering like a dog on the climbs. But I still managed to hang on, only to be left behind on the descents. The memory of my crash at Isbergues was still fresh in my mind and it scared me. I had lost my bottle. I wasn't too bad in the dry, but in the wet I was a complete disaster and I had to endure the insults from other riders as I let huge gaps open up and they were forced to come around me and close them. This depressed me, and my morale was really bad after two stages of being left behind. On the night after the second stage Thevenet came into my room and asked me what my problem was. I explained to him about the crash, expecting to receive a bit of a bollocking. But no, he was kind and understanding. He too had had the same problem during his career, and he told me to relax more and it would sort itself out. He demanded more par-ticipation from me in helping the team. 'In professional races, the individual does not matter, it is the team that counts. This is now your job, so each time you race you must try and make some sort of contribution to the team. The best way is to win races but this is not always possible so you must contribute in other ways. It may be only a small thing like fetching a bottle or waiting for a colleague who has punctured; but it's impor-tant, for at the end of the day you can get off your bike and say, "Yes I did my work today."' His talk worked wonders on me and from the next day I was riding much better.

It was strange, therefore, to get told off on a day when I felt I had made my biggest contribution. It was on the fourth stage, to Marseille. I was prominent in two early breakaway attempts and then, as we were caught, another group got away with two of our riders Regis Simon and Pierre Le Bigaut. I sat back in the bunch, delighted to have men in the front and the pressure off, but suddenly Thevenet came up in the team car and shouted that he was tired of seeing me at the back and that I was to move to the front to hinder the chasing attempts immediately. Our lads were eventually caught and that night I was given my first official bollocking. I was a bit pissed off, but had to accept it. I was made aware of the need not only to be at the front but to be seen to be at the front. It was another lesson learnt.

Two days after the Med we raced a single day-race, Nice–Alassio. I was knackered after the Med, and asked Thevenet for a day off, but he told me to start and to abandon if I felt too tired. I met Jean de Gribaldy before the start and he told me again that I was overweight and explained what a terrible handicap this was. I nodded in acceptance, but inwardly I was puzzled. These pros were so skinny and bony, almost sick-looking, yet they managed to pedal at unbelievable speeds. I was confused. The race was a disaster for us and the whole team abandoned. Thevenet was angry, but accepted the excuses given to him from the experienced campaigners Gauthier and Le Bigaut that the Med had been especially hard and we were all a little tired. But next day, some smart-arse journalist from *L'Equipe* wrote that not a single rider from the RMO team had made it to Alassio, and that Bernard Thevenet was still out looking for us. This brought an angry response from the team sponsors, who sent a telegram from head office: 'We are not in this business to be laughed at.' Monsieur Braillon, 'Mr RMO', expressed his displeasure at his team's performance to date, and suggested an immediate improvement was imperative and that the next race, the Tour of Haut Var, was a good place to start. This annoyed us greatly, for the opening races were viewed by all as preparation races, and to be criticised by the sponsor after not even three weeks' competition was unfair.

I rode well in the Haut Var, finishing about twenty-fifth, but was really tired after it. That night Emile called me for massage, and as I entered he was giving an injection to the Brazilian rider Ribeiro. He said it was just vitamins and suggested I take one to help me recover. I declined, explaining that I never took injections. He seemed surprised but did not insist. The following day we raced the Grand Prix of Cannes and I was totally shagged. I stopped after a hundred kilometres and climbed into the *soigneurs'* car at the feed. They did not say anything, but had 'I told you so' written all over their faces. I sat in the back and thought about it. My principle was that if the body was tired you gave it rest, not vitamins, and I was sure I'd be fine after a day's rest. That night the team split up, with the riders allowed home for the first time in a month. I had no fixed address in France, but Guy Mollet had offered to let me use a house in Wasquehal where he was going to lodge the foreign amateurs in his team. I felt quite ill before getting on the plane, and the assistant *directeur sportif* Jean-Claude Vallaeys, who lived in Lille, gave me two Alka-Seltzers. Emile, who was travelling on the same flight, suggested it was a problem with my liver – that I had not looked after myself and that this was the result. He produced two small pills to help my liver, and I pretended to take them. Half an hour later I told him I was feeling better, which seemed to please him. I did not want to hurt his feelings, for I knew he was only trying to help; but I just didn't trust him and was suspicious of anything he gave me.

After the glory of racing with the team for the month of February, Wasquehal was an unpleasant shock to the system. The house was totally empty. There was just a bed. No cups or saucers or anything, just a bed. I instantly regretted having come here. The Brazilian was lodged by the team at Grenoble. I had never been there, but was told it was a beautiful city that sat at the foot of the Alps. It appealed to me greatly, but I had finally chosen Wasquehal, whose greyness and Coronation

Street decor I was familiar with, having spent a year there as an amateur.

I was not picked to ride in the Paris–Nice, but I didn't mind as I knew the pressure for results would be high. Instead I was selected for Het Volk, the one-day Belgian classic. I had hated Belgium as an amateur. Too much wind and rain and too many cobbles and flat roads. I dreaded the thought of Het Volk. We stayed at a hotel at Moeskron on the eve of the race, and as I was going to bed I noticed it had started to snow. I prayed that night that it would lash down and my prayers were answered: for the next day the roads were smothered with it and the race was cancelled. I returned to the emptiness of the flat. I had not trained for two days, and it would probably be another two before I got out. As a result my physical condition would drop, which would make the next race even harder. I realised it would have been better to have raced and regretted the cancellation. Twenty-four hours earlier I had prayed for snow. It had snowed and I was now sorry. This did not make sense.

The house filled up during the week, when some Kas riders arrived. Kas was de Gribaldy's team and he had sent three men to Wasquehal to ride in some Belgian races to be held during Paris–Nice. The weather for the first race was dreadful and I abandoned after being dropped quite early. The second race was a kermesse, or circuit race, at Ostend. It was cold, sunny and windy. Former cycling 'great' Freddy Maertens was riding and I could not help noticing what a pathetic sight he was as he took his place on the start grid. He had had it all, this man. It was rumoured he had lost everything through poor investments and that he was penniless and forced to get back on the bike after years in retirement. The race started and we took off like rockets. The fast start surprised me and I was immediately in trouble. Slipping down through the bunch I had almost reached the end of it, going into this corner, when Maertens came up on my inside and nearly lifted me out of it with his elbow. I lost a length, two lengths and was dropped. This was the final straw: to be dropped after six miles was too much to take, and I abandoned and told myself I was finished. I phoned home to my parents' house to talk about my problems. They did not really understand. How could I be disheartened about something I had dreamed all my life of achieving?

The three Kas boys were kind. One of them, Jacques Decrion, offered to take me to his house in Besançon, where I could train with him in the mountains and get my morale back. We rode one more race in Belgium, which I managed to finish and then we left for Besançon. I stayed with Jacques for five days and then we all left for a race near Nantes at Mauleon, where I was to pick up my team. When we arrived at the hotel I got out of the car with my suitcase, briefcase and bicycle. When they saw me my team-mates started laughing at my briefcase. 'Ah, Paul, the briefcase, you're a real warrior all right.' I hadn't got a clue what they were talking about. On visiting the riders' rooms that night I noticed that many had briefcases, but whereas mine contained my passport, letters and writing materials, theirs contained pills, syringes and little bottles of liquids of every colour and shape. 'So that's what they were laughing at, they thought my briefcase was full of pills. They thought I was a fucking junkie. Jesus, I am guilty without even a trial.' I was shocked, and decided to leave my briefcase open in my room so that any passers by would notice it contained papers and pens and wasn't a medical cabinet. Not all the riders had briefcases. André 'Dede' (pronounced 'deaday') Chappuis used to store his gear in an old shoebox he hid in his suitcase.

I asked about the contents and Dede went through the various boxes and pills, explaining what each was for. There were pills for avoiding cramp, for cleaning out the liver, vitamins, caffeine tablets, salts, minerals and small glass tubes of a white liquid he laughed and joked about. He said it was 'du peau' ('skin') a slang word for pervitine. 'Ton ton' and 'tan tan' were slang words for tonedron. I hadn't a clue what he was talking about and my ignorance seemed to make him laugh even harder. 'Amphétamines.' This I did understand. 'But what about the controls?' I asked. 'There are never any controls at Mauleon,' he replied. This point was validated later that evening at the team meeting by Vallaeys, who was looking after us in Thevenet's absence. There were grins all around the room and we left. Vallaeys did not directly encourage us to charge up for the next day, but in reminding us that we were professionals he was giving us the green light. This was worrying.

The peloton was unusually jolly at the start next morning. In the opening kilometres where the atmosphere was relaxed and jovial I noticed a new game being played. Riders were going around and putting their hands in the back pockets of other riders' jerseys. To me it didn't seem all that funny, but they seemed to be finding it hilarious. Someone explained that a rider who was prepared to inject himself with amphetamines had to do so two to two and a half hours from the finish. A normal bike race lasted six to seven hours so it was necessary to carry the amphetamine for three to four hours before using it. It could be taken in tablet form or through injection. Tablet was handy, as it could be carried and taken discreetly; but because it had to pass through the stomach, the effects were slower and not as good. Injection straight into the muscle gave an almost instant reaction and was much stronger, but was awkward because it meant transporting a syringe for most of the race. For transport, the syringe first had to be doctored. It was cut just above the piston that pushed out the liquid and a plastic cap was placed over the needle. Then the syringe was placed in a metal tube, usually a vitamin tube, and a piece of cotton wool pressed in on top to protect it from vibration. The tube was then placed among the fruit cake and other race food in the rider's jersey pocket until the time to use it arrived.

As we rode out of Mauleon the game was to see who had the tube and who hadn't. From the guffaws and laughter it became clear to me that quite a few tubes had been found. This was very disheartening. What chance had I against guys riding on amphetamines? At the time I looked on them as cheats, and as I had always despised cheating I couldn't understand how they could be happy winning, knowing they had taken a stimulant to do so. Try as I might, I couldn't catch anyone actually taking the stuff. I was still convinced I couldn't do anything, so I was content to finish in the bunch.

Because I lived in Wasquehal, fifteen kilometres from the border, Thevenet assumed that I liked racing in Belgium. I was, therefore, a natural choice to dispute the one-day classics that were now imminent. The Tour of Flanders was the first. I raced the first 150 kilometres trying my hardest to get out of the bunch before we reached the series of cobbled climbs near the end, where the race would be blown apart. I tried, but to no avail, and I was forced to remain in the bunch until the approach to the first climb. Twenty kilometres before it the pace started hotting up. Thevenet had told us that unless we were at the front going into the first cobbles then we could forget about it. The problem was that every other rider in the bunch had been told the same thing by their respective *directeurs sportifs*, and the result was absolute mayhem. There was pushing, shoving and shoulder rubbing at forty miles an hour on narrow roads full of holes and other hidden traps such as raised shore covers and ridges. I suddenly realised that all it took was for one rider to fall in this speeding packed bunch to bring 50 per cent of the others with him. I chickened out of trying to stay in the front, and slipped down to the back, where it was much more sociable. I knew that our team car had had a bad draw, so Thevenet was seventeen cars behind and could not possibly see the tail of the field and he therefore was unaware of my presence there. I was soon dropped and I abandoned after just 150 kilometres.

Ghent-Wevelgem was next. The difficulties of this are the crosswinds which blow in from the sea when the race hugs the coastline between Zeebrugge and De Panne. On a cold

Wednesday morning the winds were gale force, blowing sand all over the road as the bunch split into ten large groups on the seafront. I was in about the seventh group but then slipped back to the eighth, the ninth and the tenth. Questioning the point of this madness, I lost contact and was passed by the different team cars. Thevenet drove alongside but it was Vallaeys who rolled down the window. 'What's the problem?' he asked. Now, with the bunch in ten groups and bodies literally everywhere, it seemed perfectly obvious to me what the problem was; but just as I was about to answer another gust of wind blew sand across the road and into his face, blinding him. He quickly rolled up the window without waiting any longer for a reply and I laughed to myself: 'I think he got the message.'

Jean-Claude Vallaeys was not liked among the riders, which made his job of assistant *directeur sportif* very difficult. His problem was that he had never raced and so did not command the same respect from us as Thevenet, who had won the Tour de France twice. Vallaeys had been secretary of the La Redoute team and at paperwork and organisation he was very efficient, but we didn't think he had a clue about pro cycling. How were we supposed to take orders from a man who chain-smoked, and ate like there was no tomorrow? I didn't like him; I found him false and insincere. He often made fun of my efforts to speak French, which I would have accepted if he spoke English – but he hadn't a word. It was a mystery to me how a guy like Vallaeys could be at the head of a professional cycling team.

Two days after Ghent I abandoned the Grand Prix Pino Cerami in Belgium. It was a vicious circle. I needed a stage race to build up strength for the classics. But as I had not ridden Paris–Nice I was unprepared for these savage one-day events and was unable to ride much further then half-way in most of them. In between races we stayed at a hotel in Moeskron, where they served the most gigantic juicy steaks, and we ate like kings; but we raced like juniors, and the result was that my condition deteriorated instead of improved. There was also the mental side of it. Not finishing races was a bad habit that was becoming addictive. When it snowed or rained or was freezing cold, as it often was for the classics, it was all too easy to abandon the bike for the warmth of the *soigneurs'* car. Once in the car the remorse would start. The self-analysis that led to deep depression. Finishing races instilled confidence and self-respect. Abandoning destroyed both.

Two days after Cerami we drove to Compiègne for Paris–Roubaix. The weather was atrocious, and I wondered if the race would be cancelled as it was snowing heavily as we went to bed. The La Vie Claire team were staying in the same hotel and during the night one of their new professionals, the American Thurlow Rogers, left his room and the hotel without saying a word. The next day the story was that he had cracked and was returning to the States. The hardened Europeans found this very amusing, but I understood how he felt and often considered doing the same. On this cold, wet morning it was easy to make such decisions. It was snowing in Compiègne when we rode out of the cobbled square and I knew there was no way I was going to make it to Roubaix. The tactic was simple: try to get the hell out of the bunch before crossing the first *pavé*. I attacked several times in the first hundred kilometres without success and as we approached the first *pavé*, the pace shot up as the big guns moved to the front, while the small fry like myself slipped to the back. I bumped into Kelly. He was on the way up and I was on the way down. For him the race was now starting; for me it was over. The enormous gap in our abilities became apparent to me.

There was a huge crash just before the first section, and I fell off without hurting myself. I met Dede at the bottom of the tangled mess. He had lumps out of him, so I waited and then we chased together. At the exit of the first *pavé* we were seven minutes behind the leaders and we abandoned almost immediately. We climbed into the broom wagon and were brought to the showers, where I washed and changed in time to see 'King Kelly' win his second Paris–Roubaix.

It was obvious to me that I needed to take drastic action to climb out of the pit into which I had fallen. Thevenet was not pleased with my performances and after a long discussion I told him I wanted to leave Wasquehal and move to Grenoble. The head office of RMO was based in the Alpine town, and five of the team's cyclists lived in the region. The only problem would be a place to stay. RMO sponsored the Grenoble football team and also a training centre for its apprentices. Thevenet rang the centre and they agreed to lodge me until I could find an apartment. The thought of getting out of Wasquehal worked wonders on me. A week after Paris–Roubaix we rode Liège–Bastogne–Liège. In freezing cold rain Bruno Huger and I were the only two riders to finish from our team. Only sixty riders finished and Thevenet praised me for my courage – it was the first good word he had had for me in a month. Not that I blamed him, for I had abandoned seven races on the trot, but I felt sure the run was at an end. For finishing forty-eighth I managed to get my name in *L'Equipe*. This may seem trivial, but it was quite important. Monsieur Braillon would buy the sports daily every morning and scrutinise the results to find where his men had finished. By having my name in print, I proved to him that I was earning my keep, which would make it easier for him to sign my pay cheque at the end of each month.

Grenoble was sunny, bright and beautiful. From the first glimpse of the city I knew I had made the right decision. Things would now get better and I felt a page had turned.

9
GRENOBLE

I like to think that I am a survivor. I've always had good survival instincts. Moving from Lille to Grenoble was not just a matter of a change of scenery: it was essential. The two months spent at Wasquehal had given me time to analyse my situation. Because I lived so close to Belgium, they thought I liked racing there. I hated it. By living so close to Vallaeys, I was under his thumb, one of his boys. I didn't like him; and, worse, he knew I disliked him, so it seemed to me he was never going to do me any favours. I had to get out. 'Go south, young man.'

Grenoble was the hub of the team. The firm's headquarters, the team's headquarters, the decision-making, all were here. France is a huge country. The flight time from Lille to Grenoble is the same as between Paris and Dublin. So to Thevenet it was all the same if I lived in Dublin or Lille; either way, I was a foreigner. Now, if I were a foreigner like Stephen Roche or Sean Kelly and could pedal my bike faster than anyone else in the world, then my sponsor and *directeur* would bend over backwards to please me, no matter where I lived. But being Paul Kimmage was different. I knew that once my two-year contract was terminated they would look at me and say, 'Well, Kimmage is Irish but he's not Roche or Kelly; he's an ordinary solid pro but why bother hiring a foreigner when we can hire a hundred Frenchmen with the same ability?' I knew this would happen, so I had to get close to them. Living in Grenoble would enable me to keep my finger on the pulse of all that was happening in the team. I had to integrate as much as possible, make them forget that I was Irish. I told them I loved France and especially Grenoble and that I was going to remain here long after my career was finished.

This wasn't a complete lie. I did like the region, and as I knew that there would be very few job opportunities in Ireland for a not too famous ex-professional cyclist, there was a good chance that I would stay on. But still, I must admit to playing the role of Uriah Heep quite well. I should have been given an Oscar.

It worked. I had only spent two days in the city when a man from the company invited me to dinner at his house. Marc Mingat worked in the firm's public relations department and was ideally placed to fill me in on Marc Braillon's moods and humours. Mingat would give me the feedback on Braillon's meetings with Thevenet, so that I always knew the temperature of the water before taking a bath. I was invited to assist at the openings of any new company offices in the area. Braillon would be present at these, and I always made sure I was well dressed without being flashy. Braillon didn't like anyone too flashy. It was rumoured that one day Braillon was looking out the window of his office and saw one of his employees arrive in a huge, flashy car. He fired him. Braillon himself drove a Mercedes 300 but it was a drab mustard colour; it was classy but not extravagant, and he expected his employees to follow suit. There was one golden rule never to be broken: in our interviews with the press we were to talk not so much of the company but of the company chief. We were to talk not of RMO but of Marc Braillon.

I shared a room at the football club with the Brazilian Mauro Ribeiro. Like me, he was a new professional. He spoke excellent French but with a very heavy Latin American accent. By moving to Grenoble at the start of the year he got to know the other French riders in the area much better than me. But this was a double-edged sword, for they also got to know him. He wasn't liked. I learnt this from Thierry Claveyrolat and Patrick Clerc. Thierry was a former team-mate of Stephen Roche's at La Redoute. He lived in the village of Vizille, twelve kilometres outside Grenoble. Patrick had raced with Sean Kelly at Sem; he lived at Brignoud, north of the city. Both had trained regularly and had travelled to races with Ribeiro since the start of the season and complained that he was always the last to put his hand in his pocket when it came to paying for coffee on the way to a race. When I told them I was sharing a room with him they gave me an awful slagging and, wanting desperately to be accepted, I abandoned any notion of defending him and decided to play along. I didn't like him anyway. When I saw him taking a vitamin injection after the Haut-Var race in February, I instantly branded him a junkie even though this was unfair. He was, however, tight with his money. It's funny but because he never spent much, I assumed he didn't have much. And because I was a better rider, I assumed I was better paid; so I was always prepared to pick up the tab when it came to buying papers, cakes and coffee. But I was wrong; he was just tight.

I learnt this in a conversation with Marc Mingat. Marc informed me that Ribeiro was paid £500 a month more than I was and had two return flights to Brazil paid for by Braillon each year. Braillon had an office in Rio de Janeiro and it was good PR to have a Brazilian on the team, so when Ribeiro came on the market he was snapped up. This revelation turned me completely against Ribeiro, and I told the others the news – which turned them against him also. This was a mistake and very petty of me, but survival was the name of the game and the revelation would gain me some extra points.

A week after moving to Grenoble we flew to Holland for the Amstel Gold Race. It was a bit like Liège–Bastogne–Liège and I rode really well, finishing as the top rider on the team, in twenty-first place. Two important stage races were approaching, the Quatre Jours de Dunkirk and the Tour de Romandie.

I knew I was starting to find good form and I desperately wanted to ride in the Romandie. Dunkirk would be cobbles and crosswinds and I knew I would be much more suited to the hard climbs and more sheltered roads of Switzerland. In stage races teams were limited in the number of riders they could enter. At Dunkirk it was eight and at Romandie six. There were eighteen riders on the team, but places for only fourteen, which meant four would remain at home without racing. Not racing meant having to train each day alone. There was no way of simulating racing so inevitably the rider's condition would drop, making it hard for him to impress when he raced again. I didn't want to ride in Dunkirk but it was better than being at home. Thevenet explained he was sending all his pure climbers to Switzerland and that I should be grateful to ride in Dunkirk, as four riders would ride in neither race. I wanted to argue that I was a pure climber, for I felt I was, but decided to say nothing. Dunkirk was better than nothing.

I rode poorly all week except for the last day, when we had a hilly circuit race around the town of Cassel. Here, I was given instructions to go up the climb as hard as possible. My team-mate Regis Simon was lying second overall to the Belgian Dirk de Wolf and we thought the heavily built Fleming might crack on the steep but short slopes of Cassel. I gave it everything I had and split the bunch to bits, but we could not get rid of De Wolf, and Regis finished second.

A week later we were in Bordeaux for the marathon Bordeaux–Paris where the format had been changed since my debut the year before. The old tradition of the twenty-minute break at Poitiers where we had stopped to link up with our motorbike pacers had been abandoned and it was to be run along the same lines as the other one-day classics. On the morning of the race we went out for a light spin in the vineyards. Wine didn't mean much to me at the time, and the team leader Bernard Vallet couldn't believe my lack of enthusiasm as we rode through Margaux past some of the best and most expensive wine châteaux in the world. His excitement about wine amused me. Back in Ireland wine was what the priest poured into the chalice every Sunday. Guinness, now, that was a real drink. I couldn't understand this Frenchman nearly bursting into tears about us riding around a few fancy houses and fields of grapes. But his passion was obviously real, and in an effort to impress on me the value of the vineyards he said, 'Polo,' (this was my nickname) 'if you owned forty feet of that land you would never have to throw your leg over a bike again.' At lunchtime he ordered a good bottle of red which I found no more than OK, but after that I started to take an interest. Now I am a wine fanatic. Margaux, Rothschild and Yquem are châteaux I cherish, although their outrageous prices mean they aren't often enjoyed in our house.

Bernard Vallet had prepared especially for Bordeaux–Paris and at the team meeting two hours before the race Thevenet insisted that all our efforts were to be directed towards helping him. We raced out of Bordeaux in the black of night, each rider with a set of front and back lamps. Visibility was a problem and our eyes were strained to distance ourselves properly from the wheel in front. The crack was good though, some of the lads would turn off their lamps and try to sneak off without being seen. It is a bastard of a race. I started to fall asleep on the bike at around seven next morning when we had ridden 300 kilometres. It seems an exaggeration, but it's not. My eyelids were so desperately heavy that my head would keep falling forward, until I realised what was happening and woke up. Caffeine tablets would have been the answer but as I was 'pure' and regarded this as doping, they were out of the question. An important break developed near the end of the race with just Patrick Clerc from our team present. Thevenet ordered Dede and me to the front to chase it down. We had to ride our eyeballs out to bring it back, but we did; and then a fresh attack developed but this time Vallet was there. Dede and I were dropped thirty kilometres from Paris and we immediately got into the team cars. As an amateur the objective had been to finish. As a professional it was to win, or help someone else to win. Our work was done and there was nothing to be gained in struggling on to Paris. To say I was tired was an understatement. I had been in the team car two minutes when I fell asleep. I showered and we got a taxi to the airport, where I slept again. I slept on the flight to Grenoble, in the taxi to the football club, and as soon as I arrived I went straight to bed. My fascination with Bordeaux–Paris was now over and it was definitely a case of never again.

The Dauphine Libérée stage race was fast approaching. Nine days long and with stages climbing some of the biggest mountains in the Alps it is the second biggest stage race in the country after the Tour. But because it took place in RMO's back garden, i.e. in the Grenoble region, it was equally important to our beloved sponsor. This was the reason Thevenet gave for leaving me out of the team. He wanted the best nine possible and I was no higher than twelfth on the team ladder. I accepted the decision, and prepared myself to ride the Tour de l'Oise, a short, three-day event which took place at the same time. A week before the Dauphine, Thevenet organised a training run over one of the Alpine stages and invited me along. It was my first opportunity to attempt the really big climbs, and I was excited to find out about what until then had only been photographs on a bedroom wall. Thierry Claveyrolat was the team's best climber, but I managed to stay with him almost to the top on three of the mountains and he was surprised I was climbing so well. Two days later one of the selections, the veteran Jean-Louis Gauthier, pulled out of the team, leaving a place vacant. Thevenet had heard that I had climbed well in the training run against Claveyrolat and offered me the berth.

The race started with a prologue time trial on the shores of the beautiful lake at Annecy, then moved across to Lyon, St Etienne and then back across to Chambéry, Albertville and Grenoble. On the third stage to St Etienne, Thierry Claveyrolat outsprinted Laurent Fignon for a prestigious stage victory. By winning a stage, Thierry had saved the team's honour on its home ground. The pressure was now off, and we could enjoy things just a little bit more. A plan was drawn up for the following stage to Charavines, where we reckoned our sprinter Francis Castaing had a good chance. Castaing was perfectly led out by Regis Simon, Vincent Barteau and Pierre Le Bigaut and looked set for the win, but then the La Vie Claire sprinter Jean-François Rault moved up on his shoulder. Sensing Rault's presence, Castaing moved across, pushing the Breton into the barriers, but Rault quite rightly refused to be intimidated and stuck his elbow into Castaing to protect himself. Castaing insisted and they both crashed at forty miles an hour. Le Bigaut, Simon and Barteau could not avoid the two bodies sprawled across the road and they fell also. That night Castaing was heavily criticised for his unprofessional behaviour. Le Bigaut and Barteau were knocked out and missed the remainder of the race. By endangering the lives of his team-mates Castaing had committed a professional fault.

I was riding very well and was lying seventeenth after the first mountain stage to Chambéry, but I cracked badly on the third climb the following day and slipped to thirty-fourth. I cracked completely on the last mountain stage from Grenoble to Puy St Vincent, but no one noticed too much for Thierry won the stage, and Thevenet waited patiently for the forty minutes it took me to finish. He patted me on the back, and then brought me to the medical caravan: I had been picked for a dope control. The seven-hour stage in the hot sun had left me dehydrated, and I found it difficult to piss. But beer and water were available and after a fifteen-minute delay I felt the urge. I was given a clear glass flask and told to strip. The prying eyes of the commissar surveyed me as I tried to piss and at first this irritated me. Then I tried not to think of him and imagined waterfalls and flushing toilets, and at last the clear yellow urine started flowing. I watched as he split my sample into two small bottles then gave each a code, which I chose, and the bottles were sealed with candle-wax, one for analysis, the other to be opened for a second analysis if the first was positive. I never heard any more about it so I presumed I was negative. Effervescent vitamin tablets and glass tubes of minerals and iron were all I had given myself, but even so I felt afraid – afraid that there would be some mix-up in the samples and I would be found positive. I could see myself outraged and proclaiming my innocence with no one listening. For no one ever listened to a 'positive' protesting his innocence. The shame of it! I imagined the headlines in the papers back in Dublin. KIMMAGE TAKES DRUGS. Oh, the shame of it! I was thankful that I was pure and sure I was negative.

The race finished next day. Clavet was leading a competition for the first rider under the 'kilometre to go' flag. Sponsored by Fiat, the winner would receive a car, a Uno. To assure victory he had to make sure he won the last sprint. I had ridden well for him throughout the race, helping him wherever I could. With ten kilometres to go on the last stage he asked me to lead him out for the sprint. Castaing, Barteau, Le Bigaut, Mas and Vallet had all abandoned, leaving just four riders from the team still in the race. I was taken aback when he asked me because bunch sprinting was not my forte, but I agreed without hesitation. My job was to bring him to the front with a kilometre to go and then open the sprint for him. It was hard trying to get to the front and I felt sure I was going to crash as I tried to squeeze my way through the tightly packed bodies, but I hit the front at just the right time and on his prompting, 'Allez!' I opened the sprint. I was so pleased at having done everything right that I nearly forgot the idea was not for *me* to win, but Claveyrolat. He was following me but having difficulty in passing. Luckily, I remembered just in time and pulled across. Thierry won the prize and was lavish in his praise for my efforts. It had been a hard nine days but I had come through it well. Thevenet was pleased with my contribution, and for the first time I started to think about the possibility of riding the Tour de France.

A week later we rode the Grand Prix de Plumelec in Brittany. Clavet, Dede and I were provided with a team car. We drove the 1,000 kilometres to Plumelec on Saturday, rode the 200-kilometre race on Sunday and then hopped straight back into the car for the long drive home, arriving at half-past four in the morning. Clavet and I both rode well; he was sixth, I was eighth and morale was high on the long return to base. This was the hardest part about being a pro – the travelling. The hours spent in cars and airports. But the Plumelec trip was great fun, for Dede was in great form and he kept us entertained with his never-ending stories of the crashes he has had in his cars. He had written off twenty cars in different accidents but each time he returned to drive as madly as ever. He is fearless and his philosophy of death is, 'The day, the date, it's all written down.'

I was given two weeks off after Plumelec so I did some light training and spent my spare time wandering around the shops in Grenoble. The football centre was starting to get me down. There was no privacy and the young footballers were a bunch of ill-mannered, undisciplined louts. Ribeiro seemed to get on quite well with them, which puzzled me and turned me against him even more.

It was at this time that we learnt that Patrick Clerc had been sacked. A few years earlier Patrick had been one of the classiest *domestiques* in the peloton. But a year before joining RMO he had had a poor season with the Spanish team Fagor, and they had not extended his contract. Thevenet contacted him about joining RMO, but on certain conditions. Before signing his one-year contract he was made to write a letter of resignation. In this way the sponsors craftily worked their way around a French Federation rule according to which the minimum length of a contract was a year. Because Patrick had not performed for the first half of the season, his letter of resignation was produced and he was fired. He was quite bitter when he rode his last race, the Midi Libre stage race, with us. I couldn't help getting the impression that in some way he resented us, as if we were responsible for what had happened.

It was during the Midi Libre that I learnt I had been selected for the Tour. I was really pleased, for I had been hoping ever since the Dauphine. Now it was official. Back in Grenoble I planned some big training spins that took in some of the Tour's biggest climbs: Lauteret, Galibier, Granon and Izoard. I took notes on the gradient, surface and gear requirement for each mountain, convinced this could be a help three weeks later. I set my heart on winning one of these mountain stages, for in my mind I was still a climber.

A week before the Tour we rode a four-day stage race in Brittany. We were told to take it easy, and to use it as training, but I was feeling good. On the first stage I managed to get into a break of seven riders and we sprinted out the stage win between us. I led into the last corner with the finish 200 metres slightly uphill. As I cornered, my right pedal hit the ground, lifting the back wheel and as it landed the rear tyre rolled off and I slid into the gutter. I escaped with a few scrapes, but I was disgusted, for I had felt sure of at least finishing third. The stage was marked by Bernard Hinault abandoning the race. He sat at the back of the bunch from the start and frowned whenever anyone came near him. The 'Blaireau' was a weird fellow: he frightened me. I was always afraid of crashing in front of him and bringing him down. Sometimes he would attack and the bunch would string out in a long line behind him. Then he would sit up and start laughing, mocking us. He had a certain presence, a sort of godlike aura. He was a great champion, but I didn't like him.

There were just five days before the start of the Tour after the Armorique. As the Tour was starting in Paris and we had to be at the hotel two days before the start, Stephen Roche invited me to stay with him for the three days between the two races. I had planned to take it easy, but it was never easy to train with Stephen and I can remember feeling very uncomfortable at his side on our training rides. He had had a lousy year, with his knee giving him all sorts of problems, and was unsure about riding the Tour until the last minute when he said 'Yes'. As the countdown to the Tour started, I began to feel more and more nervous. There would be three Irishmen in the Tour: Martin Earley riding for Fagor, Stephen for Carrera and myself riding for RMO. There should have been four, but a crash in the Tour of Switzerland had ruled out Sean Kelly. As we drove into Paris I felt my rendezvous with destiny was arriving. I had dreamt of this as a kid. Now it was here.

10

TOUR DE FRANCE

Friday, 4 July 1986
Prologue: Boulogne Billancourt (4.6 kilometres TT)
Stage winner: Thierry Marie (France)
Race leader: Thierry Marie

Today was special. The crowds, the atmosphere, the size of the race all hit me for the first time. I rode a lousy prologue – I was far too nervous. Nearly fell off the ramp as I was cycling down it, and I couldn't feel my legs. I'm rooming with Barteau, which is a bit of a pain because nobody on the team wants to room with him. Oh well, I suppose somebody had to draw the short straw. He is a bit of a mouth and is still living off his 1984 Tour, when he held the *maillot jaune* for thirteen stages. We were given five new jerseys, five new pairs of shorts and five new pairs of gloves. The waiter asked me if I could get him a pair of gloves as a souvenir. These fellows have no idea.

TOUR DE FRANCE

Saturday, 5 July
Stage 1: Nanterre to Sceaux (85 kilometres)
Stage 2: Meudon to St-Quentin-en-Yvelines (55
kilometres Team Time Trial)
Stage 1 winner: Pol Verschure (Belgium)
Stage 2 winner: Systeme U
Race leader: Thierry Marie (France)

Today was a split stage. In the morning we had an 88-kilometre road stage around the streets of Paris, and in the afternoon a 55-kilometre team time trial. The bunch is huge, 210 starters, and I found it hard to stay at the front. There were a lot of crashes but I avoided them all. I should have worn a crash hat, but it's no good for the image. The team time trial was hard. I rode strongly and never missed a turn. Barteau was dropped near the end, was outside the time limit and has been eliminated. Tonight there was a big row between Thevenet and Barteau in the hotel. Barteau was angry that the team didn't wait for him when he ran into difficulty. Thevenet replied that he must have ridden the last ten kilometres at two kilometres an hour to get eliminated. Barteau told the press that Thevenet was a bad *directeur sportif*. Thevenet replied that he might not be the world's greatest *directeur sportif*, but it was a fact that he couldn't find anyone in the team who wanted to share a room with Barteau. No one said anything at the dinner table about Barteau's elimination but secretly we were all glad. He has gone home now, and I guess that means I will be getting a new room-mate. 'It's an ill wind . . .'

Sunday, 6 July
Stage 3: Levallois-Perret to Liévin (214 kilometres)
Stage winner: Davis Phinney (USA)
Race leader: Thierry Marie

We left Paris this morning, going north to the industrial mining town of Liévin near Lille. Before the start it was bucketing down. We, the English speakers Yates, Lauritzen, Earley, were sheltering inside a tent drinking coffee. The mood was sombre as we contemplated six hours in the rain. Paul Sherwen, a veteran of seven Tours but now working for Channel 4, came over to our table and sat down. He looked at our faces and knew exactly what we were thinking. 'Never mind lads, only four more Sundays to go.' At first I laughed but then started thinking about it – and Christ, he was right: there were four more Sundays to go, and for the first time the horrific length of the race hit me. Punctured near the finish but was going well and had no trouble getting back on. The rain stopped almost as soon as we left Paris, but my gear was still filthy. Had to scrub it over the bathroom sink. It's desperately hard trying to get the stains out of these white jerseys. God, I'm starting to sound like an old one in an ad for washing powder. Am rooming with Jean-Louis Gauthier. He doesn't say much, but he showed me a great way of wringing out the wet jersey. You roll it up in a bathroom towel and wring it hard. It comes out nearly dry. Only three more Sundays.

Monday, 7 July
Stage 4: Liévin to Evreux (243 kilometres)
Stage winner: Pello Ruiz-Cabestany (Spain)
Race leader: Dominique Gaigne (France)

Our man Regis Simon made a great effort today. He broke away alone for over 100 kilometres and was caught just fifteen kilometres from the line. The finish was so incredibly hard, everyone was flat out. Tried to do some blocking for Regis and nearly got into a fight with some of Stephen's Carrera team, but Stephen told me I was in the wrong so I backed down. I noticed that the Belgian rider Eddy Schepers never leaves his side. He protects him from the wind, and when it's not windy he watches him like a faithful watchdog surveys its master, waiting for the next command. I wish I were Schepers.

Tuesday, 8 July
Stage 5: Evreux to Villers-sur-Mer (124.5 kilometres)
Stage winner: Johan Van de Velde (Netherlands)
Race leader: Johan Van de Velde

A strange thing happened tonight. There was a knock on the door just before dinner and I answered it. It was someone wanting to see Jean-Louis so I let him in. There was something about him: I knew I had seen him before somewhere. It came to me just as Jean-Louis introduced us: 'Raymond Martin'. In 1980 this man had been third best climber and won a stage in this very race. Then, he and Jean-Louis had been team-mates. Now Martin was working for a sock manufacturer. He asked Jean-Louis about his plans for the future when he retired at the end of the year. Jean-Louis had no idea what he was going to do, he just hoped something interesting would turn up. And then it dawned on me that one day I too would have to return to normal life. My childhood fantasy of earning enough money on which to live happily ever after went out of the window as Martin spoke.

Jean-Louis Gauthier. He is an extraordinary fellow, so honest. He says this will be his last Tour. In 1980 he won a stage, in 1983 he held the yellow jersey and yet he still has regrets. He regrets that he never cycled down the Champs Elysées in the service of the winner of the Tour de France.

The first night I don't think we exchanged more than two words, just 'Goodnight', and then 'Good morning'. I didn't know him too well before the race. I just knew that he was our best *domestique*, that he was the oldest rider and respected by everyone on the team. Everyone except Bernard Vallet. He didn't like Vallet and I found this hard to understand. He must have liked me for we have roomed together for three days now. I know if he disliked me I'd have been put somewhere else. The second night we talked a bit more and then a bit more and now I feel totally at ease with him. He is very helpful. When Martin left, I asked him about his decision to stop at the end of the season and if he would leave the sport content. He replied that he was unhappy with his career. In 1983 he had had a great year and received lots of good offers to move to other teams. But he was a loyal person and he stuck with his old sponsor. He realised now that this was a mistake. He said that in the last few years he had lost the will to win, had become too comfortable in the role of *domestique* and had been too satisfied helping others. I suppose it happens. If you work as a *domestique* long enough you end up losing the urge to win for yourself. I made a mental note to avoid this happening to me.

Wednesday, 9 July
Stage 6: Villers-sur-Mer to Cherbourg (200 kilometres)
Stage winner: Guido Bontempi (Italy)
Race leader: Johan Van de Velde

Today was incredible. From the drop of the flag we went like hell. At times I was hanging on by the skin of my teeth right down the back of the bunch. You know you are at the back because you hear the engines of over a hundred cars and motorbikes following the peloton. It's very irritating because you get the impression that they are all looking at you. I was more than happy to arrive in the coastal town, still in the bunch. Had tea with my cousin Theresa Byrne and her husband Mick this evening at the hotel. Nice to get a bit of support.

Thursday, 10 July
Stage 7: Cherbourg to St-Hilaire-du-Harcouet (201 kilometres)
Stage winner: Ludo Peeters (Belgium)
Race leader: Jorgen Pedersen (Denmark)

Ninth! Ninth on a stage of the Tour de France. Today I justified my existence. This was what it's all for. This was the thrill of professional cycling. To be in the front of the race in a twelve-man break. To have Messieurs Levitan and Goddet behind you in their red race directors' car. To have the helicopter buzzing over your head and the television motorbike zooming in to project your image across the world. I imagined my mother and father doing somersaults in front of the TV back in Dublin, as Phil Ligett the Channel 4 commentator shouted, 'Paul Kimmage is magnificent, this has never happened in the Tour de France before! Can he do it? Can the Dubliner win the stage?' As I pedalled my way to St-Hilaire I could hear him, and it made me pedal harder. My God, it was wonderful. I was suffering terribly in the front, but I was giving it my all. With 500 metres to go I was there, sprinting for a stage win in the Tour de France. I believed, I believed. My legs were so desperately tired, but I believed in the miracle that would propel me across the line in front of the others. But I made a mess of it. Got into a lovely position second from the front, but was caught on the hop as the others swept past and boxed me in. The crafty Belgian Ludo Peeters won the sprint. I was ninth. I was worth a place in the top five, but I had messed it up. I am now the best-placed rider in the team. Thevenet came into the room tonight and said he was very pleased with me. I blew a good chance today, but I'm sure there will be others.

Friday, 11 July
Stage 8: St-Hilaire-du-Harcouet to Nantes (204 kilometres)
Stage winner: Eddy Plankaert (Belgium)
Race leader: Jorgen Pedersen

Felt tired all day. Must have been the efforts of yesterday. Wasn't able to do much about helping the team. Felt a bit guilty and talked to Gauthier about it. He said there was no need to feel guilty if I was tired and unable to help. Liked him even more after that. He's becoming my big brother on this race.

Saturday, 12 July
Stage 9: Nantes to Nantes (61.5 kilometres TT)
Stage winner: Bernard Hinault (France)
Race leader: Jorgen Pedersen

Today I had a rendezvous with reality. I had hoped for much and came away with so little. Thevenet had warned me, but I hadn't listened: 'Don't ride too hard, save your strength for the stages to come.' Wasn't he forgetting that I was the best-placed rider in the team? Damn it, I had worked hard for the team for over a week: today was my chance to do something for myself. A good ride would have pushed me into the top thirty. I set out to give it my all. I did. I have never ridden so hard in a time trial. When it was over I almost collapsed with exhaustion. I cycled back to the hotel, but could hardly get the pedals round. I was sore all over. My buttocks ached from the effort of using the big time-trial gear. On arriving at the hotel I marched straight to my bed and threw myself on it. The top riders were finishing. Bernard Hinault had the best time. He had beaten me by eight minutes. Eight minutes in sixty-one kilometres, and here I was, exhausted on the hotel bed; and there he was, fresh as a fucking daisy, chatting out at me from the television screen. That's when I realised the world had separated us. I had been taking the usual multi-vitamins since the start of the race. I had refused all injections, but as I watched Hinault I realised that it wasn't possible to continue this way. I was on my hands and knees after nine stages: how could I possibly complete the fourteen that remained? Tonight I told Thevenet I was knackered. He asked me if I was looking after myself. He seemed surprised that I had not taken any injections. He brought me to Emile's room and suggested a B_{12} injection. Emile looked at me and smiled. He was very kind, I had expected an 'I told you so', but none came, and I was grateful for this. I dropped my shorts and abandoned my virginity without a second thought. I fought off guilt waves flowing from my brain. 'This wasn't doping, it was just getting even with the others.' However, I was a bit suspicious that the others were putting stronger stuff than B_{12} in their syringes. But B_{12} was as far as I was prepared to go, for the moment. I asked Jean-Louis about the use of hormones, for I knew that cortisone and testosterone were being widely used. He warned me off them immediately and without hesitation. 'That stuff is shit, it's dangerous, messes up the system. Stay away from it.'

Sunday, 13 July
Stage 10: Nantes to Futuroscope (184 kilometres)
Stage winner: Angel-Jose Sarrapio (Spain)
Race leader: Jorgen Pedersen

I felt really bad at the start, was sure I was going to get dropped. But as the stage went on I started coming round a bit and it was an easy enough day until the last sixty kilometres. LeMond was in trouble today. He had a bout of diarrhoea. He rode by me with thirty kilometres to go, surrounded by his *domestiques* bringing him to the front. God, the smell was terrible. It was rolling down his legs. I know if it was me I would have stopped. I mean, it's only a bike race. But then again I'm not capable of winning it. He is and I suppose that's the difference. Stephen rode a great time trial yesterday and is now third. Don't know how he does it, for a few days earlier he assured me he was having trouble with his left knee. He said he was riding on one leg. I wish I had his bad leg.

Monday, 14 July
Stage 11: Poitiers to Bordeaux (258.5 kilometres)
Stage winner: Rudy Dhaenens (Belgium)
Race leader: Jorgen Pedersen

Another long stage, 260 kilometres. They wear you out, these long flat stages, hour after hour in the saddle. Tomorrow we enter the mountains. I prefer the mountains. Jean-Louis's wife and child came to the hotel tonight. She's extremely nice and I made a special effort to be friendly, despite being totally exhausted.

Tuesday, 15 July
Stage 12: Bayonne to Pau (217.5 kilometres)
Stage winner: Pedro Delgado (Spain)
Race leader: Bernard Hinault

War. Today was war. We lost two men. Bruno Huger and Jean-Louis Gauthier both abandoned. Jean-Louis's quitting was a big blow. We started the stage at Bayonne and from the drop of the flag it was war. Attack followed attack on the roller-coaster, leg-breaking Basque roads. A large group went clear, there was a fierce pursuit and then it settled for a while. Just after it settled I talked to Jean-Louis and asked him how he felt. He looked shaken and he told me he was shagged and having a really bad day. Soon after that, we attacked the first big mountain (col) of the Tour and I never saw him again. After the stage I cycled back to the hotel with Bernard Vallet. I expressed my concern for Gauthier and it was Vallet who told me the news. Gauthier had been dropped on the first col and was chasing alone, twenty minutes behind, when he punctured. He could have taken a spare wheel from the broom wagon but decided to pack it in.

I couldn't believe it. I entered our room at the hotel and he was there, already showered and dressed in ordinary clothes. I walked over to him, put my hand on his shoulder and said, 'Shit'. I couldn't think of any other word to console him. I showered and slipped out of the room for a cup of tea and to give him time to think by himself. I went for massage and then returned to the room, and we watched the TV highlights of the stage as on any other night. But this time we watched in silence. I realised now just how upset he was. He just sat there in the same position with a sad, empty expression on his face. I rose and suggested we go down to dinner, but he didn't follow. Half way through the meal I mentioned to the lads that Jean-Louis was very upset. Claveyrolat, who had been on the same team at La Redoute, left the table to bring him down. Half an hour later he returned alone. Gauthier had told Claveyrolat that he was ashamed, that he couldn't bear to eat with the team. He didn't eat tonight. He must be starving, for his last meal was at nine thirty this morning and he had raced 150 kilometres before climbing off. Before sleeping he said only three words, 'Bonne nuit, Paul.'

Wednesday, 16 July
Stage 13: Pau to Luchon (186 kilometres)
Stage winner: Greg LeMond (USA)
Race leader: Bernard Hinault

Jean-Louis woke early and I heard him sneak down for breakfast. When I eventually dragged myself out of bed he was back in the room and had his bags packed. He gave me a few vitamin tablets he said he would no longer be needing and then we shook hands and said goodbye. I felt we were close friends. Here was a guy who had ridden seven Tours and finished them all. But all that seemed to be no consolation to him now. Before coming into the race I was 100 per cent determined to finish. Thinking of Gauthier I feel almost ashamed of myself. My 100 per cent determination is not nearly enough.

Today was desperately hard again. I felt dead at the bottom of the first col, the Tourmalet, and was instantly left behind. But after three kilometres of struggling I suddenly felt the strength to pedal faster and I upped the pace. I caught a group, left them behind and caught another. I couldn't believe it when I saw Stephen in a group of stragglers. He was suffering really badly and I felt desperately sorry for him. Damn it, I was getting used to being left behind on the big climbs but this was a new experience for him. I threw my arm around him and tried to console him. I should have waited with him, but I felt a new thrust of power and I wanted to see just how far it could carry me. I went across to the next group and rode really strongly up the rest of the Tourmalet. I got a bit of a fright on the descent. I was going too fast as I entered a long, sweeping bend in a sort of half tunnel. I bounced off the wall but incredibly managed to stay up. I rode hard in the valley that brought us to the bottom of the second col, the Aspin. I climbed this with the same vigour as I had climbed Tourmalet but it was on the third climb, Peyresourde, that I started running out of steam. The final two kilometres were never-ending and I crawled over the top. Stephen's group caught me as we were about to start the last climb, the thirteen-kilometre rise to the ski station, Super-bagnères, with the stage finishing at the top. This time Stephen was encouraging me and I realised I had made a big mistake. It would have been much wiser to have stayed with Stephen's group on the Tourmalet, but instead I had set off like an idiot on the glory trail and burnt off the small reserves my body still possessed. Superbagnères was Calvary, but I made it. Tonight we are staying in an old school dormitory. It's an awful kip, but I'm so tired I don't mind where I sleep.

Thursday, 17 July
Stage 14: Luchon to Blagnac (154 kilometres)
Stage winner: Niki Ruttiman (Switzerland)
Race leader: Bernard Hinault

Today I realised just how tired I am. Some idiot attacked just before the feeding station and there was chaos. I grabbed my feeding bag and threw it over my back. The attack split the bunch into one long line and I was the last man and too occupied to transfer the food from the bag to my jersey pockets. Thevenet drove up beside me and told me to move quickly to the front. I pulled out and started making my way up the line. I passed five guys when all of a sudden I realised I hadn't got the strength to go any further and I started slipping back, only to end up back where I had started from. The five guys I passed started laughing when they saw me going backwards, and I couldn't blame them. The chase lasted over twenty-five kilometres, and it was a half an hour before I could empty my musette and we all settled down. I'm looking forward to the rest day, but it's another four hard stages away.

Friday, 18 July
Stage 15: Carcassonne to Nîmes (225.5 kilometres)
Stage winner: Frank Hoste (Belgium)
Race leader: Bernard Hinault

It's dreadfully hot tonight. My body is sweating all the time and I know I won't sleep too well. After dinner I went out for an ice-cream with Clavet, Castaing and Dede. We had to sneak out of the hotel, as Thevenet doesn't take too kindly to us eating ice-cream. It was good fun, but irritating to watch the holiday-makers enjoying themselves in the bars and cafés of this bright, ancient Roman town. How many times have we cycled by lake-shores, crammed with people enjoying themselves? Or been applauded by sunbathers in scanty bathing costumes? Is it worth it?

Saturday, 19 July
Stage 16: Nîmes to Gap (246.5 kilometres)
Stage winner: Jean-François Bernard (France)
Race leader: Bernard Hinault

Today we arrived in the Alps and tomorrow is the first Alpine stage. The air is cooler and cleaner here than the hot and sticky stuff in Nîmes. Castaing's face is all bloated. I am not sure what it is, but perhaps he has been dabbling with cortisone and got his doses wrong? The other lads are giving him a hard time about it. Phoned my parents in Dublin. Da was out, so I talked to my mother. She says my father has bought a plane ticket for Paris and is coming over to the finish. This made me angry. He should know better than to presume I will finish this race. At the moment I am not sure of anything. I take it day by day. I've been surviving ever since the time trial at Nantes. Getting to Paris is all Thevenet expects of me, but I'm not sure if I can.

Sunday, 20 July
Stage 17: Gap to Col du Granon (190 kilometres)
Stage winner: Eduardo Chozas (Spain)
Race leader: Greg LeMond

This was to have been my stage. The one I trained specially for. What a joke. What a cruel joke. At least I know now that I'm not a climber and never will be. A strange thing happened at the finish. I crossed the line and Thevenet was waiting for me. He put his arm around me and told me I had made it, I was inside the time limit. And for a few seconds I was disappointed. I was so exhausted, so knackered that I would gladly have accepted being eliminated. Elimination would end the nightmare of getting up each day to face another six hours of this bloody, endless torture. Today was easily the hardest day of my life. I was in trouble from the start, on an insignificant little third-category climb which was nothing compared to the three giants, Vars, Izoard and Granon, which awaited us.

I tried to get myself together for Vars. I talked to Stephen just before it and he told me to start the climb at the front of the bunch. I followed him and attacked the first hairpins in the best possible position. Then the pressure went on, not a big attack, just an increase in pressure. I felt for the gear lever, pushing it downwards, trying to make things easier. But I was going backwards. I tried to hold on, but it was no use. I looked for the top of the mountain and the lines of spectators showed me exactly how far I had to go. 'Christ, I'm not sure I can make it.' I kept slipping backwards and all the time one minor detail was troubling my brain. Of the three giants Vars was the easiest.

But curiously I felt much better on Izoard. I was in a big group of twenty-five riders and I could have left them behind on the fifteen-kilometre monster. But I remembered the Tourmalet and decided to stay with them until the bottom of the Granon. We descended into Briançon and then rode out to the bottom of the last mountain. The Granon was desperately steep. Out training I had sailed up it but now I was dying. The training reconnaissance was now a big disadvantage, for I knew exactly how hard it was. I said to myself, 'I can't make this.' The good sensations I had had on the Izoard had now disappeared, and I slipped to last in the group. Our second team car was behind me. At the bottom of the climb they had stopped to pick up a fellow called Robert, who works with RMO in Grenoble. He was standing on the front seat shouting at me through the sun roof. Three of the twelve kilometres had passed, I was dying. Spectators started to push me. Robert, who knew nothing about cycling shouted at the people not to push me. It is illegal to take a push and Robert thought he was doing the right thing. I turned around to face him in a rage. I said, 'Robert, for fuck's sake, let them push me.' He was stunned, then realised his error and started shouting at the people to push me. I was pushed all the way up the climb but the last kilometre was still hell. My two hands on the tops of the handlebars, my head had dropped between my arms and I could hardly lift it to seek out the line. When I crossed the line, Thevenet was waiting. 'You made it Paul, a couple of minutes inside the limit.' 'Fuck.' I was sorry I had made it. Tomorrow I must start all over again.

Monday, 21 July
Stage 18: Briançon to L'Alpe D'Huez (162.5 kilometres)
Stage winner: Bernard Hinault
Race leader: Greg LeMond

Emile gave it to me before the start. A caffeine tablet. He told me to take it immediately the stage started at the bottom of the highest climb of the race, the Col de Galibier. Normally I would have thrown it away, but this time I put it in my pocket. Some bastard attacked as soon as we left the town, and I had absolutely nothing in my legs and was instantly dropped. I panicked and reached for the tablet in my pocket hoping for some miracle; but nothing happened. I wanted to stop. I wanted to get off the bike and kiss the road and sit down and weep my tears of defeat, but I remembered Stephen's words, spoken to me before the start: 'Whatever happens, finish. If you are eliminated there is no shame – but don't abandon.' So I pedalled on.

I started feeling better after the Galibier. Was it the caffeine? I don't know. I just know I was going better. I caught the French rider Bruno Cornillet in the valley before the day's second climb, 'Croix de Fer'. At the start of the race Cornillet had worn the white jersey of the best Tour *débutant*. Now, like me, he was on his last legs. Although I had never spoken a word to him in my life, it turned out he knew my name. It was 'Paul this, and Paul that'. All because he wanted me to ride with him, he didn't want to be left on his own. I knew how lousy it was to be left alone and so I decided to stay with him. There was a small third-category climb just before Croix de Fer. I was going much better than him and began to pull away. He was desperate and started begging me to stay, saying that there was a long valley up ahead and that it would be better if we stayed together. I knew there was no such valley and that he was lying, but I understood why, so I waited. On Croix de Fer he was crawling, totally wasted. Every time I turned the pedals I pulled away from him. A spectator at the side of the road shouted that we were twenty-five minutes behind the leaders, Hinault and LeMond. I realised it would be touch and go for the time limit.

I looked at Bruno, he had raced a good race for sixteen days but was now reduced to this – a crawling, begging shadow. I was surprised he didn't abandon and let me get on with it. My look said I had to go, and he understood. 'Allez Paul,' he said and I left him. I rode as hard as I could till the finish at Alpe D'Huez. I had a fierce urge to piss on the descent of the Croix, but I knew that every second was now precious if I was to beat the time limit so I pissed off the bike at sixty kilometres an hour. I arrived at the Alpe just three minutes inside the time limit. Cornillet arrived fourteen minutes behind me. He was eliminated.

Tuesday, 22 July
Rest day: L'Alpe D'Huez

I feel so pleased I have made it this far. It feels wonderful still to be part of the race. Rode for an hour this morning to stop the legs getting stiff. The afternoon was spent hand-washing my gear for I have no more clean shorts or jerseys. Had a good chat with Martin. He told me he was knackered at the bottom of the Alpe yesterday when this large German *fraulein* came to his rescue. She grabbed him and started pushing him up the mountain. She had huge breasts, which swung freely as she ran. But she was crouched over Martin and her left breast kept hitting him in the face. 'Schnell, schnell!' she cried, and Martin kept encouraging her. He didn't know whether to laugh or cry.

Only five more stages to go. I must hang on.

Wednesday, 23 July
Stage 19: Villard de Lans to St Etienne (179.5 kilometres)
Stage winner: Julian Gorospe (Spain)
Race leader: Greg LeMond

Thank God, Hinault controlled things today. He went to the front of the bunch and no one dared attack. The rest day hasn't done me much good. I felt desperately tired. Was left behind when the pressure went on with thirty kilometres to go, but finished in a big group.

Thursday, 24 July
Stage 20: St Etienne to St Etienne (58 kilometres TT)
Stage winner: Bernard Hinault
Race leader: Greg LeMond

I paced myself well over the thirty-five kilometres, hurting but not flogging myself. Today was almost a second rest day. Only three more stages. If I get over tomorrow's mountain stage to the Puy de Dôme I should make it to Paris.

Friday, 25 July
Stage 21: St Etienne to Le Puy de Dôme (190 kilometres)
Stage winner: Eric Maechler (Switzerland)
Race leader: Greg LeMond

Hinault controlled things again today and the race started with just fifty kilometres to go, which suited me fine. The Puy is a savagely steep five-kilometre ramp but I rode up it OK. I think I can make it now.

TOUR DE FRANCE

Saturday, 26 July
Stage 22: Clermont-Ferrand to Nevers (194 kilometres)
Stage winner: Guido Bontempi
Race leader: Greg LeMond

A nightmare. I was the only rider in the whole peloton to be left behind when the pressure went on, twenty kilometres from the finish. The shame of it, I am totally knackered. But the real problem is tomorrow. The lads have been telling me that the speed on the Champs Elysées is something incredible. What if I'm left behind in front of millions of television spectators – and, worse, in front of my father, who will be in the crowd? God, the shame of it! 'No one gets dropped on the Champs Elysées,' they said. But damn it, I was the only one to be dropped today. After dinner there was a small meeting in one of the rooms. One or two of the lads were preparing syringes. Cutting them down to size, preparing them for the white amphetamines they would use the next day. I was astonished. 'What about the controls?' They smiled. Safe smiles. 'Tomorrow is the last stage of the race. Only the stage winners and leaders will be controlled. There is no random testing. That's why no one gets dropped on the Champs Elysées.' I was tempted, desperately tempted. They offered me a charge, explaining that I could take it in tablet form if I preferred. I refused and said I needed time to think. I didn't despise them. They were my friends. I understood. Hadn't we suffered enough? They wanted to help me. I wanted to accept their help, but that bloody conscience of mine was stopping me. I had never smoked behind my father's back. Had always been dependable and good. I had an acute sense of right and wrong. Taking drugs was wrong. The only merit I had now was finishing this race. If I did it with the help of amphetamines I could never forgive myself. But it was so tempting. I badly wanted to be one of the boys.

ROUGH RIDE

Sunday, 27 July
Stage 23: Cosne-sur-Loire to Paris (252 kilometres)
Stage winner: Guido Bontempi
Race winner: Greg LeMond

It was a great stage. A fun stage. The triumphant ride into Paris.
During the long 252-kilometre ride to the capital a bottle of
champagne was passed around the bunch. There was the
singing of the Tour song 'Oh, Champs Elysées' and spirits were
high. I got more and more nervous as we approached Paris and
the speed went up. I saw one of the lads taking his stuff. It was
so simple. The metal tube was opened. The plastic cap,
protecting the needle, was taken off and held between the
teeth. The right sleeve of the jersey was rolled back and the
needle was slipped into the skin of the shoulder and with a
squeeze of the sawn-off piston the amphetamines were pushed
in. The plastic cap was replaced on the needle, the syringe was
put back in the tube and into the pocket. Beautifully done and
terribly simple. One of the lads offered me a tablet, but I
refused and lied that I was feeling fine.

We could see the Eiffel Tower. What a wonderful sight. We
raced along the bank of the Seine past the huge mass of metal,
then swung left into Place de la Concorde and on to the Champs
Elysées. The roar from the crowd sent goose pimples through
my legs and though we raced up and down at over sixty kilometres an hour I felt no pain. I was so overjoyed at having made
it, so overcome with the magnificence of it all that I didn't feel
the pedals. The finish line was crossed and we ground to a halt.
Bernard Vallet stopped beside me and embraced me. He had
tears in his eyes. 'Now you know what it is to ride the Tour de
France.' My father was standing just a little further on. He threw
his arms around me. I was so pleased he was here to share my
triumph. It was the happiest day of my life. Two hundred and
ten riders had started. One hundred and thirty-two had finished.
I was 131st. I had survived. I was a 'Giant of the Road'.

11

THE ARMS RACE

The Tour was a great education. I learnt so much about myself and the real world of professional cycling. Every race before the Tour had been almost child's play compared to 'La Grande Boucle'. The Tour was the ultimate. The 100 per cent race. Finishing it had instilled in me a certain sense of pride. It took a hard man to finish and I now had my 'hard man's licence'. I had expected it, but it had been much harder than I had imagined. I had felt like abandoning a hundred times in the last week but I didn't give in. I couldn't, for I felt my survival as a professional rider depended on getting to Paris. RMO was a small team, but at the end of the season the weak men would be sacked and new blood brought in. Monsieur Braillon was not pumping money into cycling to play in the second division. Big names would be signed and small names got rid of to make room for them. I had a contract for two years so I was assured of my place for 1987, but already I was thinking ahead to 1988. I may not have been the classiest bike rider in the world, but I had other qualities. Courage, guts and honesty. In a year's time Thevenet would remember not that I had finished the Tour on my hands and knees but that I'd finished.

I had made some bad mistakes. I had been desperately naïve in thinking I could ride a Tour de France on two multi-vitamin tablets each morning. The Tour de France was no ordinary race. It made superhuman demands on the human body.

Riding six hours a day for twenty-three days was not possible without vitamin supplements, mineral supplements, chemicals to clean out a tired liver, medication to take the hardness out of rock-hard leg muscles. Taken in tablet form the medication passed through the stomach and liver. This was extra work for already overworked organs and the result was that much of the benefit of the product was lost. Injections avoided this and were therefore much more efficient. A syringe did not always mean doping. In a perfect world it would be possible to ride the Tour without taking any medication, so long as everyone else did the same. But this was not a perfect world. We were not doping, we were taking care of ourselves, replacing what was being sweated daily out of our bodies. The substances taken were not on the proscribed list, so how could we be doping? And yet one thing was becoming clear to me: as soon as you started playing, as soon as you accepted the taking of medication, the line between what was legal and what was illegal, between taking care of yourself and doping grew very, very thin. Most fellows cross it without ever realising they have. They just follow the advice of a team-mate or *soigneur*. 'So and so swears by this, any time he wants to do a ride he takes it.' And even though the rider himself may not want to take the product, perhaps doubting its legality, the thought of being disadvantaged changes his mind. It's a bit like the arms race: 'Laurents got an intercontinental missile in his arse today, I'd better get one or I'll be blitzed.' And before they know it they are in the middle of a very dangerous game. By accepting an injection on the night of the Nantes time trial, I had indeed entered the 'dope stadium'. I was, however, firm in my commitment to stay off the playing field as far as illegal substances were concerned. Could this last? I hoped so.

On the night the Tour finished we were back on the Champs Elysées, but this time dressed in shirt and tie and pressed trousers. It felt great to be able to wear normal clothes again. For a month we had spent our days with a sweaty jersey on our backs and the greasy leather chamois of our racing shorts on our bums while at nights we were obliged to wear the drab old team tracksuit. Champagne was the beverage of the 'soirée' as we clinked our glasses to half-naked cabaret girls at the Millionaires' Club. It was a great night. Next day, I returned to Grenoble. As a way of trimming down travelling expenses it was decided that Dede and I travel home with the equipment truck. The journey was long and tedious as we had a long detour to drop Dede at his home in Rumilly before finally arriving in Grenoble. There was no tickertape welcome awaiting me. The football centre was empty as most of the apprentices were on their summer holidays, but as I entered my room I got a sharp surprise. A young black footballer was lying on Ribeiro's bed, and I noticed immediately that my personal belongings were not as I had left them. His name was Charles and he explained to me that Ribeiro had flown back to Brazil for two months and that he had been ordered to take his bed. This Charles seemed a nice enough fellow, but I was furious. After a month's suffering, what a way to travel home and what a home to come home to! I would have to look for an apartment of my own, for the centre was becoming impossible to live in. I had to get out. It would take time to find a suitable flat, but there was no question of me spending my two weeks' holidays with these arrogant brats. I decided to return home to Dublin.

I had not seen Ann for six months as she had spent the summer working in New York. I had phoned her from a coin box in Nantes on her birthday and she had spent much of the five minutes crying. New York was not working out; she was finding it hard to get work. Like thousands of others, she had gone there without a student's working visa and had no social security number. She had gone in the hope of raising money to pay for her studies, but her tears told me she would barely cover her travel expenses. I told her to fly home and she arrived two days before I did. It felt good to be back, surrounded once again by the warmth of one's family. To have your girlfriend throw her arms around you and tell you she loved you. It made it all worthwhile. The emptiness of the football centre was a million miles away. I felt like a star.

There were two city-centre 'criterium' races on in Dublin and Cork. Professional races with Kelly and Roche both riding. Sean, Stephen and Martin were all managed by a Dublin businessman called Frank Quinn. I was always sceptical about managers who scratched their backsides and demanded 10 per cent but Frank was different. He had a great human quality about him. He cared and this was important to me. At the start of the year he had offered me his services and I accepted. In my four years of professionalism I think it is the only manager–rider relationship which finished with the rider owing the manager money, but that's the way Frank is. He phoned the race organisers, informed them I was available and talked about a contract for the two races. It was very fair and on a par with what a new professional would get in France – about £250 per race. They offered him a pittance, claiming their budgets were all tied up. I felt really let down, insulted even. The organisers had flown over a load of continental pros for the events and here I was, one of only four professionals in the country, one of only five Irishmen ever to have ridden the Tour de France – and they could find no place for me. There was no place for Martin either. It was despicable. This took a lot of the good out of being home. I no longer felt quite the star and was almost looking forward to going back to France.

Thevenet phoned me in Dublin at the end of the two weeks and told me to fly straight to Amsterdam for the Tour of Holland. The flat, open plains did not suit me and I spent a very uncomfortable week. It was a huge come-down from the glories of the Tour and, not at all motivated, I abandoned with a stage to go. Of the four RMO riders present, only I had ridden the Tour. The other Tour riders were in France riding criteriums.

Criteriums were a French tradition in August. The Tour

would generate huge interest for cycle racing in July, but in August there was nothing. The criteriums were a means of avoiding the cold turkey syndrome. A placebo for an addicted public until the autumn classics. The mayor of a small village would decide he wanted the stars of the Tour de France in his town and would contact a criterium manager. The manager would submit the price of engaging thirty professionals and the mayor would hand over the money. The manager then set about contacting the riders. He would sign up three or four really big names, the Tour winner if possible, the French champion, and two or three Tour stage winners. Most of the mayor's cash would be spent on these, for these were the men who drew the crowds. The rest of the peloton was made up of usually twenty-five small-timers or *domestiques*. It was at criteriums that the poorly paid *domestique* made most of his money. For the two to three-hour street race he was paid about £350. It wasn't 100 cent profit. It was the rider's job to look after his own accommodation, travel and food. To economise most *domestiques* travelled together. It was not uncommon for them to race in Brittany, finish about midnight then jump into a car and drive to the next race at the opposite end of the country. To save time, and money, the pre-race meal was usually a bag of chips and a sausage roll bought from a chip van at the side of the road. If there was the possibility of a few hours' sleep a cheap and often sleazy hotel would be found, anything to save a few francs. As a result, on arriving at the criterium they were often in no condition to race – but this was a minor detail. Amphetamines were wonderful for motivating a tired *domestique* to climb once again into the saddle. And as there were never any controls it was at criteriums that abuse was at its highest. The drugs were never used in the pursuit of victory, because all the criteriums were fixed. The people came to see the star winning, so the star always won. That way the punters went away happy and would return next year. No, the amphetamines were an insurance. An insurance that riders would 'perform'. The small riders were expected to animate the race. The routine was to attack off the front for a few laps, milk the applause and then let the star bring you back. By doing this you felt uninhibited when, at the end of the night, you approached the manager and asked for the contract. Contracts were always paid after the event. Amphetamines ensured you got paid.

During the Tour Vallet had promised me he would find me a few contracts. He was a big name and had a lot of pull with the criterium managers, but it was like a lot of the promises he made – empty. I reckon I am the only rider to have finished the Tour in 1986 who didn't ride a single criterium that year. It was one thing being a *petit coureur* and French, but quite another being a *petit coureur* and Irish. They could ring up the criterium managers and demand favours; but I hated crawling, and besides I was afraid. I knew that the criterium would draw me close to the temptations of drugs and I didn't want that. I was afraid of being tempted, too many complications. If one of the lads offered me a charge, in good faith, before a criterium, how could I possibly refuse without offending him? I still wanted desperately to be one of the boys. If I refused a charge, I knew they would never totally accept me. And so being absent from the criteriums suited me just fine.

At the end of August we rode Paris–Bourges, a two-day stage race. It was my first contact with Gauthier since the day he had abandoned in the Tour. He was in good form and told me privately that he had received an offer to race with the Z Peugeot team in 1987. He had decided to accept. I was surprised as I felt sure he had made up his mind to retire. He had, but talking about retiring was one thing, actually doing it was another. There were not an awful lot of avenues open to a 32-year-old former *maillot jaune* of the Tour de France. He had had one or two offers of employment but none that pleased him. The local amateur club from his region had made him an attractive offer if he wore their colours for a year, but the thought of racing again as an amateur disturbed him.

There was a nice, relaxed atmosphere in the Paris–Bourges. Dede had been offered a new contract for 1987 and this cheered him up greatly. And when Dede was happy, we all were. He was always the life and soul of the party. I was knackered after the first stage and decided to go to bed early. I was not rooming with Gauthier but with one of the others, whose identity must remain secret. I had slept solidly for more than an hour when my room-mate came in and woke me. 'Paul I have a girl, and I'm on to a sure thing. In a few minutes I'm going to bring her up. You just keep your eyes closed and pretend to be asleep.' I laughed and told him I was knackered and to stop pulling my leg. He went out and five minutes later he was back with a girl. There was a slight hesitation when she saw my sleeping body in the adjoining bed. 'That's Kimmage, the Irishman, he's a very heavy sleeper,' he assured her. I was lying there with my eyes closed, paralysed. He was serious. He was going to have intercourse with this girl on a bed almost touching my own.

At first they talked. She was competing in the women's race to be held next day. She asked him about his life as a professional and marvelled at his prowess. He played her along beautifully for fifteen minutes – then the clothes came off. The two bodies flopped down on the room's second single bed. I kept my eyes glued shut. I never saw anything, I didn't have to, the noise they made left nothing to the imagination. I thought about pretending to wake up, but this would only cause embarrassment all round. During dope controls I felt embarrassed when the commissars stared at me while I was urinating. How could he possibly have intercourse with a girl when there was someone else in almost the same bed? I couldn't believe it. Then I noticed the smell, a burning smell which I couldn't quite place. What could possibly be burning?

They lay motionless for five minutes and then she asked him if she could take a shower. He escorted her to the bathroom and carefully closed the door. He ran over to my bed and shook me by the shoulder. 'What about that, Polo, do you want a go now?' I insulted him, but this only seemed to please him more. 'What the hell is burning?' To dim the light in the room, he had placed a towel over the bedside lamp. He ran over to it, lifted the smouldering remains off the bulb and threw it out of the window. His partner finished her shower and re-entered the bedroom, no doubt amazed at the sleeping powers of the Irishman still unconscious on the other bed. He bid her goodnight and she left the room.

Next day as we started the second stage he was still euphoric about his conquest. He would ride up behind me and burst into a fit of laughter. Then he would go around the bunch telling all his mates about it and bring them to me for verification. The typical reaction was, 'I wouldn't have let him into the room unless I was sure of getting a go.' Or, 'I would have woken up, pushed him off and jumped on myself.' I don't know if all sportsmen are as gross as this. Not all cyclists are, but most of them are. There is this crude, savage side to them. I don't know if it's the demands of the sport that cultivate it, but it certainly exists. A typical example is the following:

Pierre: 'What's up with Louis? He's not sprinting very well.'
Serge: 'Yes, he had a bad crash while going for the stage win last week, and as he wasn't wearing gloves he ripped all the skin off both hands.'
Pierre: 'That's bad luck, I'm sure he'd have won a few stages here, he was going really well.'
Serge: 'Yes, but the worst part is that he can't even have a wank.'

I didn't ride well in the Paris–Bourges. I didn't ride well in any of the end-of-season races. The Tour had taken a lot out of me and I was just going through the motions at races in August.

September was another quiet month. I rode three one-day French classics before lining up for Paris–Brussels, which was to be my last race of the season. I didn't want to ride, but was told I had to make up the numbers because the team needed ten starters to be paid travelling expenses by the race organisers. The night before the race I talked to Gauthier, who told me how he had abandoned the year before. The day before the race he put his bike in the car and drove to a little village fifty kilometres from the start at Senlis. He parked the car and then cycled back to the team hotel. Next day he raced the fifty kilometres from Senlis to the village, abandoned down a narrow side street as the peloton traversed the village, jumped into his car and drove home. It was too late for me to try the same stunt, but I planned something else. On the morning of the race I signed on the start sheet, dressed in my shorts and jersey. Just as the race was about to start, I hid in the toilet of a café across the road. When I was sure they had gone I discreetly slipped out of the café, jumped into the car and headed for Calais and the ferry to Dover. I crossed to England and caught another ferry to Dublin. Home. My first season was over. Well, not quite.

The Tour of Ireland, or Nissan Classic, was due to start a week late but RMO were not sending a team so I wasn't racing it. Stephen had planned to ride it in a composite team, but his knee was still giving him trouble and he pulled out. This left a place to be filled. Frank phoned the team's sponsors, Ever Ready, and proposed me as a replacement. They agreed, and on the day I arrived home Frank phoned me and told me I was riding the Nissan. I was a little bit out of condition and spent the three days before the race in frantic last-minute training. The team was made up of two Belgians, Jef Lieckens and Carlo Bomans; two Englishmen; Sean Yates, Tony Doyle and myself. On the first stage to Galway, it rained heavily. The bunch was in one long line and was being buffeted by strong crosswinds as we raced along the Oranmore road to Galway. I had bad stomach cramps and felt really weak. I was dropped. It was a cruel disappointment. I would have to ride into Galway and complete the small circuit on my own, minutes behind the whole bunch. I knew my mother and father were waiting for me and I felt quite ashamed. Just before arriving on to the circuit I rode past the team hotel. I thought very seriously about getting off and making some excuse. Any excuse. Anything to avoid the shame of riding the circuit on my own. But I kept going, Ever Ready were paying me a contract. By abandoning it, I would not be honouring it and this would not be professional. I finished the stage in a foul humour and cursed myself.

The rest of the week went off much better and I started to ride quite well. After the third stage to Cork I roomed with Sean Yates. I liked Sean. When I was an amateur he had helped me take the yellow jersey in the Tour of Britain Milk Race. He is one of the nicest and most down-to-earth blokes I have met in the game. He had a little gadget for examining blood. You pricked your finger for the sample, placed the droplet on a slide and examined it through a sort of small microscope. I asked him to test me and on examining my droplet, he said I was lacking in iron. I asked if he had any with him and he prepared me a syringe with vitamins and iron. Sean, like most of the pros, rarely went to the *soigneur* if he felt he needed something. He would simply do it himself. The idea of sticking a needle in myself repulsed me and I asked Sean if he would do it for me. He refused. 'You have to learn some time. Now is as good a time as any to start.' He gave me a piece of cottonwool with methylated spirits and the syringe, or *flèche* as it was known in the trade, and I went to the bathroom and closed the door. The door was always closed just in case anyone walked in. I often wondered about my father walking in and seeing me with a syringe in my hand. What would I have said? 'Eehh! Sorry, Da, this is not what you think.'

The syringe had to be inserted in the muscle of the buttock at about the same height as the coccyx. We had a choice of buttock, left or right, but it was equally painful. I had watched the lads do it before. There were two methods. The most painful was to place the point of the needle against the skin and slowly start pressing. Or, you could throw the syringe like a dart, so that it penetrated the flesh quickly. I decided to opt for the second method. I stood for at least ten minutes and made several efforts at throwing the syringe, but each time I was unable to release it. This infuriated me. When finally I found the courage to do it, I was so tense and my buttock muscle so contracted that the needle hit the flesh and bounced off on to the dirty bathroom floor. Furious, I picked it up, squeezed the piston and squirted the liquid down the toilet bowl. I threw the empty syringe in the bin and left the bathroom, cursing. Sean had a huge grin on his face and offered to make me another one, but I refused. I later retrieved the syringe from the bathroom bin, as it was a golden rule never to leave anything that might surprise the cleaning maid. But I was thoroughly disgusted with myself.

The Nissan finished on the Sunday in Dublin. I tried to put up a bit of show in front of my home crowd as we dashed up and down O'Connell Street, but I ultimately failed to make any real impression. Galway was forgotten, and I could at least hold my head high again. This time the season was over and I wasn't sorry. I needed a break.

12

QUALIFIED PRO

The winter months were spent in Dublin. This was the fun part of being a pro, the three months spent at home at the end of every season. I enjoyed a high profile in my native land. My notoriety had started when I was an amateur. Now, as a professional, I was part of an elite band. There were just four professional cyclists in the country. Sean Kelly was the world's number one, with Stephen Roche not far behind him. Martin Earley had won a stage in the Tour of Italy and Paul Kimmage had finished, well, 131st in the Tour de France. Cycling was becoming more and more popular with the media and as a result more familiar to the ordinary man in the street. I enjoyed cashing in on my new fame. I was invited by cycling clubs throughout the country to give coaching talks and lectures on the life of a pro. There was often a five-minute television slot here or a radio slot there and gradually I was building up a name for myself. There was no money to be made out of it, but it made me feel important, as if I was something. So at the end of my break I always found it hard to return to France, where I was nothing.

I left Ireland on 9 January after a phone call from Thevenet. He had organised a pre-season training camp at Gruissan on the French Riviera. I caught the ferry to England and drove to Stoke, where I stayed the night with Martin. The next stage saw me on a stopover at Paris with my good friends Jean and

Ginette Beaufils. And from there I drove to Gruissan. There were eight new faces on the team. Gauthier, Le Bigaut, Barteau, Russemberger, Mogore and Castaing were replaced by six Frenchmen, an Italian and an American. Jean-Claude Colotti, Jean-François Rault, Dante Rezze, Patrice Esnault, Vincent Lavenu and Michel Bibollet were the French newcomers. Pierangelo Bincolleto was the Italian and the 1984 Olympic champion Alexi Grewal the American.

Alexi was to be one of the leaders for the year. He had ridden one or two races with us on a trial basis in 1986, although it is important to point out that it was Alexi who was giving RMO the trial. He seemed to like it, so he signed up full-time for 1987. Thevenet thought very highly of him, but I knew there was no way it would work. Physically he had the capabilities to be an asset to any pro team on the continent. But mentally Alexi was never going to fit into ours or any other European team.

I shared a room with him at the training camp. He had this fear that his body would run down if he didn't eat enough. Half an hour before dinner he used to light up a small portable gas stove that he had brought with him from the States. He boiled water and cooked and ate about half a ton of spaghetti. When he had finished he would come to the dining room and eat a normal dinner with the rest of us. He was a great man for stretching and yoga. Sometimes I would walk into the room to find him standing on his head or lying on the floor on a special piece of wood that massaged his back. On the team training rides, he would often ride a hundred metres behind the group on his own because he felt he was training better. And because he was Alexi Grewal he got away with it. He was paid 35,000 dollars a month, which kind of dwarfed the £700 a month that I was earning.

I found him to be the most eccentric, obnoxious person I have ever met, and yet I liked him. I despised many of the traditional European cycling values but my survival depended on toeing the line. I could never open my mouth. That's what

I admired most about Alexi: nothing and nobody intimidated him.

I knew he wouldn't stick it. Alexi was too American, too inflexible. But his biggest problem was his fragile health. He was incredibly vulnerable to picking up colds, which would soon develop into bronchitis and put him out of action for weeks. Good health is one of the primary assets of being a pro. If Alexi had had the same health as Sean Kelly he would have gone a long way. But in the six months he spent with the team he was constantly sick, and I don't remember him ever riding well. By June he had had enough and returned to the States.

Of the other new guys, Colotti was the one I liked best. He was a year older than me but had only started to race four years earlier. I had been racing since I was eleven years old and the difference showed in our attitude to training and racing. He had a huge appetite for training and an infectious enthusiasm for the sport. It was all new and exciting to him but I had seen it all before. I was more laid back. Too laid back. In the opening months of the season, while I struggled desperately to find any sort of decent form, Colotti blossomed – earning regular top ten placings and winning the French classic, the Tour de Vendée. His success frustrated me. I didn't begrudge it him, I just couldn't understand why it never happened to me.

The start of the new season was soured by two deaths in the peloton. The Spaniard Vincente Mata lapsed into a coma and died shortly after crashing in the Trophy Luis Puig in Spain. A week later I was a witness to the second death. It was in the Tour de Haut Var. There was a short hill not long after the start, and the descent was narrow and twisting but not too dangerous. We were strung out in a long line. I was fifth from the front, on the wheel of Thierry Marie, when suddenly the Hitachi rider in front of him, Michel Goffin, fell off. We both managed to avoid running into him, and it didn't look a heavy fall. But when I looked back he was lying motionless in the middle of the road. The Belgian lapsed into a coma and died two weeks later. I was fully aware that cycling was a dangerous sport, but deaths were uncommon. The two deaths in February made us all feel uncomfortable about the risks involved. There was no way I wanted to die on the bike. I wore my crash hat for a few races after that. But the dangers were soon forgotten, and although my crash hat was always a part of my baggage it was rarely taken out of my suitcase.

The opening month of the season was a disaster. I rode pretty badly in almost every race I entered, so it was logical that I wasn't selected for Paris–Nice in March. On returning to Grenoble I immediately started looking for an apartment, as there was no way I was going to stick another year at the football centre. Clavet told me about a two-roomed flat that was vacant in his town, Vizille, which was just twelve kilometres outside Grenoble. I paid it a visit and decided to take it. The hassle of moving didn't do my physical condition any good and I missed a lot of training. As a result I was in poor condition when I returned to competition for two races in Belgium. I abandoned both of them and this started a run of seven abandonments, one after another. I managed to stop the rot at the Grand Prix of Rennes where I finished seventeenth and succeeded in getting my name in *L'Equipe*. This was important. Thevenet was starting to lose patience with me and the result at least showed that I existed. Things improved from then on. I finished fifty-first in my favourite Classic, Liège–Bastogne–Liège, and returned to Ireland shortly after for the wedding of my brother Raphael.

It was not a triumphant homecoming. Kelly, Roche and Earley had all had fantastic starts to their seasons. Mine had been a disaster. I started to worry about the future. My two-year contract with the team was up at the end of the year, and unless I improved dramatically, I'd be lucky if they offered me another one. What would I do? Jobs were almost impossible to find in Dublin. There was not much demand for ex-professional cyclists, especially unsuccessful ones. On the day before I returned to France I had lunch with my friend David Walsh. David was a journalist with the *Sunday Tribune* and also worked for *Magill*, an Irish current affairs magazine. When I finished the Tour in 1986 he asked me to write an account of the race, or more particularly my struggles in the race, for *Magill*. The story seemed to go down quite well with everyone who read it. I had written other stories for an Irish cycling magazine in my amateur days and I liked expressing myself with a pen. I often wished I had entered university and taken a degree in journalism instead of dashing off to France for a professional cyclist's contract. David suggested that there were plenty of opportunities to write freelance cycling stories on the Continent. He encouraged me to continue on the bike and made me feel much more optimistic for the future.

I made my comeback at the Frankfurt Grand Prix, where I rode quite well. Two important stage races were coming up, Quatre Jours de Dunkirk and the Tour de Romandie. The Dauphine was just a month away and I knew that my selection for it depended on a good performance in one of the two stage races. I preferred the Romandie to the Quatre Jours and managed to convince Thevenet to send me there. Stephen was riding it and this was my first opportunity to talk to him, as up until then we had rarely raced together. He was having a dream of a season and was clearly back on top after his troubles of last year. I made a special effort to impress him during the race, as my secret ambition was to ride by his side in the same team – but only if I was good enough. I was proud of my independence at RMO. I had won my contract there on my own steam without the help of either Kelly or Roche. My plan was eventually to team up with one of my famous compatriots, but on my terms. I wouldn't accept charity. If I wasn't good enough to be offered another contract by RMO then I wasn't good enough to join Kelly or Roche. Stephen's good form continued in Romandie, where he won easily.

On the night before the last stage I shared a room with

Bernard Vallet. It was the first time I had ever shared a room with him. It was almost an honour. I admired him because he was suave and classy and had always been nice to me. He told me he was pleased with my performance and that he would make sure that I had my place on the team to ride the Dauphine. Having the confidence of Vallet was a great advantage, for I knew he pulled a lot of weight with the sponsor Braillon and with Thevenet. He then asked me about my impressions of Thevenet as a *directeur sportif*. I knew they were friends but because I liked Thevenet I found no reason to lie and told him exactly what I thought.

'Bernard has one or two organisational problems but he has great human qualities which compensate largely for his faults. I like him. He is a good *directeur*.'

I was a little puzzled about his reasons for asking my impression of Thevenet. Jacques Michaud was directing the team in Switzerland, while Thevenet was looking after the Dunkirk squad. Was Vallet conducting an opinion poll behind Thevenet's back, or with his approval? I was quite unprepared for what followed.

'Braillon has asked me to take over as *directeur sportif* of the team next year.'

Silence. Ah ... all is revealed. He looked at me, trying to gauge my reaction. I was shocked, but tried not to show it. I had expected Vallet to join Thevenet next year as his assistant – but not as his replacement.

'I want to accept, but I am in a bit of bother because Thevenet and I are good friends.'

Why was he confiding in me about this? I could see he was getting high just talking about it. He must have been dying to tell someone and I just happened to be around when the dam burst. He asked me to keep our conversation secret, saying that he needed time to make his decision. But he wasn't fooling me. His decision was already made. He would take the job.

My good form in Switzerland had gained me selection for the

Dauphine. Apart from the Tour, it was my favourite race. I lived in the region and felt compelled to perform well in my own 'back yard'. There was always a lot at stake in the Dauphine, but this year especially so. A good performance meant a place in the Tour de France team. A place in the Tour team enhanced my chances of being offered a new contract, so I was not lacking in motivation. I had super form for the eight-day event, but I used my form cleverly. Even with that kind of form I knew I was not capable of winning a stage. But I was capable of helping Claveyrolat or Vallet to win one. This was what was important about being a *domestique*. It was better to put all your efforts into helping a team-mate to win than trying and failing to win yourself. Second or third. Fifth or sixth. These places have no value for a pro team. Winning is everything. I knew I was capable of getting placed on stages, but decided it was in my best interests to sacrifice myself for the leaders. Vallet and Claveyrolat were on form. Vallet would more than likely be *directeur sportif* the following year. Clavet was my friend. For the eight stages I put myself totally at their disposition. I protected them from the wind, rode at their side in the mountains, fetched their drinks, waited with them when they stopped to piss, pushed them and willed them to success. They rewarded me with praise each night in front of Thevenet at the dinner table.

'Did you see the work Paul did for us today? He was extraordinary.'

The only regret I had was for my parents. They came over from Ireland on two weeks' holiday to see the race with my youngest brother Christopher. My only bad day of the race was on the first mountain stage to Modane. It was a scorching hot day and I cracked early on the Col du Glandon. I knew my parents were waiting for me at the top. I dreaded passing them so far down the field, and in my frustration I composed a speech that explained my role of *domestique*. On seeing them at the side of the road I planned to stop and say, 'Da, I'm sorry. Look at me. This is the reality. This is what I am. I'm not a star and never will be. I am a water carrier, a *domestique*, a nothing.' I never got to say the prepared words. He was standing two kilometres from the top, with a bottle of water. I smiled, pulled in and filled my *bidon*. He said I was doing fine, and pushed me off, encouraging me further. His enthusiasm lightened my heart and my speech was cancelled.

The following day we crossed three mountains. At the summit of the second, the Izoard, I was just behind the leading group. Only Claveyrolat from our team was in front of me. Thevenet ordered me to wait on Vallet, who was chasing behind with two other team-mates, Mas and Simon. I went down the descent like a madman and we rejoined the front group in the valley. Three riders had broken clear and I was ordered to the front to chase. I rode my heart out until the first hairpins of the day's last mountain, the Col de Vars, where I soon cracked and was dropped. My work was not in vain, for Thierry won the stage and moved up to fourth overall. That night Thevenet came into the room. He praised me for my team work and told me to prepare myself for the Tour de France.

'I hope you are going to stay with us next year.'

He was offering me a contract. I was surprised and delighted.

'Bah oui, j'espère (I hope so).'

'Good. Think about your salary and come back to me next week with a figure. If you wish, you can sign on for two years.'

I was thrilled. A new contract. Lots of good amateurs turn professional but half of them never last longer then the duration of their first contract. The first contract is an apprenticeship. The second one is a confirmation of qualification. I had been offered a second contract: I was a qualified pro.

The day after the finish of the Dauphine, I left for the Tour of Luxembourg. I didn't want to go. The Dauphine had been very hard and had taken a lot out of me, but the team was committed to riding both in Luxembourg and at another stage race in Brittany so I had no choice. I don't know how I ever made it through the first stage. It was a short-circuit race in the city centre and there was lashing rain which turned the oily roads into a skating rink. I was knackered and spent the entire evening at the back of the bunch, counting down the laps to the finish. On nights like that racing a bike was not sport, but just a job. An obligation to earn an honest crust. To survive, you must put the race and the suffering out of your mind. You must think of good times. It rained every single day in Luxembourg, so I was thinking of good times for almost a week. I was climbing really strongly and finished the race in good form about fifteenth and best of our team.

I had ten days off after Luxembourg. The problem of my salary was bothering me. Thevenet had asked me how much I wanted. This was awkward. I would have preferred him to make me an offer. I am not a good businessman and don't like asking for money and had no idea of how much I was worth. One thing was very clear to me. This job was far too hard to be worth only the £700 a month I was then being paid. At a meeting with Thevenet at the team headquarters in Grenoble I asked for £1,000 a month. He scratched his head, and said I was asking for too much. He offered me £900. I accepted, but decided to sign for just one year. This was a bit of a gamble. I was sacrificing the security of a two-year contract. But if I rode really well, I would be free to negotiate a higher wage and the gamble would be worth it.

Things were going well. With my contract and Tour ticket in the bag, I returned to competition for the Midi Libre stage race. Seven riders were assured of places in the team for the Tour. Along with me there were Vallet, Claveyrolat, Colotti, Vermote, Esnault and Mas. The remaining two places were to be fought out between Dede, Simon, Rault, Pedersen and Bibolet. The Midi Libre was the final selection race for the two places. The atmosphere in the team was not good. The battle for the placings strained relationships between the five. Only a blind man could fail to notice the back-stabbing as some of the team tried to score points with Thevenet at the expense of others. I was a little disgusted at this, but then I suppose it was easy for me to talk. Perhaps if I was fighting for my place I would be the same?

For the second time in a month I was selected at random for dope control. Had I a junkie's face? I don't know: it just seemed a bit of a coincidence. It was after the third stage, and I was a little bit worried as I had taken a vitamin C and caffeine tablet before the start. But the doses would have been quickly sweated through my body and Clavet assured me I had nothing to worry about. With two stages to go, Patrice Esnault took over the race lead. I was quite pleased with myself, as I had bust a gut in the breakaway to ensure that Esnault took the leader's jersey. The next day was a time trial and he managed to hang on to his slim advantage over the Spaniard Julien Gorospe. Just one day to defend the jersey: things could not have been better. The last stage was split into two parts: 100 kilometres in the morning and 90 in the afternoon. Because it was a split stage and the last day, we knew there would be no random dope controls on either the morning or the afternoon stage. Esnault, as race leader, would be controlled. So would the winners of both the stages. But the significant thing was that there was no random control. The job of protecting the lead was not Esnault's responsibility; it was his team's. With no random control they, we, could charge up to protect his lead, knowing we wouldn't be asked to pee.

I felt most uncomfortable on learning all this. I wanted to do everything I could so that Esnault would win, but I drew the line at charging up for him. If I wasn't prepared to do it for myself then I wasn't going to do it for someone else. What disturbed me most was the attitude of some of my team-mates. Some certainly disapproved, but a few were almost rejoicing about the fact that they had a green light to be merry the next day. And to make matters worse, one in particular put pressure on me to toe the line. He said it was part of the job. That Esnault had made the supreme effort of defending his lead in the time trial and that it was the duty of his team to defend for him on the last day. I felt he was putting a gun to my head. I refused. Others refused also, but we were a minority. I felt a bit guilty, but most of all I felt angry at being placed in such a dilemma. Why on earth were there no controls? Did the organisers not realise the pressure they were putting on riders like myself? Esnault hung on and won the Midi Libre. It was the first stage race the team had ever won, but the repercussions of the last day left a bitter taste in my mouth.

My non-eligibility for the French road-race championships meant I had ten days off before the Tour. I spent them resting on the shore of the lake at Laffrey, seven kilometres above Vizille, with Ann. She had just graduated from university with a teaching degree, and had come to live with me until the end of the season. Three weeks later I would once again be at the lake shore of Laffrey, but this time as a Tour de France rider, looking at the sunbathers as I cycled by. Now I treasured every minute.

13
TOUR '87

Wednesday, 1 July
Prologue: West Berlin (6.1 kilometres TT)
Stage winner: Jelle Nijdam (Netherlands)
Race leader: Jelle Nijdam

Today I rode faster than twenty-one other pros in the six-kilometre prologue time trial. There were 185 riders who rode faster than me – so I can't say I'm exactly delighted with my first day on the race. Still, it feels wonderful to be part of it all. It's so big and colourful and exciting. A man from Irish radio interviewed me today. The Tour is getting big coverage back home this year, so I must try to keep my face up there. We haven't trained well the last two days. Most of the time has been spent trying to find quiet roads, but inevitably we end up staring at the wall or trying to ride through Checkpoint Charlie. Dede seems happy enough, though. He found this park with women sunbathing almost nude. Today was Colotti's birthday and we ate this huge cake to celebrate. I must have put on weight, for the food here in Novotel is brilliant.

Thursday, 2 July
Stage 1: West Berlin to West Berlin (105.5 kilometres)
Stage 2: West Berlin to West Berlin (40.5 kilometres
Team Time Trial)
Stage 1 winner: Nico Verhoeven (Netherlands)
Stage 2 winner: Carrera (team)
Race leader: Eric Maechler (Switzerland)

It's always a bit worrying when you discover you are not going as well as you thought. Today I discovered it. It was in the afternoon team time-trial stage. I started it with the conviction that I'd show the lads just why I was one of the best *domestiques* in France, but things didn't quite work out. I spent the last twenty kilometres swinging off the back with Clavet.

The morning stage was chaotic. Everyone was extremely nervous and the stage was incredibly fast. We covered the 105 kilometres at an average speed of forty-eight kilometres an hour. Inevitably there was a huge crash that completely blocked the road. Two riders got tangled up together and fell. Normally everyone else would have avoided them, but because we were riding so hard most people had their heads down. Again, normally we would have been alerted by the noise of metal scraping off the ground, but the television helicopter was down so low over our heads that we couldn't hear a thing. At least forty hit the deck and an Italian was carted off to hospital. One down. Jean-Claude got off to a great start and is wearing the red jersey of leader in the sprints competition. I suppose we will have to help him to defend it, as it's good publicity. He is also the French TV mascot for the race. Every day he is interviewed after the race on live TV and asked how his day went. That's more publicity. He is doing well for himself.

TOUR '87

Friday, 3 July
Transfer from West Berlin to Karlsruhe (West Germany)

Today we flew over the Wall and back to the West. Whenever we make these transfers by plane I am reminded of the Munich air disaster that wiped out the Manchester United football team. What would have happened if our jet carrying 200 of the world's best cyclists had crashed? Well, obviously, the cancellation of the Tour. But not everyone would be sorry. The riders not selected for the Tour would be jumping up and down with relief. The world-ranked 201 would be thrilled, as he would suddenly become the world's number one. And 200 bottles of champagne would simultaneously pop in the homes of until then ambitious but frustrated amateurs. It's a morbid thought, but the consequences never cease to fascinate me.

Saturday, 4 July
Stage 3: Karlsruhe to Stuttgart (219 kilometres)
Stage winner: Acasio da Silva (Portugal)
Race leader: Eric Maechler (Switzerland)

The holiday is over. What a stage! Oh, my God, what a stage! It was so unbelievably hot and so incredibly hard. Tonight I feel as if we are in the third week of the race, not the third day. It was up and down for 219 kilometres and at the finish there were bodies everywhere. One big 22-man group got away in the last hour. We had no one in it but we were all too knackered to chase. Mottet, one of the favourites for the race, was up there but his rivals did nothing to chase. They couldn't: at the end it was a case of every man for himself, just to finish. It was action all day from the gun. There was always someone on the attack and someone else ready to chase – until the end, that is. The pace was so fast that we could not go back for bottles from the cars, and near the end I had to give Kelly a drink, as he hadn't a drop in his *bidon*. I don't understand why he didn't command his *domestiques* to fetch him one. I'm sure he could, with someone like me in his team. My leaders may not be the best in the world but they are seldom thirsty. Funnily enough I was actually riding better than most of my team-mates. They all suffered from the heat. So did I. During the stage I thought of a great idea for Treets. You know, the chocolates that melt in your mouth, not in your hand. The idea was to have a Tour rider carrying a Treet in his jersey pocket and to take it out during the boiling hot stage, and it not be melted. Am I going mad?

Sunday, 5 July
Stage 4: Stuttgart to Pforzheim (79 kilometres)
Stage 5: Pforzheim to Strasbourg (112.5 kilometres)
Stage 4: winner: Hermon Frison (Belgium)
Stage 5: Marc Sergeant (Belgium)
Race leader: Eric Maechler

Another split stage. In the morning an 80-kilometre sprint to Pforzheim and in the afternoon a 112-kilometre run to Strasbourg. We didn't need a frontier to tell us we had crossed into France. We could judge from the surface of the road and from the reaction of the crowds. In Germany we had great crowds. They cheered us with air horns and shouting, just like you'd find at a football match. In France it was the traditional polite applause and accordion music as we cycled towards Strasbourg. I left home exactly a week ago and we have only just entered France. The really hot weather continues and there are already a lot of tired bodies in the peloton. Nine have quit the race after just five stages, and if we continue at this pace there won't be a hundred riders in Paris.

Monday, 6 July
Stage 6: Strasbourg to Epinal (169 kilometres)
Stage winner: Christophe Lavainne (France)
Race leader: Eric Maechler

The first mountain stage with the first-category Col de Kreuzweg and the second-category Col du Donon. I lost contact late on the Kreuzweg but managed to get back on before Donon, where I held on. But it was too far to the finish and we eased up, enabling most of those dropped to regain contact. It was the first real ceasefire of the race, so no one was complaining. The last fifty kilometres were very hard and fast and I was lucky to avoid the huge crash twenty kilometres from the finish.

We are staying in Hôtel Ibis. We hate these hotels: the rooms are so small that there is never any room to open the suitcase. The team doctors came tonight and put me on a glucose drip. I felt so tired that I wasn't refusing. I hope there was only glucose in the bottle, but I am not sure and too tired to ask. When the drip was finished they gave me a sleeping tablet. I don't like taking them, but they tell me a good night's sleep is essential to recovery and I need to recover.

Tuesday, 7 July
Stage 7: Epinal to Troyes (211 kilometres)
Stage winner: Guido Bontempi (Italy)
Race leader: Eric Maechler

I am rooming with Vallet tonight. This year we are changing almost every night, so that we are never with the same bloke two nights in a row. I don't like rooming with Vallet. I feel I must always put on a show for him. I insisted that he have the big bed because I know he expects to be offered it. I refuse to complain when he leaves the light in the room on until after eleven at night and I feel almost obliged to get up and leave the room when I feel like farting. I am nearly sure, now, that he has agreed to take over from Thevenet at the end of the year. Braillon was in our room tonight and they were talking business. I pretended not to listen.

Wednesday, 8 July
Stage 8: Troyes to Epinay-sous-Senart (205.5 kilometres)
Stage winner: Jean-Paul Van Poppel (Netherlands)
Race leader: Eric Maechler

A relatively easy day. A relatively easy day is one with a slow start, a really fast bit in the middle, a short lull and the last sixty kilometres covered in an hour. We had to drive to Orléans for tomorrow's start after the stage, which was a bit tiring. Orléans is Esnault's home town, and he has a crowd of supporters in the hotel tonight. He is supposed to be our leader here, but I am riding better than him myself. I wouldn't mind if he gave a hand with the chores. But a leader is always a leader, even when he is not riding as well as a *domestique*. Today I bust a gut to get him a bottle, and when I brought it to him he didn't want it. It is the last one he will get.

Thursday, 9 July
Stage 9: Orléans to Renaze (260 kilometres)
Stage winner: Adri Van der Poel (Netherlands)
Race leader: Eric Maechler

Colotti is still holding on to his sprint leader's jersey. Today I led him out on three occasions, and tonight we are rooming together and he gave me a jersey as a souvenir. Highlight of the day was the crash, twelve kilometres from the finish. We had been riding on good, wide roads all day, but for some inexplicable reason the organisers brought us on a criss-cross of small, narrow roads for the last thirty kilometres, so crashes were inevitable. This one was different, because there was

Above: My father winning the last stage of the Ras Tailteann 1963 in the Phoenix Park
Below left: My brother Raphael winning a stage of the Ras Tailteann in Carrick on Suir in June '83. Second is Sean Kelly's brother Vincent
Below right: Ras Tailteann '83 – my only ever ride in the race they call the 'big one'

Above: Racing towards the yellow jersey in the Milk Race '83
with Sean Yates on my wheel
Below left: Milk Race '83, the race that nearly made me
a star – accepting the yellow jersey
Below right: Milk Race '83 – crossing the finish line at Harrogate
having lost 13 minutes and the yellow jersey

Above left: On the attack with Frenchman Christian Sobota in
the colours of my French club C.C. Wasquehal, June '85
Above right: Dede Chappuis – St Etienne time trial, Tour de France, 1986
Below: Brand new anorak. Grand Bornand '86 – my first meeting with
the RMO team. LEFT TO RIGHT: Jean Louis Gauthier, myself,
Bruno Huger, Christian Mogore, Michel Vermote, Bernard Thevenet,
Thierry Claveyrolat, Simon Regis, Patrick Clerc, Marcel Russenberger,
Pierre Le Bigaut, Frances Castaing, Vincent Barteau, Gilles Mas, Per
Pedersen, Jean Claude Vallaeys, Bernard Vallet, André Chappuis

Above: Helping hand: Bernard Thevenet always stood on the
finish line until all of his riders came in. He had to wait 35 minutes
for me here at L'Alpe d'Huez – '86 Tour
Below: Tough at the top. After finishing the stage to Alpe d'Huez, '86

Above left: Alone on the mountain: struggling on the Galibier – '86 Tour

Above right: Nearing the end of my pain: 100 metres from the finish
line of the Mount Ventoux time trial – '87 Tour

Below: Claveyrolat shares his supply of food – Nissan '87

Above: Smiles before the miles: riding out with Stephen and Martin Earley in the '87 Tour

Below: Shades, suntan: I'm looking pretty cool this morning with Martin and Stephen at Orléans – '87 Tour

Above: World Road Race Championships, Belgium 1988.
The rider in dark glasses, to my left, is Jorgen Pedersen.
Below: And now the end is near: the Aubisque mountain, '89 Tour –
Stephen's last day on the race. The Fagor riders (*from left to right*):
Kimmage, Biondi, Roche, Lavenu and Schepers (his back)

Above: The heroes: without Roche and Kelly I would never have survived my four years in the professional pelaton
Below left: Tour de France '89. Montpelier, 13 July.
The evening of my last race as a professional. Hours earlier I had abandoned the Tour and my career as a pro cyclist
Below right: Hillwalking with Ann in the Alps, August '89

almost a fight after it. The Colombians are responsible for most of the crashes in the bunch. The majority have very poor bike control, and now every time there is a crash someone cries, 'Bloody Colombians!' I'm not sure today's crash was their fault, but it happened at a very bad time, when most of us were knackered and roasted by the sun. A Belgian threw his *bidon* at a Colombian, hitting him on the back of the head. He was immediately set upon by two other Colombians, and things got a bit out of control.

Friday, 10 July
Stage 10: Saumur to Futuroscope (87.5 kilometres TT)
Stage winner: Stephen Roche (Ireland)
Race leader: Charly Mottet (France)

What a long time trial: eighty-eight kilometres to be ridden alone. Lucho Herrera was off a minute behind me, and he caught me after twenty-six kilometres. I rode hard, but not flat out as the memories of Nantes were still fresh in my mind. Stephen won, and I think I lost about sixteen minutes, which is phenomenal. I think if my life had depended on it I could have ridden six minutes faster, but no more. I feel a bit small tonight. The hotel is showing pornographic videos, and you can walk into any of the rooms and it will be on. I reckon there will be a few tired bodies tomorrow.

Saturday, 11 July
Stage 11: Poitiers to Chaumeil (255 kilometres)
Stage winner: Martial Gayant (France)
Race leader: Martial Gayant

Today was probably the hardest stage of the race so far. It was 255 kilometres, but up and down all day on tiny roads with the tar melting off them from the hot sun. My feet are killing me. They expand in the heat, and the pressure of the buckle of the toe-strap left me limping after the stage. Colotti nearly cracked mentally today, and I had to nurse him through. Physically, I didn't feel too bad; but for anyone who went all out in yesterday's time trial it must have been hell.

Sunday, 12 July
Stage 12: Brive-la-Gaillarde to Bordeaux (228 kilometres)
Stage winner: Davis Phinney (USA)
Race leader: Martial Gayant

We lost Kelly today. We had ridden hard for the opening fifty kilometres, when the pace dropped. I was dying for a piss, and stopped as soon as I recognised the ceasefire. The Team cars had just started to pass me, when suddenly they all braked and I heard the word 'chute' ('crash') from the race radio. As soon as the word was spoken the team mechanics jumped from the cars with a pair of wheels and ran to the pile of tangled bodies up the road. I didn't panic, as crashes happened every day; so I finished my widdle and casually set off in pursuit. As I passed Thevenet, he told me not to hang around, as there had been an attack. The race radio was announcing the names of those who had crashed. Kelly was riding at the back and surrounded by three team-mates when I made contact. His face was screwed up in pain, and he was riding with one hand off the bars. The doctors' car drove up alongside and sprayed his shoulder with pain-killer but it didn't seem to be having much effect. The bunch slowed and we made contact, but he never stirred from the back and it was obvious to me that he could not continue in his present state. I approached him and gave him a gentle pat on the back as a gesture of solidarity, and then one by one the team leaders dropped back to pay their respects. He was distanced as soon as the road started to rise, and he abandoned in tears shortly after. I felt really disappointed for him. He was having a lousy Tour, and that morning he had made a rare appearance at the coffee table for a joke and a chat. It wasn't the same without him.

Signed a new one-year contract for £900 with Braillon at the hotel tonight.

Monday, 13 July
Stage 13: Bayonne to Pau (219 kilometres)
Stage winner: Erik Breukink (Netherlands)
Race leader: Charly Mottet

I was in good form riding out of Bayonne. I like the mountain stages and I have always a little hope in the back of my mind of one day winning one. I started badly on the first climb, the first-category Col de Burdincurutcheta, but soon found my climbing legs and went through the struggling bodies like a warm knife through butter. I was with the top group going over the top of the second-category Bargargui and felt this was going to be my day. Clavet, Mas and I were the only three from the team still up there, and I felt wonderful as we started the descent. Then it all went wrong. Someone attacked on the descent, and we went down it at a fierce pace. The tar had melted on some of the corners, making them treacherously slippy, and I knew there would soon be trouble with over-heating rims. The rims overheat from constant braking and there are two possible consequences: either the glue that sticks the tyre to the rim melts and the tyre rolls off the rim, or the heat of the rim makes the tyre explode. Three-quarters of the way down I started to feel my tyres swaying a bit on the rims, but I could hear tyres exploding all over the place. I was descending behind a Carrera when suddenly, as we entered a hairpin, his front tyre exploded off the rim and he crashed.

'Fuck. I'm going to crash.' I swung out the bars and tried to avoid him, but there was nowhere for me to go. I hit him and flipped just off the edge of the road. Five seconds of the world turning upside-down, of total lack of control, and I come to a halt. Oh, it's always a great feeling to open your eyes after a crash. My knee is stinging a bit but I'm OK. I try to get up, but I'm trapped under my bike and I burn my hand on the hot front rim. The tyre has rolled off and I will need a change. Behind, there was chaos as, one by one, riders started piling into the back of us. The Belgian Henrick De Vos didn't have time to brake: he went straight off the cliff edge, landing sixty feet below us. Team cars screeched to a halt behind, the panicking race doctors slid down the side to rescue poor De Vos – who I felt sure was dead. Thevenet and Coval both came to my rescue. Thevenet reached me first and he screamed at the mechanic, who had run further down the road, to come back and change the wheel. But the front rim was so hot that he burned his hand as he tried to get it out.

I jumped back on the bike dazed but only slightly grazed. There were bodies everywhere on the descent, absolute carnage, and I joined Kim Andersen and Miguel Indurain. We were descending a long straight bit of road at about sixty kilometres an hour when one of the team cars overtook and came so close that he clipped Indurain's handlebars with the side of the car. God knows how the Spaniard managed to stay upright. This latest incident had a strange effect on me. I sat up and decided to take no more chances on the descent. 'These people are all insane. It's only a fucking bike race. To hell with them.'

I finished the stage with one of the larger groups and am feeling fine tonight. Twelve riders abandoned, including Vermotte from our team. De Vos was lifted from the side of the mountain in a helicopter. He has a fractured skull, but his life is not in danger so he is lucky. Colotti had a really bad day today and barely scraped through. I feel a bit guilty at not having waited with him. He is the only one from the team getting any publicity, as he is still sprint leader, so I will stay with him tomorrow.

Tuesday, 14 July
Stage 14: Pau to Luz Ardiden (166 kilometres)
Stage winner: Dag-Otto Lauritzen (Norway)
Race leader: Charly Mottet

The team doctors came to the hotel last night. This morning before the stage they came into the room. They started preparing a syringe with a small ampoule of something or other. I asked what it was and was told 'synacthen'. I hadn't got a clue what that was, but I didn't like the sound of it so I said I didn't want any. It was a bit embarrassing, but the doctor bowed to my wish and didn't insist – he gave it to my room-mate instead.

(Synacthen is common, even a 'lightweight', among many of the hormonal products used in the peloton. It is a medicament that simulates 24 of the 39 amino acids which constitute a molecule of l'ACTH, which stimulate the production of cortisone in the body. It therefore commands the body to produce its own cortisone. The other way of increasing cortisone in the body is to take it directly. Kenacort is a synthetic cortisone, and a product widely used in the peloton. It is banned but detection is a problem – the body produces cortisone naturally, and some people produce more than others, so finding a norm is difficult.)

I have been sorely tempted to experiment with stuff during the race, but fear the secondary effects of cortisone abuse, so I have decided not to enter that little game. And yet I am tempted. I know I would improve, for I've seen the improvements in others, but it's doping and I'm afraid of where it will lead me. The old argument that a doped ass won't win the Derby is a true, but a dangerous one. I know that by taking stuff I'll never win the Tour. But physically I would improve. And by improving I would gain in confidence and maybe start winning races. That would earn me more money – which is all that counts at the end of the day. Maybe it's my upbringing, the terrible attacks of conscience whenever I do anything wrong.

Maybe it's an innate survival instinct: the knowledge that at the end of the day I will have to stop and find a job, and that good health is really the only wealth that we have. I suppose it's a mixture of both. Either way, it's a road I don't want to go down.

Colotti was on his hands and knees today. He was the first to be dropped on the climb of the Col de Marie Blanque just after the start. I waited with him. I felt so strong, riding at his side. Stronger than I've ever felt in any mountain stage of the Tour. But maybe I was fooling myself. Maybe it was because he was so weak that I felt so good. I don't know. Dede waited with us as well. I felt sure he was done and just wanted friendly company for the day. We dragged Colotti over the mountain and then set off in pursuit of the descent. There was thick fog on the descent, and I overshot one of the first hairpins but didn't fall off. I felt he was going to abandon the second mountain, Aubisque, but he held on. In the valley before Luz Ardiden I rode along as hard as I could at the front of the group. We caught Jean-Louis Gauthier, Adri Van der Poel and Van Poppel and I paced them to the bottom of the climb to the ski station. We made the time limit with ten minutes to spare and Colotti went on French TV and said he would never have made it without Kimmage and Chappuis.

We are staying in a real kip tonight. I think it's an old school-house.

Wednesday, 15 July
Stage 15: Tarbes to Blagnac (164 kilometres)
Stage winner: Rolf Golz (Germany)
Race leader: Charly Mottet

What a terrible day! Had trouble with my stomach, cramps. There was a cloudburst with forty kilometres to go, and I have never seen so much water on the roads. At one stage you would have drowned on toppling over. The bunch split to pieces under an attack from Mottet and Fignon. We had to ride really hard to avoid being eliminated. Bob Roll, the American who rides for Seven Eleven has a phrase that sums the race up. 'It sucks.'

Thursday, 16 July
Stage 16: Blagnac to Millau (216.5 kilometres)
Stage winner: Regis Clere (France)
Race leader: Charly Mottet

Colotti abandoned. It was early in the stage and he complained of problems with his left knee. Dede and I waited with him on two occasions when he was dropped at the start, but on the third time he decided to call it a day. He was devastated and in tears as he climbed off, and I felt sorry for him. He had tried so hard – too hard – in the first ten days and he was still wearing the sprint leader's jersey. But his lead was being eaten away and he had not won a sprint for three days. He was physically drained, but it's a pity he could not hang on, for in two days we have the rest day.

Clavet was also in trouble. He has picked up bronchitis from yesterday's bad weather, and he was dropped with forty kilometres to go. Dede waited with him.

Friday, 17 July
Stage 17: Millau to Avignon (239 kilometres)
Stage winner: Jean-Paul Van Poppel
Race leader: Charly Mottet

The stomach pains continue and are getting worse, if anything. Today was a nightmare: 240 kilometres, with a big climb just after the start. We started like rockets, and I was in big trouble on the climb and only held on by the skin of my teeth. Vallet started shouting near the end for us to attack, but the guy's dreaming. He was as quiet as a mouse for the first ten days, when he was hanging on, but now that he is going better we are supposed to attack. I didn't feel much like attacking, and got dropped near the finish in the crosswinds. Ann was at the finish. She came down with Clavet's wife Myriam. She is staying the weekend, for tomorrow is the rest day, and on Sunday there is the time trial up Mont Ventoux. Thevenet tells us that he shouldn't really be allowing the wives and girlfriends to stay in the hotel with us. At mealtimes we are forbidden to eat together. The riders eat at one table. The wives eat at another. Tradition has it so. Tradition sucks.

Saturday, 18 July
Rest day: Avignon

Thank God it's a rest day, for there is no way I would be capable of riding a stage. I spent the morning in bed: the cramps are subsiding but I feel terribly weak. Ann washed my gear and in the afternoon I went out with Paul Sherwen to turn the legs a bit. We did about forty kilometres around the vineyards of Châteauneuf du Pape. I have started to appreciate wine now, and can look around me with a new interest. Most of the lads rode up the Ventoux but I was too weak to contemplate it. The doctors are treating me, and I feel a little better tonight.

Sunday, 19 July
Stage 18: Carpentras to Mont Ventoux (36.5 kilometres TT)
Stage winner: Jean-François Bernard (France)
Race leader: Jean-François Bernard

The Giant of Provence. A mountain made famous by the death of a famous English cyclist, Tom Simpson. In between the effort of trying to ride up the mountain I tried hard to pick out the memorial statue to him as I neared the top, but it was hidden behind the thousands of spectators who had come to cheer the modern-day heroes. I felt quite OK, after a shaky start, and finished 118th of the 164 still in the race. I seem to have recovered from my stomach bug and that gives me new optimism for finishing the race

Monday, 20 July
Stage 19: Valreas to Villard-de-Lans (185 kilometres)
Stage winner: Pedro Delgado (Spain)
Race leader: Stephen Roche (Eire)

Clavet and Esnault both packed it in today. The team is down to just five men and morale is low. Poor Clavet, I feel sorry for him. Tomorrow we ride through his home town, my adopted town, Vizille. The mayor of the town sent leaflets to all the inhabitants asking them to come out to cheer the two 'local' men, Claveyrolat and Kimmage. But Clavet won't be around now for the 'party'. He has locked himself in his room, and there is no talking him out of it. The television showed his tearful abandoning this evening. I suppose it must make great television, but it's still a bit much.

I had one of my better days. I felt good from the start and was never under any serious pressure. It's a great day for the Irish for Stephen is the new *maillot jaune*. He becomes only the third Irishman ever to have worn the famous tunic. I'm very happy for him, although I would like to get to talk to him more. He is too busy trying to win the race.

Tuesday, 21 July
Stage 20: Villard-de-Lans to L'Alpe D'Heuz (201 kilometres)
Stage winner: Frederico Echave (Spain)
Race leader: Pedro Delgado (Spain)

If, in later years, I am asked what the greatest thrill in my life has been, I will hesitate between two replies. It would either be arriving on the Champs Elysées after a hard Tour, or riding through the thousands of screaming voices to the ski station of L'Alpe d'Huez. I was too knackered to appreciate it last year – so tired that all I ever saw of the thirteen-kilometre rise was the five feet of rising tarmac before me. But today was different, and I was going quite well. Martin and I both rode out of Villard de Lans at Stephen's side. Proud to be Irish sounds so corny but, damn it, I was proud to be Irish. It was one of the hardest stages of the race, with seven climbs. I got clear with a group on the day's first climb, the Placette, and as far as I remember it was my first time in twenty stages to get into a breakaway. It didn't last long, for the Carreras reeled us in on the descent. I stayed with the top men over the second-category Cucheron and the first-category Coq. I must admit to being highly motivated, for I wanted to be in a good position going through Vizille. I led through the village and crucified myself to stay at the front for two kilometres of the seven-kilometre Côte de Laffrey on the outskirts of the town. I got lots of cheers, and my name was sprayed all over the climb. I know the road to the Alpe like the back of my hand, and that's always a big help. I enjoyed the twenty-one hairpins of the mountain. I was able to settle into a rhythm and ride up at my own pace, and it was almost a pleasure to suffer in this way. At the top Stephen had lost the jersey to Pedro Delgado. 'Perico' is in the same hotel as us tonight. I like him: he is natural and has an honest smile. I didn't see Ann today, although she told me on the phone tonight that she was on the Laffrey. Frank arrived from Dublin and is a bit disappointed about Kelly.

14

22 JULY

It is 7.45 a.m. at the Hotel Christina. I have been lying awake for fifteen minutes now. It's nice to lie here and rest. Soon it will be time to get up. Another stage, another day. I didn't sleep well last night. I woke at least four times but each time managed to doze off again within five to ten minutes. I put it down to sleeping at altitude. I never noticed the problem until I heard Mas and Vallet complaining that they never slept well at altitude. This set me worrying that I wouldn't sleep well at altitude and, consequently, I don't. Frank Cronseilles, one of the team *soigneurs* enters the room and I close my eyes, pretending to sleep. He taps my shoulder and whispers softly, 'Allez Polo, c'est l'heure.' I drag myself out of bed and walk out on to the veranda. The view of the Alpe on this fresh sunny morning is breath-taking. Below, the *soigneurs* are busy loading suitcases, while the hiss of an air compressor inflating a hundred tyres announces that the mechanics too are at work. Which reminds me that it's time for me to start. After washing and shaving, I go down for breakfast. Coffee, fresh croissants and jam. It's the favourite part of my breakfast. Normally we are not allowed croissants. The myth is that they are too fattening. Typical of the French: it's OK to eat half a ton of cheese in the evenings but not OK to eat croissants in the morning. I have lost three kilos on this race, so I decide to ignore the frowning brows and reach for a second. The food here is really good. The steak is tender and the spaghetti *al dente*, so for once eating is eating and not fuelling up as is often the case. A yogurt, a fruit salad, and a stroll outside to see what's happening.

The *soigneurs* are starting to panic. They urge me to return to the room to pack my suitcase. The suitcase is a mess. I'm not a very organised person. For 'organised' you can substitute 'tidy'. I throw a day's kit on to the bed, pile everything else into the case and close it with great difficulty. It is then left outside the door to be picked up by the *soigneur* on his next passage. There is just time to study the race bible and the battleground for today's stage. Five mountains: Lauteret, Galibier, Telegraph, Madeleine and the summit finish of La Plagne. Hmmm . . . the Galibier. Visions of last year's tour and my struggling body on its steep slopes disturb my mind. But I am riding much better this year, so there shouldn't be any problem.

The stage start is in the village of Bourg d'Oisans, twenty-one hairpins below us. A few years ago it used to start here at the Alpe and be neutralised to the bottom. But the riders were forced to brake constantly behind the race director's car and the wheel rims overheated, causing dozens of punctures and blow-outs. Now everyone descends in cars. As usual I am the last to leave the hotel. Thevenet blows the car horn for me to hurry. His is the only team car left and it's full. He drives with Vallet beside him in the front seat. I am squashed in the back between the mechanic Coval and Yves Hezard, an ex-pro and a good friend of Thevenet's. With the exception of Coval, each of us has raced up the Alpe in the Tour and it is the topic of conversation as we descend.

'What used to impress me most', says Hezard, 'was arriving at the bottom and looking up to see the lines and lines of spectators almost directly above you.'

'I don't remember ever having the strength to look up,' Thevenet replies jokingly and we all laugh.

As we descend, we notice hordes of cycling tourists of every shape and size sweating and panting their way up the mountain.

'They are all timing themselves,' says Thevenet. 'They know exactly how long it took Roche and Delgado to climb yesterday and tonight they will compare times and work out exactly how many pros they'd have beaten on the stage.'

Like all Tour de France stage 'departs', Bourg d'Oisans is crammed with spectators and it is with great difficulty that we find a parking spot. The routine never changes. Get out of the car, collect the race food from the *soigneurs'* car and the bike from the mechanics. Check that the brake blocks are not too close to the wheels and that both wheels are well tightened. This is purely a personal thing. I hate having the brake blocks too close to the rims in case they rub and I'm always afraid of an untightened front wheel popping out of the forks at sixty on a mountain descent. I ride to the signing-on podium and spend the thirty minutes before the start chatting and drinking coffee with Martin at one of the hospitality tables. We meet at the same table each morning. Sean Yates, Adrian Timmis and Allan Peiper are with Martin at 'our' table as I arrive. Conversation is as it always is. Of the day before, of how knackered we all are and of how we are all looking forward to finishing in Paris. Our chief concern today is that the hostilities don't start too early on the road to La Plagne. But then again that's our chief concern every day. Pedro Delgado, the race leader, arrives at an adjoining table: the table where all the Spanish riders sit. He is pestered by autograph hunters and requests from journalists and has no time to drink coffee. Being famous can be such a pain. The high pitch of the race starter's whistle beckons us to line up. The excited spectators shout the names of their favourites. 'Tiens, il y a Roche! Allez Roche!' 'Le voilà Delgado! Bravo Pedro!' No one ever shouts my name but this morning a spectator taps me on the shoulder.

'Bonjour, I'm a friend of Dante Rezze,' he said, shaking my hand.

'Ah, OK,' I reply.

What being a friend of Dante Rezze has to do with shaking my hand is beyond me, but these things often happen on the Tour. The starter's flag drops, and I ride out through the valley talking to Martin. He is changing teams at the end of the year and is getting a bit of hassle from Fagor, his current employers, so his morale is low. My own worries are of a different nature. The amazing thing about being a bike rider is that you always know from the first turn of the pedals what sort of a day you are going to have. Or is it the same in every sport? Can Serge Blanco tell by pulling on his rugger boots if he is going to score five tries or play a stinker? It's something I must find out. This morning, I was in no doubt. My legs were tired and very heavy. It would be a bad day.

'Have you ridden up the Lauteret from this side before?'

Martin shakes his head for 'no'.

'It's a long bastard.'

Soon we turn left and the climb begins. There are climbs you like and climbs you hate. I like the Alpe d'Huez. I hate the Lauteret. It is thirty-three kilometres long, is badly surfaced and I never ride well on it. After just one kilometre I am sweating. My arms and face are dripping and I feel most uncomfortable.

'Shit, I should have brought a caffeine tablet.'

The pace is fast but bearable when we enter the first of five tunnels on the climb. It is unlit. The riders in the front accelerate, safe from all obstruction. Behind, it is chaos. It is almost impossible to see the wheel in front and we are forced to ride through at a snail's pace. Coming out of the tunnel we are forty-five seconds behind the *tête* of the peloton. I chase hard for two kilometres with Peiper to rejoin. The chase confirms my earlier impressions. I am having a really bad day. Others are suffering too.

'Did you see the guy that crashed in the tunnel?'

I look across. It's Dede.

'No, didn't see a thing.'

'He was covered in blood.'

A race official's motorbike moves up alongside and we learn that the Dutch rider Nijboer has abandoned and is being taken to hospital. We enter another tunnel and another Dutchman, Solleveld, falls off just in front of me – but this time without serious injury. Fignon stops for a pee. Martin decides it's a good idea and stops with him. Jean-François Bernard stops, and with him his watchdog Dominique Garde. And for two kilometres we ramble along and I am thankful for the common sense being shown. Then it happens. The attack. Shouts and whistles go round the bunch and I look up to see who it is. Yes it's him. Chozas. He does this every year, the Spanish bastard. Takes off at the start of a hard mountain stage when everyone is content to take it easy. The million dollar question is: will they chase him? If they do, it will blow the race apart. If they don't, we shall ramble along for a good bit longer until someone decides it's a reasonable time to start racing. I look up, waiting for a reaction. I can hear it. The imaginary fuse burning on the end of the imaginary dynamite. More cries. Two more riders dash off the front. The chase is on. Badooom!

The peloton stretches out in one long line, and all I can do is try to hang on. Those with tired legs are soon in difficulty. The points leader, Van Poppel, is dropped along with eight others including Peiper and the Swiss Zimmerman. The chase intensifies. I am directly behind Dede. He lets the gap open.

'Allez Dede!'

'I am sick of this bloody race.'

I ride past. I look around and he is twenty or thirty metres behind. I'm suffering but am surprised and encouraged at my ability to close the gaps opening all over the place. There are just five kilometres to the top of the Lauteret, then we swing left immediately to start the eight-kilometre ascent of the Galibier. Martin is in trouble. He lets the gap open and I ride up behind him.

'Hang on, it's too early to lose contact.'

We take turns at trying to reduce the deficit. We close to

thirty metres, twenty, then I pass him and grit my teeth in one last effort to make the junction. But suddenly I run out of gas. I can't make it and can no longer stay with Martin. My legs are turning, but without power. The tiredness mounts from my legs to my arms, and soon it has paralysed my whole body. I look up just as Martin makes contact. And then the group pulls away.

The Van Poppel group catches me. I grit my teeth and take my place in the slipstream of the last rider. We pass the café at the top of the Lauteret and turn left to start the Galibier. I am finding it harder and harder to stay with the group. My body feels empty and my morale is tumbling. One length, two, and I lose contact with the group. Panic, desperation and the realisation that I am in big trouble. Rault catches me and shouts for me to stay with him.

'Go on, the Tour is finished for me.'

Why did I say that? Thevenet passes me in the team car.

'Paul you must try to get up to Van Poppel's group.'

I look across to him and shake my head and he drives past. The pedals turn but with no conviction. Self-pity is now the abiding sentiment, and once that starts there is no hope. I am doomed. I see a banner, 'ROCHE EARLEY KIMMAGE', and my friend Seamus Downey standing under it. I look to him and shake my head, and then feel angry with myself for giving up. Dede catches me.

'Allez Paul!'

'No Dede, go on leave me.'

But he insists on staying with me, so I scream abuse at him to leave me alone. He does. Michaud is behind now, in the second team car. Tears fill my eyes. I decide to try again. I begin to ride faster, deciding not to give up. But the effort lasts just one kilometre. My legs are just empty. A rider passes me on the right at twice my speed. I look across to see who it is. It's a bearded tourist, riding up the mountain with pannier bags on his bike. A bloody Fred. Michaud drives up alongside and tells the tourist to get off his bike. But the damage is done, and I am now completely demoralised. Spectators are now pushing me, and Michaud realises that I'm cooked and drives past saying that he will shortly return. I look behind. The broom wagon is just 500 metres back, with just two riders in front of it. It is drawing me in like a giant magnet.

I am resigned now to abandon, as I know there is no way I will make the time limit in my present state. I pass the statue of the Tour founder Henri Desgrange. It's as good a place as any to get off, but there are too many spectators. Allochio, an Italian and Gorospe, a Spaniard pass me just before the summit and leave me. The broom wagon is now directly behind. The descent of the Galibier is twisting and dangerous but I take no risks. There is an icy wind blowing up from the valley below and it freezes me as I drop. Down through the village of Valloire and then the short five kilometre climb of the Telegraph. Oh God, that feeling of jadedness when I am asked once again for effort. There is nothing in my legs. I look for a place to end it. A place void of people so that I can retire with dignity. I stop on the right-hand side of the road after a kilometre of climbing. I have cracked. It is over. The broom wagon and ambulance stop behind me. I stand, head bent down over my bike, as a nurse descends from the ambulance and offers her sympathies. A commissar gets out of the broom wagon and unpins the two race numbers from my back. 'C'est dure,' he sighs, as he completes this unpleasant duty. People further up the mountain come running down to witness the excitement. There are ohs and ahs as I climb into the bus, and then cheers as I am driven away. I feel numb and dazed and cold. I wrap myself in a blanket and ask the commissar how many abandonments there have been. Four.

We catch Gorospe and Allochio at the feeding station at St Jean de Maurienne. Gorospe abandons. The commissar gets out to remove his numbers. He gets into one of his team cars. Michaud is waiting for me. He tells me I must stay in the broom wagon until the end of the stage. I nod, accepting my punishment. He gives me a bag of food and drives off. We catch Allochio at the bottom of the Madeleine. My eyelids are so heavy and I must fight to stay awake, but there is no fight left in me and exhausted I fall asleep. I wake half an hour later near the summit of the mountain. It's like waking from a bad dream and encountering a nightmare. I can't come to terms with the fact that I am in the bus. What am I doing here? How the fuck could I have abandoned the Tour de France? Oh God, what have I done?

My body has warmed up now, so I discard the blanket. Some spectators recognise my jersey in the back of the broom wagon. 'Look, an RMO has abandoned.' I pull the blanket around myself again, this time to hide my identity. I am in disgrace.

The final climb to La Plagne seems unending. The nearer we get to the finish the worse I feel. We drive past a huge Irish tricolour flag with the names of the four Irishmen on it. Ashamed, I look away. We pass the little red triangle that signifies the last kilometre and arrive at the finish line. As usual it's chaotic. The race announcer Daniel Mangeas announces the list of the day's abandonments. His voice is soft and sad. The tones are those you would expect from a man announcing a list of soldiers killed in a war. I leave the bus and walk, head down, to the team car. Coval is at the wheel. 'Thevenet is gone looking for you.' I sit in the front seat and Thevenet returns five minutes later. He knows exactly how I am feeling and his words are chosen carefully.

'Ah Polo. You gave it all you could. We can ask no more of you.'

The kind words have the effect of an aquarium just shattered by the blows of a hammer. Three hours of caged-in disappointment, anguish and shame come flowing out as I break down and weep as I have not done for a long, long time. There is a short drive to the hotel. Thankfully I am rooming with Dede. He tries his hardest to sympathise, but it really isn't easy and I realise exactly how Gauthier felt at Pau a year earlier. Dede goes off for massage and I am happy to be left alone. Alone with my thoughts. I have failed.

I left La Plagne the very next morning about half an hour before the start of the stage. The team equipment truck was to leave me at the station at Albertville, where I could catch a train to Grenoble. There were cars everywhere and we got stuck in a traffic jam just outside La Plagne. Some teams had stayed in the valley below and had to drive back up the mountain. The Carrera car stopped opposite us and Stephen was in the front seat. I tried to hide, hoping he would not see me but he did and immediately rolled down the window. I smiled a false smile. He grinned that typical Roche grin and shouted playfully.

'Oh, Kimmage, what are you doing there?'

This hurt. It hurt badly, but I tried not to show it. He recognised the hurt.

'Take it easy for a few days, Paul, but get back on your bike as quickly as possible.'

The words were sincere and greatly appreciated. The cars in front started to move, and our conversation was interrupted.

'Good luck to you Stephen.'

Although it was only seventy kilometres away, it was two train rides and a bus journey back to Vizille. Ann was waiting at the flat. I hadn't phoned and this had hurt her. I was narky and tired. She felt hurt and upset. We had a huge row as soon as I entered the flat. She was quite right to be angry, but my disappointment had been so complete that I could not bring myself to pick up a phone to talk about it.

Back in Ireland the whole country was following Stephen's bid to win cycling's biggest prize. I couldn't bear to watch any of it during those final three days. On the day of the race-deciding time trial at Dijon I was out shopping with Ann. I remember walking by a furniture shop with a television set in the window. It was the live broadcast of the time trial that drew my attention. I had left the house to avoid watching it, but as I passed the shop the temptation was too much. I stood in front of the window and watched as the screen split showing Delgado and Roche and the time gap that separated them. Stephen was winning the Tour. The next day, Sunday, we took the train to Paris. I had promised Thevenet I would come up for the end-of-Tour team night out. But as I arrived at the Sofitel I was sorry I had come. It wasn't the same. I couldn't rid myself of the feeling of guilt. The feeling that I had sinned.

Just before we went out to dinner Stephen, the triumphant Tour winner, arrived back at the hotel. He was surrounded by a million people, which suited me because I wanted to avoid him. I felt compelled to approach him and congratulate him, but the revulsion I felt about having quit was stronger. But there was another factor. I was happy he had won, but I was also jealous. Jealous that he had made it to the top of the world, while I had just fallen off it. He was a star now, and I could find no likeness to the Roche I had adored as a youngster. So I decided to stay clear of him. But the most incredible thing happened. He was being jostled from all sides and was pushed and shoved across the marble floor until he was right under my nose. He had a warm greeting for me, and I felt instantly ashamed. I put my arms around him and congratulated him as best I could. And then he was whisked away on a tidal wave of handshakes.

Five days later when we had returned to Vizille, I got a call from Jacques Chevegneon, a criterium manager. He said he had a place for me at a criterium at Château Chinon on Monday and would pay me £250 if I turned up. I agreed and put the phone down. I was sorry I had agreed. I had been off the bike for nine days. I would surely get the hell knocked out of me at a criterium where 90 per cent of the guys would be charged up. I dreaded facing another hammering – another humiliating slap on the face in front of thousands of spectators. But I had given my word. Early on Monday morning I loaded the car and headed for Château Chinon.

15

ONE OF THE BOYS

Château Chinon is a four-hour drive from the flat in Vizille. I arrived at 11.30, three and a half hours before the race, but I like giving myself plenty of time. The town is smothered in a thick, wet fog and it's hard to avoid the Monday morning blues. I expected it to be much bigger, but it's really quite small. Too small to accommodate the hundreds of spectators' cars already choking the streets. Still, the locals don't mind, especially *les commerçants*: it's the only traffic jam of the year, and the bars and cafés are full. I park in the main street and wait. I don't really know what to do, but Vallet and Claveyrolat will arrive soon and I plan to follow them. After spending half an hour in the car I recognise their two cars driving through the town. They have come from Bordeaux, where they raced a criterium the day before. Vallet has not been home for nearly six weeks now. The day after the Tour finished he set off from Paris and has ridden a criterium a day for eight days. Nine days and thousands of kilometres of driving from one small village to another. I'm not sure how much he gets per race but I know he will go home with about six grand in his pocket – which is not far off what I earn in a year. His wife and two daughters are travelling with him and they look almost as tired as he does. Claveyrolat is travelling with Colotti. Jean-Claude is completely shagged and has also had a hard week.

The greeting is as it always is, a handshake and a smile. I

follow them to a small hotel at the end of the main street. It's a typical criterium hotel. Run-down and cheap, but clean. Two rooms have been reserved and we will also eat lunch here before the race. Most of the riders are eating and changing here. But first the bikes must be prepared. I take mine from the car boot and put the wheels in and inflate the tyres. The bike is spotless. I washed it yesterday, to make sure it was shining for my first criterium race. Appearances are everything. If I make a good impression today then the criterium manager might offer me one or two others. The other lads' bikes are not so clean, still caked in the grime of the Bordeaux criterium. But a wipe with a cloth makes them presentable. It feels strange, being responsible once again for the cleanliness and good working order of your own bike.

Lunch is simple and light and digestion is helped by the constant good humour to be found whenever cyclists eat together. Outside the fog is lifting and the roads are starting to dry. The Château Chinon criterium, Le Critérium de France, is one of the most prestigious in the country. It is one of the few modern-day criteriums where spectators have to pay an entry fee on to the circuit to watch, thirty-five francs. They are still coming into the town in droves and as I look down on them from the hotel bedroom I feel pressure. Today I am not just a professional cyclist: I'm a performer. These people are paying to see me perform. In a normal race you don't give a damn about what the guy at the side of the road thinks. Some are very abusive. It's not uncommon to be insulted as a lazy bastard or an over-paid lout by a spectator peeved by the fact that we are taking it easy. People are not happy unless they see us riding by at sixty kilometres an hour with our eyes in the backs of our heads. Or grovelling up some mountain on our hands and knees. If they insult us, then we feel justified in insulting them in return. I mean, nobody forced them to stand at the side of the road. Today is different: today they are paying to see a spectacle, and therefore we are obliged to perform. What if I can't? What if

I'm unable to follow the others? The lads say that Château Chinon is one of the hardest criteriums with a climb each time on the short two-kilometre lap. The Tour left me feeling terribly bitter. Didn't ride my bike for nine days after it. Couldn't face it. But I will surely pay the price today. I'll probably be dropped. Will the manager still pay me my contract? Will I have the neck to approach him for it? I shouldn't have come here – but hell, I need the money. Ann is living with me now. There's more expense, more responsibility. I have never had that responsibility before. We won nothing in the Tour this year, a pittance. I need the money. It's the only reason I'm here.

We change into our strip. There are five of us in the room. I apply grease to the chamois leather of my racing shorts and pull them on to my bare bum, the cold grease sending a shiver up through my body. A bit like putting on wet swimming gear. I pull on a short-sleeved woollen vest, a pair of white ankle socks, two short-fingered leather mitts, cycling shoes and finally the white RMO jersey of my sponsor. I sit on the bed watching the others get ready, waiting for the moment. I know it has to happen. I'm waiting for it to happen. Fuck it, I want it to happen. The pressure – I can't take this pressure. It happens: the smiles . . . a bag is produced. In it small white ampoules of amphetamines and a handful of short syringes. A glance is thrown in my direction. My 'chastity' is well known within the team but it is only polite to offer. I scratch my head and breathe in deeply. If I walk out through the door with only the hotel lunch in my system I will crack mentally. As a result I will probably be dropped and ridiculed after two laps. I can't face any more humiliation. The pressure. I need the money. I nod in acceptance.

My syringe is prepared. As it's my first time it is decided that 7cc will be enough. Ten to fifteen is the average dose, but the real hard men often use double or treble this. Amphetamines work strongly for about two to three hours, after which the effects diminish. The criterium will last just two hours, which means we can take them in the privacy of the hotel room before going out to the start. I roll back the sleeve of my jersey. No turning back now. The needle is slipped under the skin of my left shoulder. I'm charged. One of my ambitions had always been to leave the sport without ever having taken anything. I got a certain satisfaction in casting myself as the pure white hero fighting to hold on to my virginity in an evil black world. But that was over now. To hell with the past.

They tell me to remain perfectly still. They say I will soon feel the urge to talk and jump around the place, but that I must refrain from talking and gesturing excessively. People have eyes. If they see the normally calm and withdrawn Paul Kimmage arrive on the street shaking hands and patting everyone on the back they will put two and two together. I don't want that. My mind is clear and lucid, but after five minutes I start to feel the first effects. A little buzz. It gets stronger and stronger and is soon a big buzz. It turns my head a bit at first, but then it manifests itself in a new way: aggression. I feel a terrible urge to get on the bike and make it bend under me. I feel invincible, that nothing can defeat me. The lads start joking about the effects the charge will have on me.

'You will drive back to Vizille like Fangio and tonight you won't be able to sleep a wink. Your girlfriend will have a great time.'

I laugh with them. Someone says he will give me a sleeping tablet for later. But sleeping is the last thing on my mind. I'm ready for action.

'Come on lads, let's get to the start.'

More laughter. We pick up the machines from the hotel garage and cycle the two kilometres to the start. My head is clear. I can't let anyone notice anything different. I must remain calm. I must remain calm. I must remain calm. Then I hear it. The voice. The voice calling out my name. An Irish voice. Jesus, an Irish voice calling for me, and here I am charged up to the gills. Stay calm. Stay calm. I turn around to see who it is. He is young, and, yes, I recognise him from somewhere but can't quite place him. We start talking. Paul, don't look him in the eye. If he sees the dilated pupils he will cop it straight away. I try not to look him in the eye. The name comes to me: Gareth Donahue, a young Irish amateur cyclist racing with a local French team. I said I had to rush and would talk to him again after the race. Of all the luck. The one time in my life I charge up, I run into someone who knows me. The finish line is crowded. We must sign on at the podium and collect our numbers. There is a metal crowd-control barrier blocking the entrance to the podium. I am in full buzz and, feeling full of energy, I decide to jump it. I clear it by at least ten feet but land on my backside. I look up to see if anyone has noticed. Thierry Clavet is fighting hard to hold back his laughter. 'For God's sake, take it easy, Polo.'

I sign on at the podium, making a special effort at calmness. Most of the lads are sitting on the chairs pinning their numbers on, so I join them. My fingers are rattling a bit as I try to pin mine on, but eventually I manage to do it. We are called to the line. The peloton is made up of twenty-five pros and six of the best local amateurs. Charly Mottet and Jean-François Bernard are the two stars – the men the crowd have come to see. I presume one of them is to win, but no one has said anything to me. I ask Clavet what the story is, but even he's confused. There seems to be a bit of a problem between Mottet and Bernard – both want to win. Because he rode in the Tour, Jean-François Bernard would normally have been designated to win. But 'Jeff' lives in the region and there's an unwritten rule that the local man never wins in front of his home crowd. This is to avoid any crowd suspicion of race-rigging. The Peugeot rider Gilbert Duclos is boss. He acts as mediator between the different leaders and then informs the smaller riders how the race is to be won. He controls things during the race. If a small rider steps out of line by attacking when he isn't supposed to attack, Duclos will kick his arse. Punishment for a big offence is a word in the ear of the criterium manager. The offender will then have to wait for a while before he is offered another criterium contract. First, second and third are always designated, but anyone can race for the other placings. Sometimes the leaders don't agree and a free-for-all is announced, resulting in the victory of a smaller rider. Fathers don't always appreciate explaining to their sons how Joe Bloggs managed to beat Charly Mottet when Charly Mottet is supposed to be the best. So it is in the interests of all the riders to toe the line by having a good, 'organised' race, so everyone goes away happy. But although the race is organised this doesn't necessarily make it easier. It's not that easy to fool the crowd. Unless they see the stars whizzing by at sixty kilometres an hour they won't be happy. There is nothing false about the average lap speed, which rarely falls below fifty kilometres an hour. There is nothing false about the grimacing faces. It is just the result that is, well, 'doctored'. Duclos rides up to me on the first lap.

'It's Mottet in front of Bernard and Colotti. D'accord (OK)?'
'D'accord.'

There is no way I'm going to rock the boat. If he tells me to dive off and fake crashing, I'll do it. If he wants me to make a spectacle by riding around with my shorts around my ankles I'll do it. I just want the money. I just want to be one of the boys.

The race is one of the easiest I have ever ridden. I am never under pressure. I have such absolute confidence that I won't get dropped, and I'm able to attack off the front and contribute to the spectacle. This is all that matters to me. To be able to perform. To merit the few quid I have come for. I am prominent in several breakaways. Each time we ride hard to build up a good lead and then ease up without making it look too obvious. Duclos controls things masterfully. Physically I feel the effort. I feel the pedals, the shortness of breath on the climb, but mentally I'm so strong that it's never a problem. My mind has been stimulated. Stimulated by amphetamines. I believe I'm invincible therefore I am.

Bernard and Mottet break clear with three laps to go.

Bernard is still not happy about not being allowed to win so they fight out a straight sprint and he just edges Charly out. The gap between them is so close that I'm wondering if indeed it was a straight sprint, but anyway this is unimportant. The crowd have been given a good race and go away happy. We ride back to the hotel. After showering and changing we divide the room and lunch bill between us. I offer to pay for the 'charge'. Amphetamines are hard to come by and very expensive. An average charge costs about fifty pounds, but I'm not surprised when the offer is refused. It is rare that money passes hands between the riders. It's a case of 'See me right today, and I'll see you right tomorrow.' I have joined the club, and it feels almost satisfying to have done so.

The club contract cheques are distributed in a room at the town hall. We line up to enter one by one and receive our envelope from a member of the organising committee, under the watchful eye of the criterium manager. Sometimes the bastards make you wait until after the race reception. They know full well that you might have 300 kilometres to drive home, but expect you to shake hands and talk small talk to the locals before they hand over the hard-earned few bob. This is the fault of the criterium manager. They cream off 10 to 12 per cent of all the riders' contracts, and also demand a large chunk from the race budget of the organising committee. They are parasites and I despise them. They exploit the smaller riders, paying them small amounts, knowing only too well that the poor sod has no choice but to accept. Real scum.

A large crowd of enthusiasts gathers outside the town hall, and I sign a hundred autographs on the way back to the car. Clavet and Colotti are also going home, but Vallet is engaged at a criterium somewhere else next day. Clavet gives me some advice as I get into the car. 'You will probably feel guilty later on. It happens to us all, but you must not blame yourself. It's just part of the job.'

I thank him but forget to ask for the sleeping tablet. He

catches me an hour later and we race for five minutes, but I don't feel comfortable driving at speed so I let him go. The drive back seems much shorter but not short enough to avoid the pangs of conscience stinging my brain. After the upper there is inevitably the downer. It is after twelve when I arrive home, and Ann is in bed but awake. I decide to tell her of my day's activities. All of them. She is lenient.

'You did what you thought was best. As long as it does not become a habit there is no harm done.'

This is said to comfort me, to ease the guilt. But her attitude annoys me. It's too casual. I mean, I took drugs and cheated myself of my honour. How can she be so casual about something so serious? I want to be told off, to be chastised. We have a row, and she turns her back to me and falls asleep. I lie there, my two eyes glaring out of my head like headlights. I'm a million miles from sleep. The events of the day are turning in my head, the arguments for and against crossing my head like a tennis ball in a seemingly never-ending rally. The 'againsts' are hitting beautifully.

'Where was the logic in taking a charge for a race that was fixed? Where was the benefit? You realise that now you'll never be able to ride a criterium without taking something? And more than likely they'll find you dead in some hotel room in five years' time with a syringe sticking out of your arm and your eyes bulging out of your head. And the lads will crowd around your tombstone and later raise a glass to you and praise you for being one of them. One of the boys.'

But the 'fors' return with some lovely volleys.

'No, that's rubbish. You've sat on the fence for long enough. Aren't you forgetting how vulnerable you felt before the race? If you hadn't taken it you would have been slaughtered. You didn't do it to cheat. You did it to survive. To fight the battle with the same arms as everyone else.'

Over and back. Over and back. The last thing I remember is the 'fors' being two sets up and then the lights going out.

16

THE FAB FOUR

The repression of amphetamines through dope controls has had varying consequences. The use of the drug in the major tours and championships is minimal, almost non-existent. It is number one on the controllers' list and is easily detectable. The current trend is towards a different area of doping: hormones. They are natural, the body produces them and so detection of hormone abuse is difficult. The 'sin' lies not in taking illegal products, but in getting caught. Hormones, when used intelligently, offer the security of undetectability. The abuse is frightening.

An amphetamine charge lasts roughly three hours and is then flushed out of the system. Frequent use can result in addiction and maybe one or two problems with heart rhythm – but nothing too serious. Hormones are different. They don't flush out after three hours. They screw up the body's chemistry, lingering in the system for months, even years. Abuse can result in cancer and death. I was tempted many times to try hormones. I could see their beneficial effects on other members of the team, but the consequences of abuse scared me and I never touched them. I did, however, dabble with amphetamines.

I used them twice in criteriums shortly after Château Chinon. In twenty months of professionalism I had stayed clean but, incredibly, in the space of two weeks I charged on three occasions. It becomes so easy to slip into a routine. Once you experience the feeling of invincibility it is hard to race with just Vittel in your bottle, especially when you see other riders taking stuff.

I had always taken pride in my strength of character and my new habit started to worry me. I was losing control of my ability to say no, and on analysing the problem I decided never again to put myself in the position of riding a criterium without having trained. It was difficult at first but I managed to hold out. Even so, I never felt comfortable starting a criterium without at least two vitamin C tablets in my drinking bottle. I suppose it was doping, but at least it was legal. In my two final years in the peloton I stayed clean, but I am not particularly proud of this. There were many reasons why I never again touched it – a guilty conscience was the principal one, but there were other factors. I suppose you could say I was 'chicken'. The fear of being caught terrified me. The scandal it would have caused back in good old Catholic Ireland would have ruined me for life. I couldn't bear to bring that shame on my parents. But there was another factor. I was not prepared actually to stick the needle into my own arm. When my team-mates did it, I would look away. It was not a fear of pain or of needles, it was just the act of doping oneself that I found repellent. Another reason was the acquisition of the amphetamines. I had heard stories of police raids on riders' cars, and this scared me. I hadn't the balls to purchase and transport the stuff myself, and there was no way I could continue to borrow it from others. This would have given me a bad name among them and, above all, I wanted to be liked.

Back in Ireland, Stephen's Tour triumph was celebrated as a national victory. He was welcomed home to scenes of incredible adulation in an open-top bus tour of Dublin. Cycling was 'the' sport, and winning the Tour made Stephen the greatest sportsman the country had ever produced – and one of the most popular. I felt sorry for Kelly. Before Roche's Tour win Kelly had always been regarded as the country's number one cyclist. July 1987 must have been the most miserable month of his life. On the 12th he crashed out of the Tour, and to have sat at home injured and watch another Irishman wipe out everything he had ever done with one triumph must have been unbearable.

If Kelly was in agony then Roche was very much in ecstasy. For years he had played second fiddle to the 'King', but every dog has his day and this was Stephen's. He could have been forgiven for making the most of it, but he refrained from proclaiming himself as the country's greatest, which was admirable.

'People shouldn't say I have won this race and Sean had won that. They should look at our careers and say that between us we have won every race on the continent worth winning.'

When I look back on the nice things he has said and done throughout his career, it is to his eternal credit that he was nicest in his finest hour.

I met up with Kelly again in August. He was making his return to competition in the five-day Kelloggs Tour of Britain. My first words to him were those of consolation and encouragement, which I think he appreciated. I liked him and admired him more than any other rider in the peloton. It hadn't always been this way. Before I turned professional I never understood him: I'm still not quite sure that I do, but I'd go as far as saying that in those early days I actually disliked him. I found him solemn, a machine with no heart and no personality. He was the world's number one who could have helped me when I was struggling for my contract, but didn't. Ireland was split between the 'Kelly' men and the 'Roche' men. I was definitely a Roche man. It has taken me four years of professional cycling to break down the complex layers of Kelly. Talking to him was never easy. It still isn't. You have to make an effort to reach him, but once you do then the effort is worth it. He is colourful; he has a caring heart and a great personality. I am grateful now that he didn't help with my contract when I was struggling as an amateur. It made me fight harder. I earned it under my own steam, which is the only way.

I remember riding the Criterium International in my first year. I was eliminated in the Sunday morning mountain stage and as a result was exempt from the final-stage time trial in the afternoon. I left for the airport to fly back to Lille before the time trial finished and as the plane was about to close its door Kelly ran in, still in his racing gear. He had just won the final time trial, clinching the race, but had no time to change – there was just one evening flight to Lille, and his wife Linda was picking him up and driving him to their home in Brussels. We had to change flights at Lyon and he bought me dinner. We dined and talked and being with him was such a thrill that I completely forgot about the lousy weekend I'd had.

My justification for writing this book was that it would describe the unglamorous life of the 'back-room' boy. The account of the life of an unknown among many unknowns who pass most of their lives in the professional peloton without ever making a name for themselves. But, on reflection, I realise that I was not a *domestique* like the others. I had one great advantage. I shared a friendship and a comradeship with two of cycling's greatest-ever riders. It is a privilege that only now becomes apparent to me as I look back on August 1987.

Martin and I both profited enormously from the euphoria of Stephen's triumph when we returned to Ireland for three city-centre races at the end of that month. I will remember for the rest of my life the night of the first race in Dublin.

It wasn't easy. I hate city-centre races – one-hour dashes on tight circuits – and we were totally unused to this type of racing on the Continent. I just hadn't the speed to perform well in them. None of us had – except Sean. But because it was Dublin, and Stephen had just won the Tour, I expected that the opposition, all British apart from the Aussie Allan Peiper, would have no objections to fixing it for Stephen to win. I was wrong. We had a meeting among riders before the race. Sean spoke on our behalf and suggested we come to an arrangement for Stephen to win. He was backed up by Peiper and by Paul Sherwen. Paul had been a pro for seven years on the Continent, but was riding his last season with Raleigh in England. He tried to convince his compatriots that everyone would benefit from a Roche win. The spectators would applaud it and the future of the event would be assured. But the appeals fell on deaf ears. The 'English pros' argued that city-centre races were their bread and butter. They wanted financial compensation in return for a Roche victory.

Their attitude disgusted me. I walked out of the room before a solution had been reached. I had never liked the English pros, big-headed sods who thought having a pro licence made them professional. I despised them for their pettiness. They were not fit to polish Roche's shoes, and yet here they were laying down the law, in Dublin. Pathetic. I waited for the three lads to come out of the meeting. The English pros had agreed to let Stephen win in return for £1,000. The race was incredibly fast and I remember gritting my teeth so hard that I chipped one, sprinting out of the last corner and going into the finishing straight. Stephen won and most people went away happy, but not all of them went away.

After the finish we showered in one of the Georgian houses directly behind the finishing line on St Stephen's Green. There was a post-race reception at Jury's Hotel, but the view from our room told us that getting there would be a problem. Hundreds of people were banked at the entrance to the house waiting for us to come down. When we did, it was chaos. They all wanted autographs and they were shouting, screaming, touching. I felt like one of the 'fab four' coming out of a concert in the 1960s. We needed protection from the Gardai to get from the house to our manager Frank Quinn's car, and flashing blue lights and screaming sirens cleared the road for our drive to the hotel.

The second race was held in Wexford the following evening. We left Dublin in the morning and rode some of the way for training. The world championships were just twelve days away. Again, as in Dublin, there was a riders' meeting before the race. We weren't invited, and the English lads met among themselves to divide up the spoils. No one approached us about it, which we felt was most unreasonable. Stephen had paid to win in Dublin, and we felt it only right that we be recompensed in a similar way for an English triumph in Wexford. Being ignored irritated the two lads and we decided to pull out all the stops for an Irish win. At the end of another fast race Stephen led Sean out along the Wexford seafront, and Kelly swept by for the victory. It is questionable whether Kelly got as much pleasure out of winning two Paris–Roubaix races as he did in sprinting to victory that night on the seafront, for he was truly delighted and we all shared his pleasure. After showering at the hotel, we decided that a celebration was in order. A few pints in some quiet bar would have suited us fine, but it was impossible to leave the hotel. There was no such thing as a quiet bar for Kelly and Roche. They were instantly recognised anywhere they went, so we stayed at the hotel. We ordered fresh fruit salad, sandwiches, tea and coffee and a few drinks to be brought up to the rooms. I roomed with Martin and Sean with Stephen, but our entourage included Frank Quinn, his assistant Margaret Walsh, Kelly's brother-in-law Gerard Grant and Stephen's brother-in-law Peter. The bedrooms were too small to hold a party, so we laid out the trays of food and drink in the corridor outside and sat together on the carpeted floor. It was a great night. We talked and joked and made plans for Cork.

I don't know if the English riders saw it as we did, but for us the three-race series had developed into Ireland versus England – especially now that we were winning two nil. We were outnumbered ten to one, but this sweetened the challenge for two aces were always going to beat forty jokers. We did indeed look on them as jokers, with the exception of Sherwen and John Herety, who had both served hard apprenticeships on the Continent and so knew what real pro racing was about. They had 'played in the first division'. But it was never easy beating the jokers in these city-centre races. I wasn't capable of it, neither was Martin. Stephen could win only by breaking clear alone and there was no way they would let him away in Cork. Kelly was our only hope, and all our efforts would go to help him.

We rode some of the way down next morning and talked about the next challenge. Martin and I were to control the race for as long as possible by keeping the pace high and closing down any breakaway attempts. Stephen was to save himself for a lone assault in the last few laps and, that failing, would act as lead-out man for Kelly in the final sprint. The tactics worked well, right up to the last lap. Stephen hit the front, riding as hard as he could, with Kelly on his wheel. Sean came through going into the last corner and Roche followed him round. Kelly started sprinting, Roche made no effort to follow him, and, realising the danger Englishman Mark Walsham tried to go past; but in his haste he rode into the Tour de France winner. There was a huge crash, bodies everywhere. I cornered seconds after the impact and couldn't believe it. I picked out the yellow jersey of Stephen in the middle of the tangled bodies and gingerly picked my way around the groaning heap. Walsham and some of the other crash victims threatened violence towards Stephen, claiming he had closed the door and had deliberately caused the crash. Walsham and Co. were forgetting that they were in Ireland and that Stephen Roche was sacred here. If they had put a finger on him they'd have been lynched. In the turmoil of the crash, Kelly's victory almost went unnoticed. Unnoticed to all except Roche, that is. He made a fake effort at cooling tempers on both sides.

'After all, lads, the score is Ireland three England nil, and the match is over.'

Talk about adding fuel to the flames!

Martin returned to Dublin after the race, and from there took a flight back to Manchester to get to his home near Stoke.

Stephen, Sean and I flew back to the Continent early next morning. We had spent five days together and those five days will remain in my memory as my happiest five days in professional cycling. We teamed up again twelve days later in Villach, Austria for the world championships.

Villach was more serious. Sean wanted badly to save a disastrous season by winning the rainbow jersey. It was the one single-day race which had always eluded him and he trained particularly hard for it. Stephen was much more relaxed about it all. When you have just won the Giro and the Tour de France, nobody expects another performance in the world championships. His life had turned into a perpetual series of product promotion, press interviews, autograph signing and hand shaking. He had come to Villach to get back into serious racing and to give Kelly a bit of a dig-out. The difference in attitudes showed at the hotel on the day before the race. In the morning we trained on the circuit. World championships are very special. There is a great atmosphere generated among the thousands of bike lovers who have congregated from all over Europe to cheer on their favourites in the annual feast of cycling. The circuit was hard, and the long drag after the finish was more difficult than first announced. I liked it and knew I could ride well here. I felt very proud riding with the three lads. Sean and Stephen rode at the front, flanked by Martin and me. I could not help noticing the ease with which Stephen pedalled. Kelly noticed it too, but neither of us thought he had the form to be world champion. Lunch was followed by a long discussion on the choice of gear to be used. We spent most of the afternoon in bed snoozing and reading – except for Stephen, that is. Some journalists had come looking for interviews and he spent his afternoon talking to them in the garden of the hotel. At meal times he would leave his food to answer telephone calls and other requests, and he wasn't a bit serious about the race. I started to feel the pressure in the evening. None of the Irish supporters came to the hotel. It was the night before battle and they knew better.

THE FAB FOUR

The rooming arrangements were the same as in Ireland. Sean shared with Stephen and Martin with me. I liked rooming with Martin. As amateurs we had roomed many times together on Irish teams, but then we were rivals and it was often difficult to be honest. Now it was different. We were both professionals and no longer rivals. I had the edge on him as an amateur, but he was now the better professional. I was unbelievably nervous before going to bed. Two of my brothers, Raphael and Kevin, had come over from Ireland. They would be on the circuit tomorrow and I did not want to let them down by riding badly. But I was also very excited. My last appearance at a world championship was two years after my sixth place in the amateur race in Italy. I had lost any illusions about ever winning the Tour de France, but I secretly dreamed about one day being world champion. I polished my shoes before getting into bed, and had them shining. Normally I am not one for polishing shoes, but this was the world championships, and in my excitement I brushed them till they were sparkling. My enthusiasm irritated Martin, who was trying not to let the build-up start until the morning of the race. He offered me a sleeping tablet. I accepted. We slept like logs.

I love the sound of rain splattering off the windows when I'm cosy in bed. For a while I enjoyed the sound. My senses were still numbed with sleep and I could have been anywhere. In my childhood bed back in Dublin. In bed with Ann back in Grenoble. All I knew was that I was in bed and that it was raining outside and that I liked being in bed when it was raining outside. But slowly the messages from my ear found a receptive brain cell and the splattering sounds were analysed more carefully. I wasn't just anywhere: I was in the Hotel Piber in Villach. The rain that was battering the window would soon be making its way into every pore of my skin, chilling me, making me uncomfortable. 'Oh, my God, it's the morning of the world championships . . . FUCK, IT'S RAINING . . . I HATE RAIN.'

How unlucky can you get? In the run-up we had three days

157

of beautiful sunny weather, but now it was not simply raining but bucketing down. All my enthusiasm went out of the wet window. I hate rain. I never ride well in it. I'm not sure I talked over breakfast.

I was in serious difficulty for the first half of the race. I had been given new wheels and the rims were smooth, making it hard for my brake pads to get any sort of grip. Slowing on the descent was a problem, and for a while I felt very insecure. The other three sat near the front of the bunch, watching, controlling, waiting. Stephen came back to me to encourage me to come to the front. My only wish was to abandon, but I couldn't let my brothers down. They had spent their hard-earned money on coming over to see me, so I tried to follow him. The ease with which he cut his way through the bunch was heart-breaking. His incredibly efficient style. So graceful, so beautiful to watch – like a long-legged woman walking down the street. It was as if the bicycle was an extension of his hips. The rain stopped after about three hours, and slowly my stiffened leg muscles started to heat up again and I at last felt the urge to race. After eighteen laps the hill after the finish line started to feel like a small col. Cracks started appearing in the diminishing bunch, and amazingly I found myself closing gaps instead of opening them. With sixty kilometres to go a four-man group which included two favourites, the Dutchman Teun Van Vliet and reigning champion Moreno Argentin, went clear. The French took up the chase, aided by a quarter of the Irish team, Martin Earley, and the gap started to narrow. I sat near the front, waiting for a sign of weakness from Martin. The four were retrieved and the attacks followed. Martin, exhausted from his chase, retired – he had done his work. I moved up on Kelly's shoulder and told him I was available for short-range chasing. He nodded, and I set about closing down any serious break without a green jersey. As the bell rang, announcing the last lap, the decisive move went clear. It was on the climb, and I was shattered and really suffering. I looked up to the glorious sight of two green jerseys bridging the gap. Behind, the race was over, and we all knew it. I tuned my ear to the p.a. system and tried to work out what was happening up front. I said a prayer that Kelly might win. With both of them up front they had a great chance. The logical tactic was for Stephen to hold it together for Sean in the sprint. I strained my ears as we turned into the finishing straight. The p.a. announced the winner.

'Steven Rooks, Champion du Monde.'

There was a huge roar from the crowd. 'Did he say Roche or Rooks?' I wasn't sure. Rooks, the Dutchman, was also in the break. 'I think he said Rooks.' I didn't bother to sprint. It was seconds after crossing the line that I discovered the truth. I bumped into Irish journalist John Brennan as he scurried across for a few words from the new world champion.

'He's done it. The bastard's done it.'

'Who?'

'Roche.'

'No. You're joking.'

He wasn't.

I made my way through the crowd to our pit area. Stephen had been whisked off for the medal ceremony, but our pit was still crowded. Kelly was giving his story to journalists, Martin was having the back patted off him by almost every Irish supporter on the circuit and there were scenes of great joy all around the pit. I too wacked him across the back and then threw my arms around Kelly and congratulated him on his fine performance. I really wished it could have been him on the winner's rostrum, but I suppose it's the one title he is destined never to win. We pulled on some warm clothes and cycled back to the hotel, where it took some solid scrubbing under the shower to remove the grime and dirt from seven hours of racing from my legs. Stephen arrived about an hour later. He looked resplendent in his new rainbow jersey, but the magnitude of his achievement had not yet sunk in. He had done something that only one other man in the whole world had done. In winning

the Tour of Italy, the Tour de France and the world championships in the same year he had equalled Eddy Merckx.

The celebrations went on late into the next morning. Most
of the supporters came round to the hotel and it was a great
night to be Irish. I felt very privileged to be part of it all, as it's
something I can tell my children and my grandchildren. I can
see myself in my rocking chair by the fire, forty years from now
with grandson on my knee.

'Tell me about the day you helped Stephen Roche become
world champion, Granda.'

And I will tell it, without doubt exaggerating my contribution to the victory.

'And where did you finish, Granda?'

'Well, son, I was so tired after all my work that I could only
finish forty-fourth.'

My good performance at the world championships gave me
great confidence for the end-of-season races. I particularly
wanted to do well in the Nissan Classic in Ireland in October.
Thevenet was kind. He allowed me to choose the four riders to
accompany me in the race as a reward for my good year. I chose
the four who I was closest to: André Chappuis, Jean-Claude
Colotti, Thierry Claveyrolat and Per Pedersen.

I went into the race as team leader, the only time in my life
that I held such a responsibility. On the second stage I asked
Thierry and Jean-Claude to ride over the Vee climb as hard as
possible in an effort to break up the race. I sat in their slipstream
and they set a pace which blew the race apart. This was a new
kind of pressure, one I had not experienced before. My normal
role was to do what they were now doing for me – the donkey
work. But the pace they set was so fierce that I began to wonder
if I had the legs to continue the effort, once they finished their
effort. If I cracked, then I would be the laughing stock of the
bunch. Joel Pelier attacked just after the hairpin, and I bridged
the gap. Eleven others joined us, and for those behind it was
curtains, for we soon had a gap of over ten minutes – I had

detonated the vital move in the five-day race. I so wanted the break to succeed that I did too much work and was knackered by the time I got to the stage finish at St Patrick's Hill in Cork, so I was not placed highly on the stage. The following day was a hard loop around the Ring of Kerry to Tralee and I did another good ride, moving to seventh overall. The stage was won by Sean Yates in a solo break which I rate as one of the best rides I ever saw in my time with the pros. The fourth stage was a team time trial. Dede and Clavet packed it in after getting dropped after the Vee on the second stage, and spent the rest of the week buying Aran sweaters and drinking pints of Guinness. So we were down to just three men for the trial. I slipped a place to eighth, which I held on to until the finish of the race in O'Connell Street in Dublin. I felt very satisfied with my performance, for the organisers had put together a high-class field. Sean won, Stephen was second, Martin was sixth and I was eighth – it was another week of being 'fab'.

Your wedding day is supposed to be a great day in a couple's life. I enjoyed mine, but only after the church ceremony; for I was so nervous that I bungled the 'for richer, for poorer, in sickness and in health' bit – still, it got a good laugh. We were married in Ann's parish church in Balscadden in North County Dublin on 23 October. Most bike riders get married in October. It's the month that the season ends, the time for drink and fun and relaxation and, well, marriages. I had been going out with Ann for five years and I was twenty-five years old and she was twenty-two so we both reckoned we were 'ripe'. I invited the other 'Beatles' to the wedding. Sean was tied up and couldn't come, but Martin and Stephen were both present. From RMO I asked the four who had ridden with me on the Nissan, but Dede was the only one to come. Stephen's presence was a big surprise. He was besieged with requests for functions and promotions all over the country, and I honestly didn't expect him to turn up. While we were being married word got round that Stephen Roche was in Balscadden church, and village kids and housewives from the area converged on us when the ceremony was over, looking for his autograph. Stephen felt a bit worried that his popularity might detract from what was essentially 'our day', but on the contrary his presence created a carnival atmosphere that made it all more enjoyable.

We honeymooned in Connemara and Clare and I returned to France two weeks later to spend the winter in our flat in Vizille. 1987 had been very satisfying. I was sure I would continue to improve. I was wrong: it was the summit of my career.

17

COFFEE AT ELEVEN

The village of Vizille lies twelve kilometres outside Grenoble on the road to Gap. It's a typically rural French village but can claim a certain notoriety because it was here that the French Revolution started two hundred years before. A magnificent château, a former residence of French presidents, dominates the village square, and life and traffic circulation in the village revolve around it. The Café de la Gare is ideally placed, being fifty metres opposite the château and its magnificent park. It's a typically French café. From seven to eight in the morning it serves mostly coffee, nearly always black, and croissants. Just before twelve there will be a rush on *pastis*, the aniseed drink which is the French labourer's aperitif. From one to two it's coffee time again; but the afternoons are calm until just before seven, when there will be another rush on *pastis*.

I got to study the patterns quite well during 1988. There was a great view from the terrace and I studied Vizille, its inhabitants and its château in falling snow and falling rain, in grey skies and in blue. I watched green leaves turn to falling leaves – always from the terrace. From my chair and an empty row of coffee cups I studied them. The old men playing *boules* in the shade of the sixteen sycamore trees. The old woman hastily loading a basket of groceries on to her bicycle as the rain started to fall. The village idlers doing the rounds from one café to another, scrounging drink. The buzz of traffic clogging up the square. At every hour of the day, on every day of the year, you could be sure there was something happening in the village square. Which is precisely why I went there so often. It was an escape. I found immense tranquillity in buying a cup of coffee and sitting on the terrace with it. Watching, analysing, thinking and inevitably searching for a way out. A job. I spent more time on the terrace of the Café de la Gare that year than I did racing my bike. It was a bad year.

Everything had been rosy at the end of 1987 – too rosy. It was in the months of November and December that I let it slip. Because I had had a hard season I felt I needed a good break. I did, but I got carried away. When I should have been sweating it out in the weights room, I was off touring the wine cellars of the vineyard round Avignon. Wine was a passion: smelling it, tasting it, buying it and especially drinking it. I had the reputation in the team of being a 'gourmet' – a connoisseur of good food and wine. A hard man for the drink and the crack. I impressed with my knowledge of *grands crus*, and I found a new pleasure in being impressive. I got too cocky. I became great friends with Colotti. He advised me to watch my weight and to train hard. I advised him on the wines he should stock his cellar with. I rode the odd cyclo-cross, did a little jogging; but it wasn't enough.

The year started with a training camp and a 'let's get to know each other' week just before Christmas. It was Bernard Vallet's opening act as the new *directeur sportif* of the team. Thevenet had been disposed of ever so tidily and ruthlessly. He was first offered the job of team manager. The manager is in charge of team administration. He co-ordinates travel to races, deals with race organisers for expenses and acts as public relations officer. It's a cosy number, and although he would have preferred to stay on as *directeur sportif* the post of manager held a certain attraction for Thevenet. He accepted and Vallet's promotion to *directeur sportif* was announced to the French press. The dust was allowed to settle for six weeks, then Monsieur Braillon informed Thevenet that he had reconsidered and that his services were no longer required. Thevenet claimed unfair dismissal and won his case before the courts. Monsieur Braillon was forced to pay him a year's salary, about £30,000.

The training camp at Autrans, a cross-country ski resort in the Vercors mountains, was fun even though there was no snow. The core of the team remained the same and there were just five changes. Bincoletto, Lavenu, Grewal, Peillon and Huger were replaced by Frank Pineau, Eric Salomon, Hartmut Bolts, Alex Pedersen and Patrick Vallet (no relation to Bernard). We played indoor football, swam at the local pool, jogged and did some mountain biking. In between sports outings we were photographed, measured for our new clothes and examined by doctors. At night we had team talks from the new chief. Vallet gave some great team talks.

He told us he was confident that we were going to have a great year. He intended to run the team like the captain of a ship. We were all in the same boat, and we must all row together for the team's success. If he'd known the words of 'The Soldier's Song' I'm sure he'd have sung them.

And it worked. We believed him. We left Autrans convinced we had a good *directeur sportif* and that everything was fine. A day later our opinion had changed.

Looking back on it I am reminded of those gory 'Friday the Thirteenth' movies. You know, the 'just when you thought it was safe to go back in the water' stuff. In our case Freddie, or Carrie, or Gory attacked us in the shape of a newspaper article.

L'Equipe, the French sports daily, had sent a journalist to Autrans to cover the training week. The journalist, Guy Roger, did a half-page interview with Vallet, which was published a day after we returned home. To say it shocked me is an understatement. It was a question-and-answer piece, no room for misinterpretation. Vallet was questioned about the *faiblesse*, or 'weakness', of his new team. He replied.

I will be frank. Of the eighteen riders in the team, half were signed before I took control [i.e. by Thevenet]. I personally wouldn't have done it. I believe also that none of the eight would have found jobs in any other French team either.

I remember reading the interview over breakfast. I interrupted my bowl of porridge and did a quick calculation. I was one of those who had signed under Thevenet. Was he referring to me? Surely not.

He didn't criticise everyone. He had glowing praise for two of his signings, two of the new pros.

I am pleased to have signed Hartmut Bolts and Alex Pedersen, who finished second and third respectively, in the last amateur world championships. These two have the right approach. I haven't seen them pedal yet but their mentality and behaviour are those of real pros. They will help the others to get the finger out.

I had expected criticism from Vallet at some stage in the year but not before we had even turned a pedal. I picked up the phone and rang headquarters for an explanation. Vallet was not around but Jacques Michaud the assistant *directeur sportif* was. Yes, he had seen *L'Equipe*. No, there was no need to worry about it, all lies. He said that a letter of explanation from Vallet was already in the post and to make no further comments to anyone until reading the letter.

Sure enough, the letter arrived next day. Vallet told us to pay no attention to the lies written by Guy Roger, whose only interest was to upset the normal running of the team.

I didn't believe him. Any advantage Guy Roger could gain from rocking the RMO boat was beyond my comprehension. No, I was quite sure that Vallet had said it all right. Not intentionally, of course, and perhaps he just got carried away.

Being in *L'Equipe* is all that ever matters to a lot of French pros. Vallet could now give them half-page interviews and in my view he loved it. He loved the power, being the centre of attention. It seemed to me that in his first interview as a *directeur sportif* he wanted to make an 'I'm a tough guy' impression. He made an impression all right.

Two days before writing this chapter I met up with Guy Roger at the Grenoble Six, a track event. I had always wondered about the famous interview and asked him if he had altered any of Vallet's words. Roger assured me over the heads of his two children that he had written the piece word for word. When Bolts and Pedersen came to the end of their two-year contracts, signed with Vallet, he fired them both.

I accept that the job of *directeur sportif* is difficult and that harsh decisions are often necessary for the good of the team. I don't blame Bernard Vallet for my failure at RMO in 1988. He was the epitome of what a good *directeur sportif* should be. A superb organiser, he has a total understanding of professional racing and is a good motivator. He was certainly better at the job than Thevenet. But Thevenet had a quality that made up for his organisational faults, his sincerity. In my opinion Vallet didn't know the meaning of the word. I think he was as two-faced as they come.

I was fully prepared for a hard start to the 1988 season. I knew I would have problems, but it didn't worry me too much. I had had problems early in 1986 and 1987, but each time I had hit form at the right moment to win a place in the team for the Tour. I felt that 1988 would be the same, that it would take me two months to hit form.

February, March and April were disastrous months. I just couldn't get going, found it impossible even to finish races and abandoned one after another. But in May, in the Grand Prix of Wallonie in Belgium, I started putting it together. I could feel good form coming on. I had trained really hard for it, and felt good except for one thing – I had this maddening itch around my arse. I couldn't understand it, but put off getting it seen to, as it was a bit embarrassing. The day after Wallonie, we lined up for a three-stage two-day race, the Tour de L'Oise just north of Paris. It opened with a short eighty-kilometre stage but I was totally knackered, and suffered from stomach trouble. I was dropped with thirty kilometres to go and lost nine minutes. I was terribly depressed at this latest setback, and couldn't understand it as I had ridden so well in Wallonie the day before. I was rooming with Frank Pineau. I had a shit at about nine and left the most dreadful smell behind me. Frank complained that he had never experienced anything like it. He assured me there was something wrong with my insides. This got me thinking. The itch around my anal passage was driving me insane and had developed into a rash. Perhaps there was something wrong.

I started the stage next day but I had this persistent stomach cramp and was completely drained of strength, so I abandoned. I flew to Grenoble that night and on Monday morning paid a visit to the doctor. He looked at my bum and asked me to stick out my tongue.

'Champignons (mushrooms).'

'What's that?'

'It's a fungus that develops in the digestive tract. It's gone right through you from your tongue to your bum.'

I was told to stay off the bike until the rash had disappeared and he advised a break from competition for ten days. It was almost a relief to have been told there was something wrong with me. Until then I just couldn't understand what was going wrong. Now I had a reason, an excuse. Even if the mushrooms were not totally responsible for my lack of form I had no problem convincing myself that they were. Coffee sales were up that week at the Café de la Gare.

I made a return to competition at the Tour de l'Armorique. I was still undergoing treatment but was feeling brand new if a little behind physically. There was one place left to be filled in the team to ride the Dauphine, to be filled either by me or by Eric Salomon. I wanted to ride the Dauphine. It was my ticket for the Tour. But the mushrooms had set me back in my preparation. I rode with little flair at Armorique and Vallet offered the ride to Salomon.

I was disappointed, but had expected it. The day after the Armorique we stayed in Brittany for the Grand Prix of Plumelec. A single-day race, Plumelec is one of a series of French classics where there are never any controls. These races are know among the pros as the Grands Prix des Chaudières. *Chaud* means warm. The word *chaudière* is used for someone who heats, who warms up, who takes a charge. Mauleon–Moulin, Châteauroux–Limoges, the Grand Prix Plumelec, the Grand Prix of Plouay, the Grand Prix of Cannes – all are Grands Prix des Chaudières. At the team meetings on the night before these classics the dialogue from the *directeur sportif* was always the same. 'Now lads, I can't say there won't be a control tomorrow but this is Plumelec.'

And there would be spontaneous laughter.

'We are all professionals, so it's up to each of us to conduct ourselves as such. If there is a surprise control and anyone is caught, I will do my best to protect you as far as the sponsor is concerned.'

I could never bring myself to charge up for the Chaudières races and always went into them with an inferiority complex. As a result of not taking anything I felt disadvantaged and never bothered even to try to win. It was those high principles of mine: there was no way I could be happy winning a race, knowing I had charged for it. And yet I am forced to admit that a lot of it was purely psychological. In my first year I was as green as grass starting the Grand Prix of Plumelec. I didn't realise it was a Chaudières. I felt I was riding on the same level as everyone else, so it didn't bother me. I finished eighth. But three years later I was a man of the world. I knew what was going on but wasn't mentally strong enough to still try and win.

Plumelec is a five and a half hour race. It was a foul day, raining and miserable. Tired from the Armorique stage race, I was never going well. Half-way through, on one of the small back roads of the circuit, we were strung out in one long line. I was second to last and Dede last. I knew he was getting it rough so I looked around to see how he was. His body and face were wet and mucky from the spray from the back wheels. He had something between his teeth – a needle. He bit the plastic cap off and I immediately understood what he was going to do next. I dropped behind him to push him as he injected himself with the white liquid, most probably amphetamine. This was to help him to get it over as quickly as possible so no one would see him.

To see him dirty, suffering and with that needle between his teeth turned my stomach. I wanted to get off and just leave the bike there and then. I abandoned the race and rode straight to the showers. I was disgusted. Not at Dede, he was simply playing by their rules, another innocent victim. No, I blamed the system. The race organisers, the *directeurs sportifs*, the sponsors – the men in power who knew what was going on but turned a blind eye to it. And when his career ended the system would spit him out – a penniless ex-pro. The incident strengthened my conviction never to enter the drugs stadium. I would go as far as I could for as long as possible, but if it wasn't good enough then it was just too bad. If someone had offered me a decent job that Sunday in Plumelec I'd have taken it, there and then. But I had to keep trying. There were bills to be paid, responsibilities to be met – and a little flicker of hope about riding the Tour.

I believed right up until the last minute that I could still make the Tour team. It became almost an obsession. I used to take out this team poster and with a pen place crosses on the heads of those I felt had blown it. The heads of the fellows still in with a chance were marked with a question. With two weeks to go there were eight ticks on the poster. I was one of three question marks fighting for the last place. The other two were Frank Pineau and the German Hartmut Bolts.

The Midi Libre stage race was my last chance to prove myself. I worked like a Trojan for the others for the week and finished it off with third place on the final stage – a mountain stage. I was sure I had done enough. The decision was Vallet's. He said he'd make up his mind after the national championships a week before the start of the Tour. All the European and Scandinavian countries hold their professional championships on the same date. Ireland does not hold a professional championship as we are only a handful of pros. I spent the day at home, hoping against hope that neither Pineau nor Bolts would ride well. Pineau didn't. Bolts became the professional champion of Germany. On Monday I drove to a meeting with Vallet to hear the decision. I don't know why I bothered. In the morning's *L'Equipe*, Vallet had lavished glowing praise on the new German champion. I should have read between the lines and realised that I hadn't made it. But I wanted the waiting to end. I wanted to be told. And I was.

It was to be a month's holiday at the Café de la Gare.

Vallet told me to have a short break and to prepare myself for a good end of season. I was shattered. I cried on my way back to Vizille and the depth of my disappointment surprised me. I phoned the news home to my parents and also to David Walsh at the *Sunday Tribune*. We had planned to write a book on the Tour together, a 'from the saddle' account of the three-week race; but with my non-selection the project went out the window. David asked me if I'd consider writing a short column for the *Tribune* on the four Sundays of the Tour. I had been writing on and off for *Irish Cycling Review* for two years, but had never written for a newspaper before. David was taking a bit of a chance in getting me to write the column and stressed that I keep it short, about 500 words. If it was rubbish, then it would be just 500 words of rubbish and no one would notice too much. It was still a big responsibility, and on the morning

I wrote the piece I regretted ever having agreed. I was unbearable. I ordered Ann out of the house and the slightest noise drove me nuts. But writing it was only half the battle. I then had to read the piece over the phone to a copy-taker at the paper. Evelyn Bracken was very patient and understanding but even then I hated it. I kept waiting for her to say, 'Now, hold on a minute, son, this is rubbish.' But she never did and my pieces got a good response. The first one was about being left out of the Tour. The second week I wrote about my hopes for Kelly doing well. And on the third week I did a piece which the *Sunday Tribune* entitled 'A picnicker's view of the Alpe d'Huez':

Alpe d'Huez. Thirteen kilometres of strength-sapping ascensions. Twenty-one hairpin bends that climb to almost 6,000 feet. The blue riband of the Tour, a monument to its glorious history.

Driving up the Romanche Valley, or the Valley of the Dead as it is better known, I was filled with remorse. For this morning I was going to that famous battleground, not as rider but as spectator. My wife Ann and I set out at nine, convinced that the thirty-two kilometres from our house to the foot of the Alpe would take no more than an hour to drive. I had forgotten it was Bastille Day.

All of France was on holiday and we found ourselves stuck in a traffic jam fifteen kilometres from Bourg d'Oisans, the town at the bottom of the climb. For twenty-five minutes we sat there without budging. Word came filtering back that the Gendarmes had closed the road early because of the huge volume of traffic.

We abandoned the car and walked the four kilometres to the police roadblock. It was too far to walk to the Alpe so we set up camp on a boring 300-metre flat stretch of road, a kilometre from the town of Rochatailee.

Sitting by the side of the road I soon realised that as a

tour spectator I was a bit of a greenhorn. We had no fold-up chairs to sit on. No white cotton caps to keep the sun off our heads and no transistor to keep us informed on how the race was going.

We did however remember the picnic basket. It soon became evident to me that many other people had lost hope of getting to the Alpe, as little by little our anonymous piece of road started to fill with picnicking families.

The hours passed slowly and I found myself becoming more and more frustrated at the lack of race information. I spotted a veteran Tour spectator across the road. He had the vital equipment and I decided to ask him if he had heard anything. He told me that Fignon had not started the stage and that Jean-François Bernard had lost contact on the Col de la Madeleine and was trailing the leaders by five minutes.

I was amazed. Bernard had been my Tour favourite. The old spectator had no news of Kelly. I went back to Ann and we began eating lunch. I dropped my baguette when the old man raised his arm to me. Kelly was four minutes down. *Merde*! I was really disappointed.

Kelly had lost the Tour, for I knew that those four minutes would soon double and maybe even triple for they had not yet crossed the Glandon and there was still the Alpe to come. I thanked the old man for the last time. I had no more interest in crossing the road.

The publicity caravan arrived. I recognised the co-*directeur sportif* that I had had in 1986, Jean-Claude Valaeys. He was throwing plastic bags and paper hats out of the window of his brightly coloured Peugeot. Never liked the guy.

The roadside nicely littered, we waited for the main act. Rooks and Delgado duly obliged and for fifteen seconds we watched as the two heroes battled their way up the road, dwarfed by the swarm of TV cameras and photo-graphers and race organisation vehicles. Group after group the shattered faces rolled by.

I shouted encouragement at Claveyrolat and Colotti, the two team-mates I regarded as friends. But as my other team-mates passed I held my breath in disrespectful silence.

Another group appeared. Three yellow and blue jerseys riding at the front. I knew immediately this was the Kelly group. I looked at my watch. Fifteen minutes had ticked past since Delgado and Rooks had gone by. Martin Earley was riding at the front of the group. I was pleased, for it was his place. It is ungraceful and unjust that the giants of the road be left isolated on the days they are ordinary men.

Sean was in the middle of the group. In our best Irish accents we shouted at the two of them but they did not look up.

Ann had seen what she had come to see and she started the long walk back to the car. Strangely, I found myself not wanting to leave. Two years previously I had ridden along this very stretch of road on this very same stage of the race. I was thirty-five minutes down and alone.

I can remember the encouragement that I received from those spectators who had waited. I felt duty bound to wait a while. If I had been riding I would have been in one of these groups. On a good day I might have been with the Kelly group. A bad day and I would have been in one of the groups that were now passing before my eyes, forty-two minutes down.

I watched in silent homage. Still no sign of the last rider. I decided I would have to go as Ann would be waiting for me and I thought I felt a drop of rain. I felt guilty. I should not have left. The cock crowed three times as I walked back to my car.

I liked the Alpe piece. I was starting to relax a bit more and was even managing to sleep a little on the night before writing an article. But a day after the Alpe stage something happened that put an abrupt end to my series of articles on the race. The race leader Pedro Delgado was found positive at dope control.

18

RESCUED

The scandal rocked all France. Pedro Delgado, *maillot jaune – positif.* Riders testing positive was a not uncommon event in the Tour, but it was rare that the 'big fish' were caught. Delgado was the biggest fish in the pond. He had taken control of the race in the Alps, was second to Rooks on the Alpe D'Huez and he smashed all his rivals in the following day's 38-kilometre mountain time trial to Villard de Lans. Few doubted he would win the race when they entered the Pyrenees, no one did when they left. He was untouchable in the mountains – the tour had found its new champion. Or so we thought.

At Bordeaux, with just four stages to go before arriving on the Champs Elysées the bomb dropped. Jacques Chancel, a television journalist working on Antenne 2's nightly review of the race, screwed up his face at the end of the Bordeaux emission. He had something serious to tell us. He had heard, from a good source, of a positive dope test involving race leader Pedro Delgado. When a rider is called to dope control, the sample of urine he gives is put into two separate sealed bottles. The bottles are sent to a laboratory, where one is tested. If traces of illegal substances are found, the rider is informed. The rider has the right to either accept the analysis or appeal. If he appeals, then the second bottle of urine is tested. If this second testing confirms the initial results, then, and only then, can news of the positive test be released to the press.

This was not how it happened in the Delgado affair. Someone leaked news to Chancel that Delgado's first bottle had been positive *before* Delgado himself had even been told. Perhaps Chancel thought he was honouring his profession, but even so in my opinion it was still a despicable thing to do. Half the world knew of the findings of the first bottle before Delgado did. Journalists descended on him like vultures, but he professed total innocence in the affair.

Next day, the race *commissaires* were forced to clarify matters. They denied having leaked anything to Chancel, but confirmed that traces of Probenacide, a masking drug for steroids, had been found in Delgado's urine after the Villard de Lans time-trial stage. Delgado immediately appealed, and the second bottle was examined. For two days Delgado raced under tremendous pressure. The second bottle was opened and traces of Probenacide were again found, but the race leader was cleared. Incredibly, no one had consulted the UCI's (Union des Cyclistes Internationals) list of proscribed substances. They had consulted the IOC's (International Olympic Committee's) list. Probenacide was on the IOC list but was not due to enter the UCI list till August, a month after the race ended. Delgado could not be found positive for taking a medicament that wasn't yet proscribed – he was *blanchi*, cleared.

It was a most unsavoury affair, and the race was ruined. Even though Delgado had been cleared, the presence of Probenacide in his urine was still unexplained. He had escaped on a technicality, but for many he was still guilty. It was a difficult time to be a professional cyclist. In the café in Vizille I was bombarded by the bar's clientèle with demands for information. When I sat down for coffee the jokes would start.

'Hey Polo, you are used to something stronger than coffee for riding your bike.'

And they would all laugh. Few of them held any grudge against Delgado: 'Poor Pedro', that's what they all said, 'Poor

Pedro'. The consensus among the *pastis* drinkers of the Café de la Gare was that it was humanly impossible to ride a race like the Tour without taking stuff. Most ordinary people in France were of the same opinion. Delgado was encouraged like never before from the roadside: 'Poor Pedro'.

He is one of the most likeable 'leaders' in the peloton, and I was greatly surprised when news of his positive testing broke – surprised he had been caught, that is. The affair left me in an awkward situation. How could I possibly write another Tour article for the *Tribune* without mentioning the Delgado affair? Oh, I could have done it all right. A piece on my shock and horror that a fine rider like Delgado would do such a despicable thing and 'cheat' by taking drugs would probably have fitted in quite nicely. But I wasn't shocked, I knew what went on, and as soon as I picked up my pen I would have to be honest. I was not ready to write about the drug problems in the sport. They could not be explained in five hundred words. I talked it over with David and we decided that the best way out was to abandon the column. I forgot about journalism and went back to being a cyclist.

I got terribly depressed watching the Tour on television. I loved the race. Riding it, being part of the glorious circus, made the hardship and sacrifice of the pro life worthwhile. But watching it from an armchair was an act of self-destruction. Always the same old questions. What future have I in the game? I am not good enough to ride the Tour. Will they sack me at the end of the year? Will anyone else give me a job? What else can I do but cycle? The conclusion was always the same – I had no choice. Bills had to be paid and riding my bike was the only way of paying them. I dragged myself out training, and tried to get back into some sort of physical shape. Mentally it was very difficult and on the weekend that the Tour finished I hit rock bottom. I had arranged with Kelly to stay with him for a week to ride some kermesse races in Belgium. I stopped for lunch at a motorway café near Lille which was half an hour's drive from the border. It was an awful hole, really grotty, and I didn't eat too much. While eating I suddenly felt terribly alone. I started to think about the race. I hated racing in Belgium and knew I was going to get a terrible stuffing. This depressed me, and the more I thought about it the more it annoyed me that I had to go. I was desperately short of racing practice and without competition there was no way I was going to have a good end of season. But I still didn't want to go. I even started to feel physically sick about it. I needed time to think, to work it all out. I went to a near-by shopping centre to try and get myself together. No, there was no way I could go to Belgium. I needed to talk to someone, I felt so terribly alone. Who could I ring? Ann was out. My parents in Dublin would not understand. I tried to ring David, but he wasn't at home. I rang Frank Quinn in Dublin and talked to his assistant Margaret. I don't know if anything I said to her made sense but I remember asking her to phone Kelly and to inform him I wouldn't be coming. I put down the phone and got into the car. I turned down the motorway and drove 300 kilometres back to my friends in Paris. It was as near as I have ever come to a nervous breakdown.

Frank phoned me later that night. He persuaded me to keep at it, and convinced me I should drive to Kelly's house in Brussels next day. I felt like a right idiot, knocking on Kelly's door, but I was welcomed as if nothing had happened. Sean and Linda were very kind and I raced next day and was back on the rails. During my stay, I made some interesting discoveries about the 'iron man'. One night we went for a sauna in a health club in Volvoorde. I never liked saunas, and Kelly insisted on rising the temperature by throwing water on the stones. We lasted fifteen minutes but had to get out. It had been incredibly hot and we were both so drained that we could hardly stand.

'Jaysus, Kelly, you look like death warmed up.'

And he laughed, but then said, 'Did you never feel this tired after finishing a race?'

I thought about it. Yes I had, but only once. It was in a prologue time trial of the Coors Classic in Boulder, Colorado a few weeks before the Olympic road race in Los Angeles. The finish was at the top of a hard climb, and I remember losing consciousness about fifty metres before the line and waking up with a blanket around me five minutes later. It was the only time in my life I ever pushed myself beyond my limits.

'Yes,' I replied, 'once. What about you?'

'Yes, regularly.'

I looked at him: he wasn't lying.

After a week of kermesse racing in Belgium I rejoined the team for a race in Montreal. I loved the circuit, which was the Olympic road race circuit of 1976, and rode well on it. I was in the thick of the action right from the start and got myself into the winning break, but I didn't have the distance in my legs so I abandoned before the finish. Still, I won over 1,500 dollars in sprint prizes so my team-mates were very pleased with me. Unfortunately, neither Vallet nor his assistant Jacques Michaud were at the race to witness my performance.

On returning to Grenoble, I visited team headquarters to ask about my programme of races for the end of the year. The team had ridden a lousy Tour. In its last week, Giles Mas, Regis Simon and Michel Bibollet were told by Vallet to look for a new job for the following year. Bibollet was particularly upset. At the start of the Tour, Vallet had told him not to go looking for another team, and that he would be signing him later in the race. Michel was delighted – security for another year. But signing-on day never arrived, and at the end of the race Michel was shown the door.

I didn't know if he was going to get rid of me. I asked him. He said he wasn't sure. He assured me that he personally wanted to keep me in the team, that I was a great team rider but that the sponsor Monsieur Braillon wanted only winners on the team. He told me of a new team that Patrick Valke and Stephen Roche were setting up. He said that Valke had assured him that he would take me on if Monsieur Braillon didn't want me. He told me that the ball was in my court, that it was up to me to convince Braillon in the two months of racing that remained that I was worthy of my place. So that was it: Vallet wanted me, Braillon didn't. Could I believe him? I was disappointed and confused. I desperately wanted to believe that Vallet wanted me in the team, but couldn't convince myself that he did. I told Colotti and Claveyrolat of my situation and both said they would canvass on my behalf. Colotti was very supportive, and argued with Vallet to keep me on. Vallet wouldn't commit himself, and for the month of August I lived in uncertainty. André had also been told to look for new employment. The news did not surprise him. He had ridden poorly all year and he was resigned to the fact his career was at an end, but he was still bitter.

I too became bitter. I resented the riders on the team who had signed contracts. Their 'I'm all right Jack' attitude sickened me, even though I fully realised that I had acted in the same way previously. I started to panic. What the hell was I going to do? A rider's career was measured in results. I had given three years of mine to helping others obtain results. Only RMO knew my worth as a team rider. I thought of asking Kelly or Roche for a dig-out, but decided against it. If they offered I would accept, but I would never go begging. My relationship with Vallet deteriorated. A week after returning from Montreal I got a new dose of *champignons*. We were riding a two-day, Paris–Bourges, and I was so uncomfortable that I could hardly sit on the saddle, never mind race. Vallet was not very understanding, and I knew straight away there was no way I would be in an RMO jersey in 1989.

I treated the *champignons* and they quickly disappeared; but I couldn't find decent form. I went to the world championships in Belgium in September determined to do the ride of my life. I failed miserably and abandoned with five laps to go. As in Austria the year before, I cried on entering our pit. But this time the tears were of bitterness and not joy. The season had been a complete and utter disaster.

It was Roche who came to my rescue. We went back to the hotel after the world championships ended and he called me into his room. 'Don't worry about next year, Paul, I'll look after you.' I thanked him and accepted gratefully. Stephen was that type of fellow. If he promised, he delivered, and even though he didn't know who he'd be riding with I never once doubted that we'd be riding together for 1989. Some of my sacked team-mates got word that I had found a saviour. They knew Stephen and I were good friends and asked me to talk with him on their behalf. I didn't like Frank Pineau and told him to his face that I wouldn't speak for him. The two others, Mas and Rault, I liked. I just hadn't the heart to tell them that I couldn't canvass on my own behalf, never mind theirs, and promised them both I would talk to Stephen for them. I never did, just hadn't the balls. I was afraid he would think I was asking too much, so I said nothing. Jean-François Rault rang Ann a few times and left his number for me to return the call, but I never did. He never found a job. I would have liked to help him, but I was powerless.

I felt sorry for him. Six months earlier he had won the marathon classic Bordeaux–Paris. He was promised the post of assistant *directeur sportif* for 1989. Jacques Michaud would be promoted to team manager. The squad needed a manager, as Vallet had signed Charly Mottet and was strengthening the squad. The French national champion Eric Caritoux came on the market, and Vallet offered him a deal. Caritoux agreed, but insisted that his former *directeur sportif* Christian Rumeau be given a job with the team. Caritoux signed, Rumeau was made assistant *directeur sportif*, Rault was given his marching orders. I thought they should have had the decency to keep him on for another year as a rider.

The Nissan Classic was my last race with the team. Unlike 1987, I wasn't allowed the pleasure of selecting the team and simply felt thankful to be in it myself. As a result, André and Clavet stayed at home. Jean-Claude was picked, but his wife lost a baby the day before we travelled, so he couldn't come. He was replaced by Esnault, and the others on the team were the Belgian sprinter Michel Vermotte and the two Danes Alex and Per Pedersen. The day before the race I was visited at the hotel by the sports editor of the *Sunday Tribune*, Stephen Ryan. He wanted me to write a diary of the week for Sunday's paper. I agreed.

The Nissan Classic is a five-day race. For four days I rode my arse off. I desperately wanted to succeed in front of the home crowd, and I tried hard on every single stage. Nothing went right. I punctured at the worst possible times, fell off on the climbs when my gears wouldn't work properly – and some little bastard stole a pair of brand-new sunglasses from my hotel room. After two stages I was starting to feel pretty pissed off. On the morning of the third day I met a girl in a wheelchair just before the start. Her name was Deborah Kane. Her father Dave had raced with my father, and Deborah had once been the top female cyclist in the country. She was racing in England when she rode into a parked lorry. She suffered horrific injuries and was paralysed. We had a good chat before the third stage and she smiled radiantly. I could not believe she could still smile. Her smile did something to me. I suddenly felt terribly fortunate and greatly moved by her enormous courage.

The last stage was a seventy-mile loop around the streets of Dublin, to be televised live by RTE. The stage passed five miles from Coolock, where I had grown up as a kid, and the highlight of the day was the three laps around the beautiful Howth Head. I have always loved Howth Head. When I was a fourteen-year-old schoolboy with a head full of dreams I would train around it three times a week with my pal, Martin Earley. We dreamed on that hill. It was the Alpe d'Huez or the Galibier or the Tourmalet and we were Merckx and Thevenet and Van Impe. As we lined up for the start, Martin turned to Kelly and said,

'Watch Kimmage today.' The flag dropped and I had but one aim: no one, but no one, was going to beat me over Howth Head.

Because of the live television coverage, attacks started from the gun and the first loop in south side Dublin was really fast. By the time we crossed the Liffey the first selection had already been made and I was part of a forty-man leading group. I knew something was going to give as we dashed out along the seafront at Clontarf – it was just a matter of choosing the right attack. When Allan Peiper took off with Pascal Poisson, I didn't hesitate. These were two drivers, two strong men. I jumped across. We rode really hard, and I had a lead of about a minute approaching Howth harbour. We swung left up through the village and started the climb. There was a great crowd all the way up and I was cheered like I had never been cheered in my life. The cheers sent goose-pimples all over my body, and I didn't feel the pedals. I went to the front at the bottom and stayed there until we reached the summit. I was first over the Head. Vallet drove up alongside for the first time on the descent. He told me I was doing too much work and should ease up. I nodded in agreement but immediately forgot his orders. He was absolutely right. I was riding too hard, but he didn't understand. This was Howth. This was part of me. Nothing else mattered.

We completed three laps of the Head and headed east, and then south towards the finish in the city centre. I started to feel the pinch with twenty miles to go. We were joined by two Fagor riders, Sean Yates and John Carlsen. They were riding like trains, and immediately I knew there was no way we could be caught. On the run into the city centre Vallet drove up and told me to do some 'talking' to try and win the stage. I approached Sean, who was a good friend, and asked him if he was interested in doing a deal. He never answered me, so I understood that to mean 'No'. I wasn't surprised. Yates and Peiper were great mates. I knew they would be working together so I didn't bother talking to Carlsen or Poisson. I was knackered when we got on to the circuit. Peiper broke clear and won on his own. I was fifth, but the television exposure had made me a hero. I was interviewed after the stage and next day on a popular radio programme.

Dublin was my last race for RMO. Of my three years with the team the first two under Thevenet are the ones I will remember most. If Stephen hadn't rescued me I'm sure I'd have left the sport very, very, bitter; but joining a new team, Fagor, changed all that, and I could afford to be nostalgic.

It had always been my ambition to ride for at least one year on the same team as Kelly or Roche. By finding a place for me at Fagor, Stephen had saved my career. But I would never have accepted a place if I hadn't believed that I could be of some service to him. I wanted to survive on my own merit and didn't want to spend the rest of my cycling days feeding off Roche's generosity. To succeed I needed a good winter and I spent it in France. I was determined not to make the mistakes of the previous year, so I set myself a strict training schedule involving diet, weights, jogging and mountain biking. Ann and I returned to Dublin for two weeks at Christmas. I was careful not to eat too much and continued to train hard. During our two-week stay I met the editor of the *Sunday Tribune*, Vincent Browne. To my great surprise, he offered me a job with the paper. I tried not to show it, but I was secretly delighted. I had to refuse, however. I just didn't have the confidence to write full time and I wanted to devote just one last year completely to the bike. But I was delighted he had asked me. The thought of one day going into journalism excited me. At last I had an escape route. It would be easier now to accept the hardship and suffering, knowing that at the end of it all I could find a good job. I returned to France very pleased.

I trained hard in January. One morning I was out early in the suburbs of Grenoble. There was an icy fog and it was freezing cold. I came across a Ford transit van driving slowly in the opposite direction. It was painted black and had black glass on its two sides. It took a few seconds for me to realise it was a hearse. There was a coffin inside and two people followed behind in a car. The scene chilled me to the bones. I decided there and then to leave the country as soon as my career as a bike rider was over. I didn't want to die in this place, to be brought to my resting place in a clapped-out old Ford with just two people crying over me. My family and friends were in Ireland. As soon as it was over I would return there.

I met up with Fagor for a training camp at the end of the month. It was a very weak team. Most of the good riders had left after disagreements with the team's management. My old RMO team-mates Regis Simon and Vincent Lavenu had also found jobs here so the ambience wasn't too bad. We rode six hours on our first spin and I was pretty knackered when it was over. Next day I was stuck to the road and turned home after just two hours. I felt drained and run-down. When I went for massage that night, the *soigneur* asked me if I wanted to take a B_{12} injection. I did. Silvano Davo was Italian. He had looked after Stephen at Carerra and had left with Stephen for Fagor. He was temperamental, as only Italians can be, but I liked him and was confident he would never give me any illegal medicaments or shit. Normally I would take my first vitamin injection three months into the season, but, damn it, I needed it. So I took it and next day felt much better. While at the training camp I roomed with Stephen. It was great. I enjoyed being Roche's man, and wanted to be at his side at all times. I was surprised he wasn't sharing a room with Eddy Schepers, his loyal lieutenant of three years. Eddy was a rider of class, in his own right, and he was very level-headed and straight. I liked him.

On the last evening of the training camp a group of Belgian tourists sat down at the table next to us. As soon as they realised they were sitting with Stephen Roche they started pestering us. One fellow in particular was obnoxious. He was drunk and smoking like a trooper. I couldn't understand Stephen talking to them all night. When he came up to the room I asked him about it.

'Why didn't you tell them to fuck off?'

And he laughed.

'Paul, you just can't turn round and tell people to fuck off. And anyway did you see the big tanned guy? That was the Mexican Pancho Rodriguez, a former world middleweight champ. He's the Belgians' bodyguard.'

'Jaysus, just as well I kept my mouth shut.'

Next day we drove to Arles for the first race of the season. We were staying in the same hotel as RMO, and instinctively I found myself going to their list pinned to the wall beside the lift and examining it to see who was sharing with who. Clavet was sharing with Ribeiro, Colotti was sharing with a new guy, Gilles Sanders. I paid a call to his room but as usual he was spaced out, his head up in the clouds, his mind already on the following day's race – Colotti loved racing. My first race with Fagor went off much better than I expected even though I didn't finish. It wasn't my fault: a bolt in my handlebars came loose near the finish and I was forced to stop. The second race was more disappointing. I relaxed too much near the end of it and got left behind when a crosswind split the bunch to bits.

After the second race, the team split into two. Half were to spend the month racing in the south of France, the others were returning to their homes for a week and then flying to Venezuela and Miami for a stage race, the Tour of the Americas. Stephen was crossing the Atlantic, and as I was now part of his baggage I too was selected to travel. Before leaving I had a week back in Grenoble. David phoned me from the *Sunday Tribune* and asked me how the opening races had gone. He suggested that I do a weekly diary for the paper over the whole season. I hesitated. If I had won the two opening races of the year, there is no doubt in my mind that I would have turned him down. But I had made more sacrifices at Christmas than in any other year, I had trained harder than in any other winter, I had even taken a vitamin injection in the run-up to the race. And for what? I had abandoned the two opening races of the season. The writing was on the wall for me. As a pro cyclist I was Mr Bloody Average. Also-rans were nothing in this game, they are nothing in this world. You don't see too many sporting greats in dole queues, but they are often full of queuing also-rans. Writing a weekly column might open a few doors in journalism. It might keep me from the dole queue. I agreed.

19

JOURNALIST

It didn't take me long to start questioning my commitment to writing a weekly column for the *Sunday Tribune*. The first 'diary' was a piece of cake, 500 words on the opening races in the south of France, which I sent back by reading it over the phone. It was more difficult in Venezuela. I had never been to South America and had, on just two occasions, been to countries where bidets and telephones were not ordinary instruments of daily life. Venezuela was ghastly. The capital, Caracas, exuded wealth, but ten miles into the suburbs I witnessed the most incredible poverty. The residential areas were acres of tin-roofed and, in some cases walled, sheds that a 'civilised' Western man would not use for a lavatory. I saw young kids with no clothing, just a piece of sack-cloth to cover them. It made me wonder about the morality of being paid to race a bicycle while people lived in squalor.

Riding a bike wasn't easy here. The streets were covered in oil, making them dirty and incredibly slippery in the wet. Petrol was cheaper than water, and it was more economical to let a leaking tank drip than to have it repaired. Election posters littered walls and shop windows. The candidates' names pushed their credibility to the limit. How can people seriously vote for a man called 'El Tigre'? There were dead dogs everywhere, and the vile smell of rotting carcasses choked the lungs and made me want to puke. The dreadful scenes moved me and I wanted to write about them. Writing about it wasn't a problem, but trying to send it home was a nightmare. Our hotel had no direct lines, so phoning it back was out of the question. Our team interpreter informed me there was a fax machine in the press room. I knew nothing about fax machines and was unsure that a handwritten document could be sent. But it was worth a try, so I gave him a copy and he sent it off.

The first stage of the race was a long road stage from Valencia to Caracas. The second was a criterium up and down one of the principal boulevards of the capital and the third a circuit race in Maracay. The first two days went well: I was riding, dare I say it, averagely. The third stage was to have been a circuit race, but as we lined up waiting for the off I noticed a group of protesters blocking the road ahead. It was totally chaotic but the tense atmosphere provided the backbone for the piece I wrote for the *Sunday Tribune*.

Professional cycling races have, in recent times, become an easy target for the demonstrator looking for publicity for his cause. Paris–Nice, the Tour de France, the Giro d'Italia, all have suffered at the protests of striking miners, of about to be laid off ship builders, of struggling farmers.

The demonstrations are an accepted nuisance that an unlucky race organiser must face. He will listen, sympathise with their problems and do almost anything to get them off the road.

When a bunch of students blocked the road three hundred metres from the start line at Maracay on the third day of the 'Tour de los Americas', nobody noticed. But then the fire started . . . The long finishing straight was adjoined by a huge field full of high grasses and scorched weeds. These weeds were only too accommodating as the students lit their matches and a huge fire rapidly spread.

A fire engine arrived. The firemen started hosing down the flames and soon had the initial section under control.

But when it came to reversing to follow the direction of the fire, the thirty-year-old truck broke down and we were treated to the ridiculous sight of the truck being pushed down the road by the embarrassed firemen and a handful of spectators.

Race director Germain Blanco decided that the time had come to do a deal. The students were protesting about the death of a young Caracas student at the hands of the local police the day before. Signor Blanco assured them that their protest had been noted, then asked them to clear the road. The students thought about it. They decided to kidnap him.

We had been standing on the start line for fifteen minutes. No one knew what was going on. The fire engine breaking down gave us all a great laugh, but there was no sign of a replacement and we watched as the huge orange flames grew closer and listened as the students' protests grew louder. And for the first time I started to feel uncomfortable.

Stephen (Roche) was standing talking to Fabio Parra when one of the bikini-clad promotion girls walked by. He took out his feeding bottles and playfully squirted some water at her. He missed.

There was a young police officer standing facing the crowd three feet in front of them. The cold water hit him on the back of the neck. The water hit a panic button in his brain that made him draw the four-foot-long butcher's knife he was wearing and turn to face his aggressor.

Stephen saw the anger in the man's face and the sword in his hand. His mouth dropped. Parra, a Spanish-speaking Colombian, quickly gave an explanation to the confused cop. The bomb was defused but the tension remained . . . Most of the riders then abandoned the start line. Some climbed on to the roofs of their team cars to try and get a better view. The second fire engine still hadn't arrived as the flames blazed, rapidly approaching the large metal fence that separated the field from the road – and us.

And then the rats started running.

Out under the fence they ran, big ones, small ones, dirty ones. Their ship, a weedy field, was sinking and as is their great tradition they were deserting. Not all of them made it to safety. Some were crushed by cars, others had their heads stood on by amused spectators – hard men, these Venezuelans.

And then the rocks started flying.

The students pelted the line of riot police facing them with anything they could get their hands on. This was the final straw. The organisers, still minus their race director, cancelled the stage.

We were ordered on our bikes and it was decided that we ride the fifty kilometres back to the hotel. So we left that place and the angry young men. They had won. But as I rode out of the town I wondered at the price they would have to pay.

The peloton were in a jovial mood as we rode back to the hotel: 'It was good of those students to give us the day off.'

One guy even suggested putting them on the flight to Miami so they could do the same there.

All through the protest the jokes and wisecracks were flying. No one seemed to give a damn that the students were risking their lives 300 metres in front of them. This attitude disturbs me, for I too am guilty.

And there was of course the ride back to the hotel. How many noticed the barefooted sackcloth-knickered kids that lined the road? How many give a damn? Do I? I don't know. All this disturbs me. I don't feel comfortable here, and all of a sudden bike racing seems so trivial, so wasteful. I will be happy to leave.

Tomorrow we fly to Miami for two more races. Ah,

Miami. Former Olympic champion Alexi Grewal calls it the sin capital of the world. It's full of rich people and lovely women and sandy beaches. I can't wait.

I liked the piece. It gave me a huge buzz of satisfaction. Of having hit the button, done it right. It was definitely better than average and this is what pleased me most. Perhaps I did have a future in journalism.

Miami was clean and sunny and lovely. There was a different smell here, money. Miami reeked of wealth. I hated it. It came too quickly after Venezuela, and the culture shock was too brutal for my conscience to bear.

I returned to Europe in good physical condition, but was still left off the team for Paris–Nice. I didn't mind too much, and tried to train as hard as I could at home during the week-long race. My next race was to have been the French classic Mauleon–Moulin (a Grand Prix des Chaudières) but on the day before I was due to leave I received a most disturbing phone call. It was the team doctor, Monsieur Navarro. During Paris–Nice I had flown to Toulouse Hospital to do some medical tests for the team. Dr Navarro was ringing me with the results. They had found an abnormality in my heartbeat and prohibited me from racing at Mauleon.

'It might be nothing at all or it might mean you have to give up cycling.'

I was shocked and quite frightened. Three days later I returned to Toulouse for more tests. A tape recorder that monitored heartbeats was strapped to my chest for twenty-four hours, and the results were fed into a computer and analysed by the doctors. The result – nothing. They had made a mistake, there was nothing wrong with me. I was delighted: for more than a week I had been fully convinced I was going to snuff it prematurely. But then I became angry. I had not touched the bike for nine days, had not raced for three weeks and was not due to race for another two. I was back to square one. The sacrifices I had made all winter, the benefits I had acquired from racing hard in Venezuela, were now all for nothing. And all because some stupid doctor couldn't read a computer correctly. I could have cried. I did.

I don't know how I kept my sanity as I struggled to regain good physical shape. My weekly articles for the *Sunday Tribune* certainly helped. So too did the encouragement of a phone call from Stephen. But the most helpful of all was my *directeur sportif*, Patrick Valke. Fagor, like most teams, had two *directeurs sportifs*: Pierre Bazzo, an ex-pro, was the principal *directeur*, while Patrick Valke was the assistant. Patrick and Stephen go back a long way. For seven years Patrick was his mechanic, but during the Giro of 1987 the roles changed. The wars with Visentini split the Carrera team into two camps. Stephen had just two men in his, Eddy Schepers and Patrick Valke. Eddy helped him on the road, but Patrick took over as *directeur sportif* of the two-man team and they won. When Fagor came looking for his signature later that year, one of the stipulations of the contract was that Patrick be made *directeur sportif*.

Patrick's greatest fault in his new job was his lack of diplomacy. With Patrick, a spade was always a spade. But some of the management at Fagor didn't take kindly to being addressed as spades, and half-way through the year he was sacked. The man he had replaced, Pierre Bazzo, was brought back and the Roche–Valke tandem spent the last four months of the year trying to find a way out of their marriage with the Basque electrical appliance firm. Contracts are signed to be honoured. Stephen needed a team, and Fagor were unable to find a leader of Roche's calibre and both parties decided to bury the hatchet and try again in 1989. Patrick was reinstated as *directeur*, but this time as assistant to Bazzo. This created one major problem – they hated each other. Splitting the team into two at the start of the year was a blessing in disguise. Bazzo and Valke never saw each other, and for a while the union seemed to work.

I started the year under Bazzo with an open mind. It didn't last. After the 'heart' incident, I badly needed racing, but Bazzo didn't want to know. I formed the impression that he would have left me at home until the end of the season; that he didn't rate me and wasn't prepared to give me a fair trial. One of the team mechanics told me he used to insult me, and others on the team, behind our backs. True or not, the revelation turned me completely against him. After that, I never phoned him for information, and our conversations never extended beyond 'hello' and 'goodbye', and even that was an effort.

Thank God I had Patrick. He arranged for me to race in Belgium and was very encouraging. My form was terribly slow in coming at first, but the racing got me going and gradually I started feeling better. The four days of Dunkirk were my first real stage race of the year. Stephen won a stage and finished third overall, and his form was so good he decided to have a go at the Tour of Italy. I had never ridden a 'Giro' before and asked Patrick for a place in the team; Italy would be make or break. A good performance would put me in the Tour team, a bad ride would mean the end. I wanted to push myself to the limits one more time to see if I could do it. On Friday 19 May we flew to Palermo, Sicily.

20

GIRO D'ITALIA

Sunday, 21 May 1989
Stage 1: Taormina to Catania (123 kilometres)
Stage winner: Jean-Paul Van Poppel (Netherlands)
Race leader: Jean-Paul Van Poppel

The Tour of Italy, second biggest stage race in the world. Three weeks of racing, 3,709 kilometres of cycling. I was nervous before the start. This is not just another bike race: it's history, legendary. And I'm here, doing it, participating in history. Starting out from Taormina this morning, I felt as if I was heading out on a great adventure. God knows what lies ahead. God knows how far I will go.

The first stage, a short one of 123 kilometres, was like all opening stages of big tours. Everyone was highly strung, and there were a lot of crashes. Everyone wanted to get to the front, to stay out of trouble, but also for another reason. The first stage is the only stage when any rider in the peloton can lead the Giro D'Italia. I was conscious of this as I took my place at the front. It's another tale for my grandchildren: 'the day Grandad led the Tour of Italy'. As a first stage it wasn't too bad, except for the finishing circuits, which were very fast. Some stupid Italian *gregario* (an Italian *domestique*) ran into me with three laps to go, and we both nearly fell. The bastard had the cheek to accuse me of swaying into him. He was short, dark, very ugly, and as I insisted on insulting him back we nearly came to blows. Typical Italian – they're gods in their own back garden.

A journalist came up to me after the finish. My face was blackened from street dust, and sweaty. My lungs were still heaving from the effort of the final sprint. And he looked at me and said, cool as a breeze, 'Oh, I suppose today was only a gallop?'

And I looked at him and thought seriously about telling him to fuck off. But I remembered what Roche had said and decided to be diplomatic: 'Yes I suppose it was, really.'

Monday, 22 May
Stage 2: Catania to Etna (132 kilometres)
Stage winner: Acasio da Silva (Portugal)
Race leader: Acasio da Silva

Today the stage finished on the slopes of the famous volcano. It used to terrify me as a child, this fiery mountain. I imagined it erupting and the lava rolling across the seas to the doorstep of Kilmore Avenue. It was another short stage, just 132 kilometres, but it was hard, with the climb to Etna at the finish. I didn't drink enough during the stage and was dehydrated on the climb – which was a pity, as I was going quite well. I lost three minutes to stage winner Acacio da Silva and finished on my hands and knees, absolutely cooked. There were others much worse than me: Greg LeMond was miles back and going really badly. Before getting into the team car after the finish, I picked up a piece of volcanic rock as a souvenir. I will take it home to Kilmore Avenue and the childhood fantasy will come true.

Tuesday, 23 May
Stage 3: Villafranca to Messina (32.5 kilometres Team
Time Trial)
Stage winner: Ariostea (team)
Race leader: Silvano Contini (Italy)

Team time-trial day, a bit of a disaster for me. Didn't recover
from the efforts of yesterday and spent most of the time sitting
at the back. The lads rode quite well and we finished tenth. We
showered and changed at a hotel beside the finish line which
also housed the press room. The atmosphere of typewriters
clacking and journalists scratching their heads intrigued me.
Will I be one of them next year? As soon as we had changed, we
left by car ferry for mainland Italy. I had expected an
improvement, but if anything it's poorer and even more dirty.

Wednesday, 24 May
Stage 4: Scilla to Cosenza (204 kilometres)
Stage winner: Rolf Jarmann (Switzerland)
Race leader: Silvano Contini

A great day, fifteenth on the stage, I'm really delighted with
myself. It was up and down, up and down, all day – a really hard
stage. I love it when it's like that. I was particularly strong near
the finish, and able to close a lot of gaps for Stephen. I should
have done better, really. I came out of the final hairpin in race
leader da Silva's slipstream and he had two riders leading him
out for the sprint. God, I couldn't believe it, I thought all my
Christmases had come at once, an armchair ride to the line –
this is it, I'm going to win. But then, 300 metres out, this six-
foot Italian bastard from the Jolly team elbowed his way in on
top of me and pushed me off da Silva's back wheel. I should
have pushed him back, but we were doing sixty kilometres an
hour and I hadn't got the bottle at that speed. As soon as I lost
the wheel I got boxed in and started slipping back to fifteenth

on the line. The Italian with the big elbows crashed as we crossed it, and ripped all the skin off his arse. Can't say I was sorry.

Thursday, 25 May
Stage 5: Cosenza to Potenza (275 kilometres)
Stage winner: Stefano Giuliani (Italy)
Race leader: Silvano Contini

My flirtation with journalism is getting out of hand. I am not sure I have ever been this tired after a stage, and I can't even rest, as I'm typing out the final pages of this week's diary to fax it home tomorrow. But I'm totally knackered and it's a real strain. My eyes keep blurring and I have never made as many mistakes with the typing. We were up at six, for the longest stage of the race, 275 kilometres. But the race organiser, Vincente Torriani, got his sums wrong and the correct stage distance was 290 kilometres. After the stage we had an hour's drive to the hotel, where there was no hot water for showering. I think I can be excused for feeling a little hard done by tonight. We suffer like dogs, are treated like dogs – and all for few quid and some glory. Am I mad? I am continuing to ride well, and I hope it lasts. Morale in the team is great with Patrick as *directeur sportif*. I get on really well with him, although he can be a ruthless bastard at times.

Friday, 26 May
Stage 6: Potenza to Campobasso (223 kilometres)
Stage winner: Stefan Joho (Switzerland)
Race leader: Silvano Contini

Some bastard Italian attacked from the gun today. The first five kilometres were up a mountain and the attack split the field to bits. Before I knew what was happening, the three cups of Colombian coffee, swallowed just before the off, were coming back up my throat. My muscles, sore and stiff from yesterday's marathon, took their time before responding and the climb was sheer hell. It was the ultimate in bad taste. This race is beginning to stink. Where was the Giro of legend, where riders laughed and joked for five hours and raced for two?

Managed to get my fax away. Gave it to English journalist John Wilcockson who will send it tonight from the press room. It's a big weight off my shoulders, which is a bit ridiculous. I mean, I shouldn't be bothered with the hassle, and yet I am. It would kill me if I didn't get it away, and I am beginning to wonder if this has become a new motivation for finishing the race. I mean, if I'm not racing, then I can't write, and it's got to the stage now where I actually love writing.

I didn't ride as well today and cracked a bit towards the end on a long crosswind section which split the peloton. I'm not really surprised, as the last two days were so demanding. I've been having regular vitamin injections from Silvano. One, sometimes two, a night. My arse is beginning to feel like a dartboard and I'm not happy about it. It bugs me to have to stick needles in myself every night just to survive.

Saturday, 27 May
Stage 7: Isernia to Rome (208 kilometres)
Stage winner: Urs Freuler (Switzerland)
Race leader: Silvano Contini

It's a pathetic sport. Here we are, in probably the most beautiful city in the world, and we don't have time to look around it. The stage finished outside the Colosseum, but we were sprinting so hard that I never got the chance to look left. On the way to the hotel we drove past the Vatican, but there wasn't even time to visit the square. The hotel was another disappointment. It was more like a factory than a hotel: too many teams there, not to mention the coachloads of tourists. We waited over an hour before they served us dinner, and when they did it wasn't worth waiting for. Tomorrow's a big day, the first mountain stage of the race.

Sunday, 28 May
Stage 8: Rome to Gran Sasso d'Italia (183 kilometres)
Stage winner: John Carlsen (Denmark)
Race leader: Erik Breukink (Netherlands)

Today we finished at the top of Gran Sasso d'Italia, Giant Stone of Italy. It was another fast start, but I was going really well and never felt under pressure. There was some fierce attacking on a long drag after sixty-five kilometres and the bunch split into bits. For once, Stephen was badly placed, but I bridged all the gaps with him in my slipstream and got the same pleasure from it as if I had won the stage. I never left his side until the final climb to the summit, where I lost the front group three kilometres from the top. It was a great day for the team, with our Dane, John Carlsen, winning the stage. Tonight, we had champagne and extra dessert as a reward, and spirits are high. The team is pulling well together under Patrick and uniting behind Stephen, who is still very much going for the win. I have been sharing a room with him since the start and I love it. Living with a champion gives me such great motivation: talking about his worries, dreaming his dreams, reliving the race as if *I* were in front.

Monday, 29 May
Stage 9: L'Aquila to Gubbio (221 kilometres)
Stage winner: Bjarne Riis (Denmark)
Race leader: Acasio da Silva

Grovelling to Gubbio. It's what I did today, grovelled. It was a bad day, a really bad day. I must have pushed too hard into my reserves yesterday for I hadn't an ounce of strength today. I cracked on the first climb after just eighty kilometres and spent the day in a big group of stragglers chasing to beat the time limit. The climb was terrible, so unbelievably hot I thought my head was going to blow open. The tar was running down the road like water in places: the tyres stuck to it, and I had the impression I was riding through a bog. The heat cracked me, and for the first time in the race I considered abandoning. That I didn't is no comfort to me tonight. The line between hanging in there and getting off can sometimes be so thin. It scares me. I want so desperately to finish this race, but heat and gradient can melt the strongest of resolves. Today I was close to the edge.

We had a long drive to the hotel when it was over. I was in a car with Robert Forest and Laurent Biondi. They had both ridden well and were chirping away like two little sparrows. They both knew I had ridden badly, and this no doubt added to their joy. In their shoes, I would undoubtedly act in the same way, so I don't hold it against them. It's just so absurd – grown men acting like children, delighted to have scored a few points against a rival. But as I say, I would have been the same.

Tuesday, 30 May
Stage 10: Pesaro to Riccione (36.8 kilometres TT)
Stage winner: Lech Piasecki (Poland)
Race leader: Erik Breukink

What a lovely place. Our hotel is fifty metres from the most beautiful beach I have ever seen in my life (my current situation is no doubt distorting its true valuation), but we can't use it. Still, the view from our terrace is just wonderful. Bare breasts and G-strings – the sexual frustration is unbearable. The mechanics have a great time: as soon as their work is done, it's off on the town for the night. And then, each morning at breakfast, they take such delight in reliving their lustful exploits. In the hotel opposite us, two elderly women are sunbathing naked on the terrace of their room. I was too embarrassed to look, but Patrick called the whole crew into the room and they gawped in disbelief before shouting obscenities. All of this took place after the time trial, of course.

It was a hard test, thirty-six kilometres of rolling coastal road, but I enjoyed it. I rode it at 80 per cent and caught a Russian from the Alfa Lum team, who had been off three minutes in front of me. Never thought I'd see the day when I'd be catching Russians in time trials. I used the free time in the afternoon to do some washing and to type some of Sunday's article.

Stephen has moved up to second overall behind Dutchman Erik Breukink. He is pleased with his performance but is getting a lot of pain from his back and tonight his doctor flew down by private plane from Germany to examine him. The doctor had just returned from Wimbledon, where he was treating another of his patients, Boris Becker. Roche doesn't do things by halves. Tonight was special. When we switched off the lights, we talked for over an hour about how he could win the race. That's something new for me – to be working out how to win a Giro – it's very exciting and motivating. He proved today he can win the race. I must be at his side at all times until the finish. I want to be his lieutenant.

Wednesday, 31 May
Stage 11: Riccione to Mantua (244 kilometres)
Stage winner: Urs Freuler
Race leader: Erik Breukink

The good weather deserted Riccione sometime during the night and when we awoke this morning, it was to blackened skies and pouring rain. We were soaked to the skin before we even left the outskirts of the town and the 240 kilometres were ridden under a constant deluge. My mood was at one with the skies. I hate racing in the rain, it makes life so uncomfortable. Spray from the wheels injects every kind of filth into your eyes and the cold wetness penetrates every pore in your skin. At Wimbledon, as soon as it rains they pull over the covers and everyone retires for tea. But the poor cyclist has always been the peasant of the sporting world: shove a fiver in his back pocket and he will do anything you ask him to.

I fell off today, which is unusual – I don't often crash. It happened thirty kilometres from the finish, the speed was up and the lads were jostling for a good position. One guy touched a wheel, so those behind tried to brake, but the brake pads don't work as efficiently in the wet and thirty of us ran up the guy's arse. I wasn't hurt, just a few cuts and bruises. I suppose it was just one of those days.

Thursday, 1 June
Stage 12: Mantua to Mira (148 kilometres)
Stage winner: Mario Cipollini (Italy)
Race leader: Erik Breukink

There was another crash today, much more serious than yesterday's. It happened 100 metres from the line at over sixty kilometres an hour and at least six riders went down. I'm not a bit surprised as they are crazy bastards here. Pulling and pushing, elbowing and shoving: my experiences at Cosenza had taught me that sprinting it out against the Italians was only for the very brave or the stupid. It was pretty horrific and the Dane Rolf Sorensen came off worse. As I passed him, he lay against the barriers, blood gushing from his head. It took the quick intervention of a race official to stop him choking on his tongue, and he was immediately rushed to hospital. Seeing him lying there makes you wonder about the risks we take. I asked Stephen about it and he agrees, so it's not just me. But then you forget it, you have to. *C'est la vie*.

Tomorrow we enter the Dolomites, where the race will be decided. It's another summit finish, to the three summits of Laverado – which is said to be incredibly steep.

Friday, 2 June
Stage 13: Padua to Tre Cime de Lavaredo (207 kilometres)
Stage winner: Luis Herrara (Colombia)
Race leader: Erik Breukink

The rain started about half-way through the 207-kilometre stage, turning heavier as we neared the final mountain. The Laverado was as steep as its reputation, and we all suffered terribly. Near the top the rain turned to sleet, then snow, and we were frozen getting off our bikes. I was ushered into the kitchen of a hotel opposite the finishing line and was given a basin of hot water and some hot tea. I had almost finished washing myself down when Greg LeMond walked in. I passed him at the bottom of the climb and he was riding really badly. He was shivering, and didn't bother to remove his shoes or socks before placing both feet in the basin of water. His words echoed the thoughts of many.

'God, that was awful.'

Stephen lost time to Breukink and is a bit disappointed tonight. He is talking about going out tomorrow and throwing down the gauntlet. An all-out attack that will win or lose him the race. Tomorrow is the race's big mountain rendezvous. It is only 130 kilometres, but we must climb five mountains.

Saturday, 3 June
Stage 14: Misurina to Corvara (131 kilometres)
Stage winner: Flavio Giupponi (Italy)
Race leader: Laurent Fignon (France)

When I think of the hundreds of thousands of kilometres I have ridden since my Da, Christy, gave me my first racing bicycle, the 130 between Misurina and Corvara are those I will remember longest. I remember every single kilometre, every single metre. It was an incredible day.

It was overcast but dry on the morning of the stage, but we all knew the rain was coming. I asked Silvano for a caffeine suppository, just as an insurance in case of emergency. As we lined up, the first drops of rain started falling. Most of the lads immediately turned around and rushed back to their team cars for extra clothing. I pulled on a pair of woollen leg-warmers but couldn't find my gloves; I had left them at the hotel. Before leaving the car, I took the tin foil from the caffeine suppository, and shoved it up. There were just five minutes to the start and I hoped it might take effect immediately. I needed a lift, boy did I need a lift.

Sunday Tribune,
11 June 1989

How do I explain today? A day quite unlike any other that I have known in the sixteen years I have been racing. Looking back it all seems so unreal. The 130 kilometres stage from Misurina to Corvara was one of the shortest of the race, but with five mountains to be climbed it promised to be one of the hardest. It was.

As we approach the Marmolada, the third and hardest of the climbs, I am part of a forty-man group already ten minutes behind the leading riders. It has rained since the start. I look towards the summit but it was hidden. Hidden in a mass of angry jet black clouds.

A huge crack of thunder warns us of the dangers to come, but on we climb. The cold rain turning to sleet and then three kilometres from the summit to snow. Hundreds of spectators leave the warmth of their cars to encourage us.

Two thousand metres above sea level I stop to take out the plastic jacket from my pocket. A group of *tifosi* (fans) surround me, one sheltering me from the falling snowflakes with his umbrella. Another offers me a sheet of newspaper which I place under my jersey. And then, I set off, their cheers warming me as I go to face my Calvary.

You see climbing a mountain in snow is not really a problem. With your heart tapping at 175 beats a minute the body generates enough heat to fend off the worst of weather. The trouble starts when you go down the other side.

There is no physical effort involved here, just the mental concentration of braking and turning. The heart rate drops and the body no longer produces heat and within minutes you are not sweating but shivering.

The snow was falling at such a rate that it started to clog up the teeth of the back wheel, making the chain jump. It was difficult to see and our group had now disintegrated as we descended one by one, every man for himself.

My body got colder and colder, the leg muscles hardening and the arms now vibrating. I had no gloves. They were the last thing I had packed in my suitcase before leaving for the race, but I had forgotten them at the hotel. My fingers started freezing to the handlebars and I was finding it more and more difficult to brake.

I passed my young French team-mate Francis Moreau. He was doubled over at the side of the road trying to warm his hands. He looked at me as I passed and his eyes told me he had had enough.

This frightened me. I screamed at the top of my voice in an effort to motivate myself, but it was getting harder and harder to brake and I pulled to a halt at the side of the road.

I shook my arms and fingers, blowing my icy breath on them for warmth. The cold had gone into my bladder, giving me the urge to urinate. I was almost surprised at the steam rising from the yellow liquid flowing from my body. I placed my fingers in the hot springs and warmed them.

I still don't understand why I didn't follow Moreau into

the warmth of the team car. The conditions were inhuman. No *directeur sportif* in the world could criticise one of his riders abandoning on such a dreadful day.

But Roche was up ahead. What if he took the race lead? But no, it was not that, either. I suppose in a way it became a challenge, a survival of the fittest that appealed to the cannibal instincts in me. Absurd isn't it?

I was so happy to reach the bottom. The remaining two climbs of the day were not too hard and it was a relief to start climbing again to generate some heat. My mouth still quivered and I whined like a dog in pain until half-way up the climb, when I started to get warmer. The team car pulled alongside me. The mechanic taped two cloth feeding bags on my hands and this helped greatly on the last descents of the day.

I crossed the finish line thirty-three minutes after stage winner Flavio Giupponi. We drove to the hotel and once again there was no hot water. Well, I mean, after a day like that how could anyone expect hot water? I did not care. I just covered my filthy legs with a tracksuit bottom and climbed into bed. I turned to Stephen and said, 'Don't bother waking me for dinner, just wake me in the morning and put me on my bike.'

Tonight I am happy. Ten riders abandoned the stage. Twenty others were outside the time limit but were excused because of deplorable weather conditions. I survived. The cannibal.

GIRO D'ITALIA

Sunday, 4 June
Stage 15 (a): Corvara to Trento (131 kilometres)
Stage 15 (b): Trento to Trento (83.2 kilometres)
Stage 15 (a) winner: Jean-Paul Van Poppel (Netherlands)
Stage 15 (b) winner: Lech Piasecki
Race leader: Laurent Fignon

A split stage. The breakfast menu was a climb of Val Gardena pass, a long descent and some flat roads to Trento. It was snowing hard on Val Gardena and the sufferings of yesterday were repeated, but it wasn't quite as bad – we were prepared this time. I started the stage with so much clothing I looked like the Michelin man – but it still wasn't enough, I was still frozen on the descent. I didn't bother with caffeine today. Yesterday, my heart felt like it was going to jump out of my chest on the first climb, but after that, the effects wore off and I started to feel sick.

They should not have made us ride over Val Gardena. It would have been easy to divert us around the mountain, but yesterday's foul conditions have brought great publicity to the race and no changes were made. It's ironic really: Val Gardena is better known as a world cup downhill ski resort, but in weather like this the downhill would have been cancelled. We descended to Trento, the snow turning to sleet and then to rain. It wasn't a good day to be a pro cyclist.

The weather changed, and it was warm and sunny for the afternoon's circuit race around the town. I was knackered, riding down to the start, but an Irish voice in the crowd drew my attention. It was my wife's cousin. She is working in Milan, but it was Sunday, so she got the train across to see the race. I told her of the snow and of the dreadful conditions we had endured that morning but it didn't register with her. All she could see were the bright colours of the jerseys and the glitter of the shiny wheel spokes.

'It must be very exciting being part of it all,' she said.

'No', I replied, 'not a bit.'

I don't think she believed me.

Monday, 5 June
Stage 16: Trento to S. Caterina Valfurva (205 kilometres)
CANCELLED (Bad weather).

Oh happy day. We had woken to another fierce downpour. It was supposed to be another mountain stage, taking in the notorious Gavia climb. The mood was very sombre at breakfast time. No one in the hotel wanted to ride bikes that day. We all knew what was waiting for us. I knew there was no way I could survive another day of snow and shivering. All I knew was that I would ride as far as possible within reason. We changed into our racing kit and gathered in the *soigneurs'* room to have embrocation and protection creams applied to legs and body. Patrick had been called to a manager's meeting and returned just as we were leaving the room. We looked to him, hoping but not expecting, and there was total silence as he spoke.

'Messieurs, due to a landslide on the Gavia pass, I have the pleasure of informing you that the stage has been cancelled. Today is a rest day, you can return to bed.'

There was a wild, roaring, cheer. Serious, moody faces suddenly cracked open with huge smiles. Chaubet, Forest and Biondi started jumping up and down, dancing with joy, and within minutes jokes and wisecracks were flying. I was absolutely delighted. We showered off the embrocation and spent the morning under the warm bedclothes, while outside, sheets of cold rain dashed against the windows.

Tuesday, 6 June
Stage 17: Sondrio to Meda (137 kilometres)
Stage winner: Phil Anderson (Australia)
Race leader: Laurent Fignon

Our good fortune continues. With all roads to St. Caterina be Valfurva blocked, the start of today's stage was moved forward along the route to the town of Sondrio, which shortened our

210

day's work to a not too stressful 137 kilometres. The other positive to report was the surprise arrival by bike of the Irish 'tifosi' in the shape of George O'Rourke. George, or Big George as he is known in Dublin cycling circles, is one of the great enthusiasts of the sport. He started racing in the time of my father and although he has probably been shelled out of more bunches than any other rider alive, I don't think I have ever met a cheerier bloke. He joins us for a coffee before the start and entertains us with tales of his ride across the Alps. 'Jaysus George, it must have been tough in these conditions,' I suggest. 'It was. I was absolutely miserable,' he smiles.

Wednesday, 7 June
Stage 18: Mendrisio to Monte Generoso (10.7 kilometres TT)
Stage winner: Luis Herrara
Race leader: Laurent Fignon

A ten-kilometre mountain time trial. I rode strongly in the test without killing myself and finished forty-fourth, which is as well as I have ever ridden in a test as a pro. I finished one place in front of world champion Maurizio Fondriest – another story for the rocking chair.

Thursday, 8 June
Stage 19: Meda to Tortona (198 kilometres)
Stage winner: Jesper Skibby (Denmark)
Race leader: Laurent Fignon

A relatively easy day except for the last fifty kilometres, which were very hard. I am still riding well, which is surprising for the last week of the race. Just two more hard mountain stages to go, and then the final day's time trial. I must hang in there. I must not crack.

Friday, 9 June
Stage 20: Voghera to La Spezia (220 kilometres)
Stage winner: Laurent Fignon
Race leader: Laurent Fignon

We lost Chaubet today. He was dropped after the first climb and abandoned shortly after. It is maddening to suffer what he has suffered, to get so close and not make it. If tomorrow was an easy stage I'm sure he would have kept going, but it will be very hard. I too felt the strain today; my good form of the last two days deserted me, and I struggled near the end of the stage. I feel very tired tonight, but there is just tomorrow to get through and then I'm home.

Saturday 10 June
Stage 21: La Spezia to Prato (216 kilometres)
Stage winner: Gianni Bugno (Italy)
Race leader: Laurent Fignon

I made it but it was close. I got the hunger knock after the first climb and had it not been for two System U riders, Thierry Marie and my old RMO team-mate Jean-Louis Peillon, who gave me some food, I don't know what I'd have done. Tonight I am content. There is just one more stage, a fifty-kilometre time trial to go. For the first time in three weeks, I know I will finish.

Sunday, 11 June
Stage 22: Prato to Florence (53.8 kilometres TT)
Stage winner: Lech Piasecki
Race winner: Laurent Fignon

I had thought about that moment every day for twenty-one days: the moment, 300 metres before the line, when you look up and see the final finishing banner, *Arrivo*. I knew what I was going to do, had it all planned out. On crossing the line I took both hands off the bars and blew two kisses at the banner and then waved a clenched fist in triumph. The adventure was over, and I had survived. My inner satisfaction was enormous. The nightmare of abandoning the Tour in 1987 was now buried and I could hold my head high. I was, once again, a Giant of the Road.

21

CARNON PLAGE

A beach. A warm, sunny beach looking out on a blue Mediterranean sea. Wind, a cooling, glorious puff blowing in off the waves. Sand – hot, golden sand, scorching the naked feet.

Far from the maddening *tifosi*. A million miles from piddling on my fingers, from sticking needles in my bum, from being deafened by car klaxons and sweating, lies Carnon Plage. A twenty-kilometre drive from Montpellier, it was just the place for a pro cyclist who had recently ridden a hard Giro D'Italia. One week after returning from the Giro, Ann and I spent four of the most relaxing days of our lives there. We breakfasted late most mornings – coffee with croissants on the sunny terrace of the apartment. After breakfast I would take the bike and ride for two hours along the coastline, taking advantage of my wife's absence to admire the vast assortment of pretty girls tanning their beautiful bodies. I returned for a shower and a light lunch, and then it was down to the beach for the afternoon. It felt great to sit there and do nothing. I would sleep and read and stare and think.

I thought quite a lot.

In the evenings we dined out, strolled around the port admiring the sailing craft and sipped beers on the terrace of a café. For the first time in my career I could honestly say that everything was rosy. It had been a good Giro. Stephen had finished ninth, Carlsen had won a stage, Fagor were best team and I had finished 84th out of 198 starters. My future was secure. I was assured of employment for as long as Stephen could remain competitive. And I had been told I was riding the Tour. Yes, everything really was rosy. But on our third evening at the bar, I decided I didn't want it any more. I decided to retire at the end of the season.

From the first day I threw my leg over a bike I have always tried to be honest with myself, a quality I inherited from my father. It was true I had ridden a good solid Giro, but in my own eyes I had failed. I was incapable of staying with Roche in the mountains and wasn't strong enough to drive for him on the flat. The days when I was capable of good things were always followed by bad ones. I was sure of a job with Stephen, but did I really merit it? If we weren't friends, would he still want me in his team? I didn't think so.

I wasn't good enough: the Giro had spelled it out for me. I had given the race my best shot, had looked after myself with vitamin and mineral supplements from the start to finish. And for what? To be average! There was no way I was prepared to stick needles in my arse for the rest of my career just to survive, to be average. Not now that there was a way out – journalism.

The Tour of Italy pieces had produced a great reaction back in Ireland. The sports editor of the *Sunday Tribune*, Stephen Ryan, told me I could start with them whenever I wanted to. But the most satisfying thing was that my journalistic options were not confined to the *Tribune*. A rival paper was also interested in acquiring my services. I was thrilled. The future didn't look quite so daunting. So, in a quiet seafront bar, and after three days of examining the options, I decided to quit. I would ride the Tour, finish out the season with Fagor and then hang up my wheels.

A week before the start of Le Grand Boucle, Patrick organised two kermesse races for us in Belgium. I hadn't planned to tell them yet of my decision to retire at the end of the year, but I ended up telling them anyway. They had been negotiating with Fagor for a new contract for months and things were not working out. The deal was supposed to have been signed at the start of the Giro, then at the end of the Giro and then at the start of the Tour. But each time Fagor found a new excuse for delaying the signing of the contract. We all knew what they were playing at. They wanted to see how Stephen performed in the Tour before signing him up for another year. On the weekend of the Belgian kermesses Patrick had received news of a possible move for Stephen and seven of his team-mates to the Colombian team, Postobon. Patrick told me of the deal, and assured me that I was one of the seven Stephen would take with him. I was delighted that Stephen still wanted me in his team, but felt compelled to tell them of my decision. Their initial reaction was to advise me against doing anything hasty, but as soon as I explained about my opportunity to go into journalism, both agreed I would be foolish to turn it down. After I had told them, I felt a huge weight roll off my shoulders. I was no longer part of Stephen's plans for next year. I had taken the dive and there was no turning back.

The races in Belgium were a disaster. My legs were still heavy from the sun on Carnon Plage and my mind was totally switched off. I returned to Grenoble and did some hard rides in the mountains to prepare myself for the Tour. One of these brought me to the slopes of the Galibier. It was a real trip down memory lane, for I had not cycled its gradient since abandoning the Tour two years earlier. Riding it alone was a strange sensation, a bit like walking into an empty football stadium. I rode up the mountain locked in a trance, reliving the pedal strokes of my last visit. I saw my name on the road. It was written in fading white paint alongside the names of Roche and Earley. And as I examined other faded names I was reminded of a graveyard, the faded letters sticking out like tombstones. Would I notice my name in three weeks' time? Would I make it this far?

22

THE LAST CRUSADE

Saturday, 1 July 1989
Prologue: Luxembourg (7.8 kilometres TT)
Stage winner: Erik Breulink (Netherlands)
Race leader: Erik Breulink

It feels good to be back in the race. The Tour is changing, becoming more modern. When I first rode in 1986, it was still the era of Monsieur Levitan's reign as race director. The public address system churned out never-ending accordion music, giving the event a uniquely French flavour. That's all gone now: the race has been modernised, it's all Bon Jovi and Jean-Michel Jarre now. Paul McCartney is the flavour of the month. They played 'My Brave Face' at least ten times this morning. I hate that song.

It's going to be a very difficult three weeks, and I'm not just talking about the race. We haven't started yet, but already the ambience is at rock bottom. There are many reasons. Fagor still have not agreed Stephen's contract stipulations for next year. They were nearing verbal agreement and were originally going to sign a month ago, but it's still at status quo. None of the other riders have signed either, and some are starting to get anxious about next year.

The second problem is the appointment of Pierre Bazzo as number one *directeur sportif* for the race. One of Stephen's demands for signing for another year was that Patrick be given control of the team for the Tour. Fagor initially agreed, but backed down three days before the race. Patrick is here, but must play second fiddle to Bazzo – and it's killing him. It's killing me too: I don't respect or have any confidence in Bazzo as *directeur sportif* and he knows it.

Patrick is taking it badly. He was not allowed to follow Stephen in this morning's prologue time trial and it's the first time in nine years he hasn't followed his friend in a time trial. We watched it together in my room and he was so upset that tears started rolling down his face. Stephen didn't ride a good prologue. The mechanics gave him a front wheel with a bald tyre and a slow puncture, and forgot to bring his aerodynamic hat to the start – he was furious. When he returned to the hotel, he had a fierce row with Bazzo that nearly ended in blows. I have never seen him so mad.

My own prologue was pretty dismal. I was never going well and a dose of Tour nerves before the start didn't help either. The big news of the day was Pedro Delgado missing his start time by two minutes and forty seconds. I rang home tonight and talked to my brother Christopher. He wasn't very complimentary about my prologue performance: 'Delgado nearly beat you.' The sarcastic little swine.

Sunday, 2 July
Stage 1: Luxembourg to Luxembourg (135.5 kilometres)
Stage 2: Luxembourg to Luxembourg (46 kilometres
Team Time Trial)
Stage 1 winner: Acasio da Silva (Portugal)
Stage 2 winner: Super U (team)
Race leader: Acasio da Silva

Fame at last. Today was a split stage – 130-kilometre road stage in the morning, team time trial in the afternoon. After the time trial, I was invited to appear on French television station

Antenne 2's chat show, broadcast daily at the finish of each stage. The show usually concentrates on the stars, but this year they have introduced a daily slot where they interview the lesser lights in the race. My conversion to journalism was my *raison d'être*, and I used the time allotted to me to talk about my former team-mate André, and tried to blow the myth that it was a glamorous life. I was just warming up when they cut me short. Bible-thumping is not in mode with these people. The attitude here is: 'Don't rock the boat, for God's sake don't rock the boat. Talk about the Fignons and the LeMonds with awe and wonder, and say no more. It's what the people expect to hear.'

I rang Ann tonight. She didn't see me on TV – typical. Television apart, it was not a good day. I am riding very poorly. Maybe I took too much time off after the Giro, I don't know. I do know that I'm struggling at the moment. I rode badly in the morning's stage, so badly that I had to take a caffeine tablet for the team trial in the afternoon. We did twenty kilometres of a warm-up before it started, and I tried to shove it up as I was going along. But it was awkward because Bazzo was in the car behind and I didn't want him to notice. He'd have a field day if he saw me with my finger up my arse and I wasn't leaving myself open to his jibes. I stopped and pretended I was having a piss, and did it at the side of the road. It felt bloody degrading. I knew it wasn't going to make much difference but it was just a little insurance. It was doping, no mistake about it, but it was only pigeon shit to what some of the others were doing. It bothered me, but this was my last Tour and I didn't want to go out of it after just two days.

I rode better than in the team trials in the Giro, but I still wasn't great. I don't feel very proud of myself tonight.

Monday, 3 July
Stage 3: Luxembourg to Spa-Francorchamps (241 kilometres)
Stage winner: Raul Alcala (Mexico)
Race leader: Acasio da Silva

The first long stage, 240 kilometres. We had a really hard head-wind most of the day, which slowed us down a lot. It was a blessing in disguise, as I rode badly again. Stephen is having problems too: all this haggling and fighting is upsetting him. Team morale continues to slump. Bazzo addresses me now as *le journaliste* in a mocking tone which really winds me up. Some of the riders call me *le journaliste* too, but from them it's almost a compliment. My conversation with Bazzo is limited to 'Bonjour' and 'Bonsoir', but I'm not sure I can even keep this up. We had no disc wheels for yesterday's team time trial. They were supposed to have been delivered at Fagor headquarters the week before the Tour but they have 'gone missing'. The team's supply of jerseys and shorts has gone missing too. It's total chaos.

Tomorrow we ride over the cobbles to Wasquehal, entering France for the first time. I hate cobbles.

Tuesday, 4 July
Stage 4: Liège to Wasquehal (255 kilometres)
Stage winner: Jelle Nijdam (Netherlands)
Race leader: Acasio da Silva

Today was awful. Tonight, my body is just so sore from those horrible stones. Bouncing along them, my balls up around my ears, sore hands, sore feet.

The stage finished two hundred yards from where we lived as amateurs, at Wasquehal. When I think about it I realise what a long way I've come – and I'm still not happy.

Wednesday, 5 July
Transfer: Lille to Dinard

The morning was a right cock-up. The organisers had chartered a plane to fly us to Dinard, but there was a problem with it and we had to wait most of the morning until a replacement was found. We did two hours this evening to loosen out our legs a bit and I was able to wash and do some work on my article.

Tonight I hit the jackpot. Phillipe Brunel from *L'Equipe* phoned to ask me if he could come for an interview. He arrived just as we were finishing dinner, and the other lads couldn't believe he had come to talk to me. The French lads would give both balls for an interview with *L'Equipe*. I could sense their frustration as I left the table to talk to him.

I was quite impressed with Brunel. He was intelligent and obviously loves his job. We talked about my origins and my relationship with Stephen and Sean. I edited my comments on Kelly and Roche to a strict minimum and tried again to strike a blow for Chappuis. We talked late into the evening. He told me of his love for journalism and I enthused. My ranting over Chappuis had impressed him. He said I wasn't ruthless enough to be a pro cyclist. I took it as a compliment.

Thursday, 6 July
Stage 5: Dinard to Rennes (73 kilometres TT)
Stage winner: Greg LeMond (USA)
Race leader: Greg LeMond

Time trial day – the first of the race. Patrick insisted on following Stephen for the time trial, and Bazzo backed down and followed one of the others. Greg LeMond won, and I can't quite believe it. Three weeks ago I was dropping him on climbs of the Giro. I am happy for him. He has had a hard time of it since he won the Tour in 1986, but today bounced back in style – the real mark of a champion.

I enjoyed the solitude of racing on my own. The last few days have been terrible for crashes, and it was great to give the nerves a day off. That damned song continues to irritate me. They played it before the start, and my brain got hooked on it – playing it and replaying it during every kilometre of the time trial. Painful.

Friday, 7 July
Stage 6: Rennes to Futuroscope (255 kilometres)
Stage winner: Joel Pelier (France)
Race leader: Greg LeMond

Shit – the word that best describes the stage. I was on and off the back like a yo-yo all day. Crashes, punctures – today I had it all. I spent the last fifty kilometres of the stage grovelling like an animal in the gutter. It's dangerous in the gutter, riding so close to the edge. I hit a ridge with twenty kilometres to go and my front wheel turned sideways on it and started slicing. I got such a fright that I let out a roar of frustration – the others thought I was mad. Clavet came down in one of the many crashes and broke a bone in his hand. His days in the race are numbered. *L'Equipe* still haven't published the interview! What are they waiting for? The way things are going I might not be around much longer.

Saturday, 8 July
Stage 7: Poitiers to Bordeaux (258.8 kilometres)
Stage winner: Etienne de Wilde (Belgium)
Race leader: Greg LeMond

Today the story appeared – it looked quite well. There was a small photo of me sitting at my typewriter with my Fagor jersey and half a page of script. A lot of what I had said had been cut, but the good bits were still in. One of the most respected riders in the peloton, the System U rider Dominique Garde, told me he thought it was good. This pleased me. I feel a bit like the Lech Walesa of the peloton. A rebel with a cause.

It was the only bright note of the day. It rained heavily for most of the 260 kilometres and I was in a foul humour at the finish. A minute after I had crossed the line, Jim McArdle of the *Irish Times* approached me. The *Sunday Tribune* had asked him to contact me; they were waiting urgently for my copy to arrive. I couldn't understand why they hadn't got it. Before the stage I had paid a hotel receptionist £25 to fax off the six pages of typescript. Had the bastard pulled a fast one? Obviously. I was furious. The sprint that I made to the hotel would probably have won me the stage. I jumped off the bike and ran into reception. Had they a fax machine? Yes, my luck was in. I galloped up to my room and retrieved the original pages, which I had luckily stored in my suitcase. Another dash back to reception and into the fax machine. Pheeeew . . . !

My urgency to send away my piece made one thing suddenly clear to me. Unknown to myself, I had changed from a 'cyclist journalist' to a 'journalist cyclist'.

Sunday, 9 July
Stage 8: La Bastide d'Armagnac to Pau (157 kilometres)
Stage winner: Martin Earley (Ireland)
Race leader: Greg LeMond

Found my legs for the first time this week. I was going well when things got hot at the end and even managed an attack. To my great delight, Martin won the stage. He jumped clear of three others a kilometre from the finish and won on his own. I knew he was going to win. I said it to Kelly about an hour from the finish, I just got this gut feeling he was going to do it. As we arrived in Pau, I strained my ears to the commentary of race speaker Daniel Mangeas. When I heard him shout M-A-R-T-I-N E-A-R-L-E-Y, I waved a triumphant fist in the air. I am thrilled for him, but, 'Why must there always be a "but" whenever I talk of Martin?'

I suppose it's because we were such keen rivals as amateurs. I suppose, deep down, I always felt I was better than him. Not any more. He has done something I know I can never do. I am not jealous of him. I really am pleased he won today, but I'm so envious. Years ago, when we were two schoolboys cycling around Howth Head, we'd dream of one day winning stages of the Tour. Today, he made the dream a reality. He guaranteed his place in the history books of this great race.

Monday, 10 July
Stage 9: Pau to Cauterets (147 kilometres)
Stage winner: Miguel Indurain (Spain)
Race leader: Greg LeMond

Everything was fine. I was going OK and really looking forward to the first day in the mountains. We had ridden about twenty kilometres and were approaching the first Col, Marie Blanque, when Stephen's hand went up. I dashed to his side immediately. It's a great thrill having him in your slipstream, weaving in and out of the team cars after he has punctured. But this time it wasn't a puncture. It was his knee, the weak knee that he damaged in a six-day race in Paris in the winter of 1984. Suddenly it was giving him fierce pain, and we called the race doctor. The spray can was produced but we all knew that the solution was not to be found in an aerosol. He was cooked, it was over, the *bête noire* had struck again.

I stayed with him on Marie Blanque along with Eddy, his faithful lieutenant. Stephen was in terrible pain and riding on one leg. We were quickly distanced by the leaders, but left a lot of struggling bodies behind us – men with two good knees. I stayed at his right shoulder, Eddy on his left. I never once put my bike in front of his, riding all of the time a half-length behind – I didn't want to insult his dignity any further. Photographers and television crews surrounded us, like vultures waiting to be called to dinner. They all wanted to capture the moment when the great champion puts his foot to the ground and abandons the race. But he wasn't going to give them that pleasure. Roche's golden rule was that he never abandoned. He was riding to Cauterets.

I had always wanted to be at Stephen's side in the mountains, but not in these circumstances. I advised him not to torture himself for I could see he was in great pain. Tears welled up in his eyes as we crossed the top and I felt terribly sorry for him. If he had abandoned at the top I am sure I would have abandoned too, but he kept going. He rode better on the second Col, Aubisque, and I dropped back three-quarters of the way up the climb. Eddy remained at his side.

Tonight they were all banging on his door, looking for a story, but the door remained closed. There were just Patrick and Stephen and me to talk out his future. I have never seen him so low. He won't be starting tomorrow. Patrick has advised him to fly to Munich for treatment. I don't know how I'll get through the race without him. I don't have a great rapport with the other fellows on the team. I have noticed the way some of them are 'sneaking back to bed' with Bazzo, now that Stephen is having problems. I suppose they are worried for their futures; but even so, it never ceases to amaze me how low some will stoop to stay in a job. Stephen still hasn't signed his new contract with Fagor, and tonight Patrick saw two of the management in discussion with race leader Greg LeMond. The scum. Roche is not even out of the hotel and they are talking to other leaders.

Tuesday, 11 July
Stage 10: Cauterets to Luchon (136 kilometres)
Stage winner: Robert Millar (Scotland)
Race leader: Laurent Fignon (France)

Patrick knew what was going through my head. He saw me being passed by group after group on the first climb of the day, the giant Tourmalet, and knew I was just giving up. He drove alongside me and tried to persuade me to keep going. I looked at him and thought about it. Roche's last words to me were instructions to ride all the way to Paris. Patrick said I would be letting him down if I climbed off. This hit the right note and I sprinted after the group ahead. I was playing with fire. Physically I was going quite well, but my indecision about whether or not I was continuing in the race had cost me a lot of time. As we approached Superbagnères and its summit finish, we all knew it would be touch and go for the time limit. There were about thirty of us at the bottom but only twelve made it inside the limit. I made it by three minutes. Tonight I thanked Patrick for helping me on the Tourmalet. I am happy to be still in the race.

Wednesday, 12 July
Stage 11: Luchon to Blagnac (154.5 kilometres)
Stage winner: Mathieu Hermans (Netherlands)
Race leader: Laurent Fignon

Bazzo called a team meeting this morning at the hotel, 'to generate some team spirit'. Patrick was not invited. He told us that Fagor would definitely be sponsoring a team in 1990 and that the contracts would be signed as soon as a leader for the team was found.

I am normally passive at team meetings and it takes a lot to get me riled, but this was too much. I cracked.

'Why was this meeting not held before the start of the race, two weeks ago, because it's a bit fucking late to be talking about team spirit now? And what's wrong with Roche as a leader? For two months now Fagor have been messing us about. The contracts were supposed to have been signed at the start of the Giro.'

Bazzo didn't appreciate my comments, and immediately started criticising Stephen. Only two other riders spoke up in

Stephen's defence: Eddy and Laurent Biondi. This disgusted me.

Downstairs another war was taking place. Patrick was having a go at Julien Navarro, our team doctor. The previous evening Navarro had been interviewed on French television and spoke with great authority on the state of Stephen's knee. He claimed that modern medicine had reached its proper limits with Roche's knee. It was an amazing declaration from a doctor who had never treated the patient. Patrick was furious. He advised Navarro to keep his mouth shut regarding something he knew nothing about. Patrick has a volatile temper and has broken fingers throwing punches in Stephen's defence. That he refrained from decking the doctor was a small miracle.

I repeat that all of this took place *before* the stage. Part two took place after the 150-kilometre ride to Blagnac–Toulouse. This time Patrick called the meeting. Bazzo was invited, but didn't turn up – which was probably just as well, as it would definitely have finished in violence. It was hot enough as it was.

Patrick wanted to flush the rats out of the cupboard. He wanted the riders to commit themselves either to Stephen or to Fagor for next season. It was a bit unfair to ask riders to choose when he had nothing concrete to offer, but this was the attraction for Patrick. It was a test of loyalty. Biondi committed himself and chose Stephen. But Lavenu and Chaubet resented being cross-examined, so there was a row and a shouting match. The argument did not concern me – I was giving up at the end of the year. I said nothing. I watched and listened, but couldn't really decide who was right and who was wrong. A month earlier the same bunch of lads had been totally committed as a group. In three weeks we had been reduced to this, disharmony and bitterness. Such a pity.

Patrick was told tonight by management to pack his bags and go home. It seems that Navarro put a gun to their heads and gave them the ultimatum, 'Valke or me'. Patrick will fly home to Lille tomorrow morning.

Thursday, 13 July
Stage 12: Toulouse to Montpellier (242 kilometres)
Stage winner: Valerio Tebaldi (Italy)
Race leader: Laurent Fignon

I had no idea, riding into Toulouse before the start, that this would be my last day on the race. I was a million miles from thinking it would be the last race I would ever ride. The bickering and fighting had disgusted and disheartened me, but I had put it out of my head – there were other reasons for carrying on. If I abandoned the race it would mean the end of my race diary column for the *Sunday Tribune*. I was getting such great pleasure from writing it that it made the suffering worthwhile. I wanted another Tour medal. The 1986 medal meant more to me than anything I had ever won.

None of this even entered my head when I ran into trouble shortly after the start. I abandoned the race after fifty-five kilometres.

I don't regret it, it was almost a pleasure to leave the race. My grief on climbing into the broom wagon was nothing compared with what I had experienced in 1987 –

> where I can't hide
> my brave face
> my brave my brave
> my brave face

My intention had been still to finish my career at the Nissan Classic in Ireland in October, but I soon realised that I would never race again. As a cyclist I was broken. I had no spirit. Thinking about racing made me ill and after a week's reflection I decided enough was enough. I was not going to race again. There would be no dramatic final day, no tearful wave of adieu to my 'adoring fans'. Tearful adieus were reserved for heroes, and I was no hero. I was a *domestique*, an also-ran. Also-rans did not have tearful adieus. They raced as pros in anonymity. They quit in anonymity. And I was one of them. Adieu.

23

SPITTING IN THE SOUP

The law of silence: it exists not only in the Mafia but also in the peloton. Those who break the law, who talk to the press about the dope problems in the sport are despised. They are branded as having 'craché dans la soupe', they have 'spat in the soup'. In writing this book I have broken the law of silence. I have spat in the soup and a lot of people will resent me for it. It wasn't easy, and on numerous occasions in three months of writing I wondered if I was doing the right thing. The last attack of conscience was on 28 December, just before writing this chapter. I was banging away at my machine when the phone rang. It was Ma.

'Quick, Paul, switch on your TV. Channel 4 are showing a review of the Tour, and they've just shown the bit where you abandon.'

I followed her orders and tuned in just in time to hear Phil Ligget choking with excitement as Greg LeMond snatched the Tour from Laurent Fignon's grasp. It was riveting stuff, and my enthusiasm for a race that five months earlier had caused me so much pain surprised me. I was still in love with the sport. But was this really the same sport? I could see nothing bad on the TV screen. Was I justified in writing about my experiences? Would my shocking tales not spoil too many dreams? I was troubled for the remainder of the day.

Then I started thinking about it. Before all this, I had looked at the sweaty faces of the stars on the television screen and in photographs and seen only glory. And now what do I see? I see dilated pupils and unnatural spots. I study not what they eat but what they swallow. Where once I applauded muscle, I now question its fabrication.

What has happened in between?

Inspired by the glory, enthralled by their courage, I set out on my dream to join them. It was a hard struggle, one I gave my youth to, but I made it. I became a glorious, sweaty face. Unfortunately the promised land was not what I had dreamed it would be. It strangely resembled the world I was trying to escape. It was hard, desperately hard. It was also dirty and corrupt. I wanted to leave, but realised that leaving was almost as hard as getting there. I had donated my youth to the acquisition of cycling excellence. But what use was cycling excellence in the real world? No, there was no turning back. So I played the game by their rules. To survive, I was forced, against my will, to take drugs. It happened three times. I was never caught. If I had been caught I would have been branded, as all drug takers are branded, a cheat. Isn't that ridiculous? A cheat, 'an unfair player'. I was never a cheat. I WAS A VICTIM. A victim of a corrupt system, a system that actually *promotes* drug taking in the sport.

In 1983, in an effort to modernise the sport, the professional world cycling body, FCIP, established two new ranking tables. The first was for the riders as individuals. It was run along the same lines as the ATP ratings for tennis. Every event was awarded a set number of points to be given to the first, second, third, and so on – the number of points varying with the size of the event. The second ranking table was for teams. Too many teams wanted to ride the big events, and the massive bunches were making racing much too dangerous. Under the new system the points of the five best riders of each team were added, giving the team's total. The top twenty teams had automatic entry for all the classics and major tours. It was a good idea which had damaging repercussions. Sponsors of the weaker teams were not prepared to pay out money to play in the 'second division'. Some pulled out and their teams folded. Others merged and suddenly a lot of professionals were without a job. The *domestiques* were in big trouble. There were no world-ranking points to be gained for helping someone else, and *directeurs sportifs* were obliged to hire riders with points in order to survive. Riders became more selfish and it didn't take them long to cash in on the new system. The more points you had the more noughts you could put on the end of your salary. Points meant pounds.

The relevance of all this to the system *promoting* drug-taking becomes clear on reading the list of races where points are awarded. Throughout this book I have talked about certain French classics that never have controls, the notorious Grand Prix des Chaudières. Take just one of these, Mauleon–Moulin, as an example. To the uninformed it's a small race, worth a few paragraphs in *L'Equipe* and a nice trophy to the winner. Wrong: it's worth much more – world-ranking points. A win in Mauleon is worth the same number of points as being fifth in Paris–Roubaix, the queen of classics. And so the night before Mauleon, when the *directeur sportif* starts the pre-race meeting by stressing the points to be gained, and in the same breath reminds you that there are never any controls here, what do you do? Do you laugh with the rest, or do you cry? How can you win? And all of these races, the 'GP de Chaudières', carry points. What a ridiculous system.

In Chapter 10, I talked about my experiences in my first Tour, 1986. On the last day we all knew that there would be no random testing, just the race winner and stage winner, and so on. Whenever there is no random testing, people will always find a reason to charge up. Several of my team-mates didn't hesitate. It was a way of ensuring they would ride well on the Champs Elysées and would be mentioned on TV. Publicity automatically increases your market value. Nothing much, mind: the sports shop owner in your local village sees you breaking clear on the Champs Elysées and asks you around for some promotion. Or the criterium manager notices, and offers you a few contracts. But it all adds up. It's all cash in the bank.

In Chapter 12 I described riding on an RMO team in the Midi Libre stage race. One of our riders, Patrick Esnault, was race leader at the start of the last day, a split stage. Because it was a split stage there was no random testing after the morning stage. And because the afternoon stage was the last stage it meant there was no random testing in the afternoon either. This gave us the green light to charge up on both stages to defend our team-mate's lead. And provided we didn't win the stage we would get away scot-free (not winning really is child's play, believe me). Esnault duly won and his loyal team-mates were rewarded with a big lump of prize money and a nice bonus from the sponsor.

In 1989 my season opened with two races in the south of France but I then flew off to a race in Venezuela. My good friend, Jean-Claude Colotti, spent the best part of six weeks racing on the Côte d'Azur with his team, RMO. He rode the usual season's openers: Bessèges, the Tour of the Mediterranean, the Grand Prix of Cannes, the Tour of Haut Var. All prestigious races, all carrying world-ranking points. NOT ONE CONTROL. In March he lined up for Paris–Nice and Criterium International, ten days of stage racing. There were controls on just three of those days.

In May I rode in the Trophée des Grimpeurs. It's a circuit race held at Chanteloup les Vignes, north-west of Paris near Pontoise. The Grimpeurs is a *chaudières* race that has always received good coverage on French television. This year the organisers had trouble finding a sponsor, but with the help of French Prime Minister, Michel Rocard, who lives in the region, the necessary finance was raised – on one condition: Stephen Roche, another 'local boy' *had* to ride. Stephen agreed, but imposed his own condition – he insisted on dope control after the race. The organiser agreed.

On the night before the race, Patrick Valke conducted his team meeting around the dinner table. He emphasised that there would be dope control after the race and warned us not to take any chances. On the morning of the event, Patrick attended a meeting for the *directeurs sportifs*. After the meeting the race organiser discreetly pulled him aside. She had a slight problem, no doctor to conduct the test. The French Federation designate certain doctors to conduct controls in the different regions. Patrick was told that the official regional doctor could not attend because it was his child's Communion day. Please don't laugh.

Patrick returned from the meeting and told us there would be no control. Perhaps he should have said nothing, but in a way it was his duty. Most of the other teams would know there was no control. Some of the riders would charge up and our lads would be at a disadvantage. It was Patrick's duty to tell us, even though it disgusted him to have to do so. This is what we are up against: we play with the rules we have been given to play with.

We are not to blame.

Perhaps that's not totally correct. One of the most frustrating parts of it all is the reluctance of the riders to change things. Too many are unwilling to breach the law of silence. The big men never talk and to be honest I don't really blame them – what have they to gain? They too were once young and innocent. Why should they jeopardise their hard-earned respect? If they took illegal substances it was only because everyone else was doing it. It's not their fault. If races were tightly controlled they would still come out on top. Why *should* they talk? So that some smutty columnist can label them 'cheats'? No, we must not wait for confessions from the champions before taking action. They won't be painted as devils. I respect this. But I don't respect them when they start passing the buck, pointing the finger, promoting themselves as angels, as is often the case.

On 21 November 1989 the French television channel TF1

broadcast a special programme on the problems of drugs in sport. A large panel of invited French sportsmen was present, including one professional cyclist, Marc Madiot. Madiot, a former winner of Paris–Roubaix, is one of the stars of French cycling. He knows what goes on and he has seen what I have seen. By agreeing to appear he knew exactly what he was getting himself into. He knew he would be questioned.

The panel were shown pre-recorded declarations from sportsmen and women whose lives were almost destroyed by drugs abuse. Didier Garcia was one of those interviewed. In 1985 Didier turned professional with the old System-U team and raced with them for two years. He was just nineteen years old when he was thrown into Mauleon–Moulin and other 'chaudières' races. They were unbelievably fast, and he couldn't understand this at first. It didn't take him long to realise why, and he was faced with the choice of doing the same as everyone else or being fired at the end of the year. He started taking amphetamines for the *chaudières* races, but also started on a course of corticoids. Each cure lasted ten days, and he would do four cures a year. In the winter he rode six-day races. It was worse on the track. He needed amphetamines every night to race, and Valium to sleep once the races were over. He once saw a rider go completely berserk at three o'clock in the morning: he smashed his room to pieces, broke the toilet bowl and was unapproachable for fifteen minutes. The drugs started to affect Didier also. His personality changed, his friends deserted him. In 1987 his employer, Kas, did not renew his contract. He was out of a job. It was hard at first and he went into depression. For three months he continued using amphetamines for kicks, but with help from his girlfriend he gradually returned to a sane lifestyle. He now earns £700 a month working in a hospital. It's three times less than he was earning on a bike, but he's happy.

When the interview ended the spotlight turned to the invited panel for their reaction. Marc Madiot was asked to comment. He looked straight at the camera.

'Well, this is a typical comment from a guy who was never any good.'

I was furious. I could identify with everything Garcia had said and agreed with him. It was the ideal occasion for Madiot to stand up and explain the problems we endure when organisers refuse to enforce dope controls, and what it can lead to. But what did we get?

'Typical comment from a guy who was never any good.'

Thank you Saint Marc, protector of the professional peloton. I won't bother phoning to ask his impressions of my book. I know exactly what he will say about it: 'Typical comment from a guy who was never any good.'

A lot of my former colleagues won't be pleased with what I have written. In particular I refer to two French team-mates I raced with at Fagor. They are two smashing guys, but they have strange views on the drugs issue. They believe in the law of silence. Whenever a big fish was caught in the drugs net they would always say: 'Encore un sale coup pour le vélo' ('Another dirty blow for cycling'). They love cycling, never see anything bad in the game. It's their life, their passion. Both use amphetamines liberally whenever the occasion demands it – part of the job. One of them told me an interesting story about the 1988 Paris Six. The story gives an insight into how he views the drugs question.

On the third night, a medical team from the French Ministry of Sport arrived at the track. They had a ministerial order to perform controls on the top ten riders. It was supposed to have been a surprise swoop, but there was a leak. All the riders knew and all those tested were clean. Now if I had been riding, I would have been delighted with a control that kept everyone clean, but my team-mate objected to it.

'Is it any wonder the crowds don't come to the six days any more? I mean, we have just come from a hard season on the road, all of us totally knackered. The people expect to see a performance, a show. How can we be expected to put on a show with just Vittel in our bottles?'

Hard as I try, I just can't come to terms with his argument. I know what he is saying but I simply can't find any justification in it. Perhaps I don't love the game as he does.

There are others who believe that the fairest way is to abolish dope controls completely. 'Let guys take what they want to take, and if they want to kill themselves then so be it – we're all grown men.'

Time Out: 3 January, 16.14

This chapter really is heavy going, can't quite take all this analysis. I'm typing it out in David's office in the wilds of Kinnegad in County Westmeath. It's a nice office, he must have a hundred sports books. They tempt me each time I lift my head from the page. I've just picked one up called *Running in the Distance*, written by an athlete, Jack Buckner. Interesting fellow, a lot more famous than me: in 1986 he was European 5,000 metres champion. I'm glancing through its pages, a diary of a year in athletics, Olympic year. 'Hmmm now that's interesting. We all know what happened at Seoul, don't we? Ben got caught. Jack should have something to say about that but the Johnson affair only gets half a page.' He writes:

> Johnson's positive test once again throws the spotlight back on the problem of drugs in sport. No doubt there will be endless discussion and suggestions on what action should be taken. What I find most frustrating is how every athlete is smeared by the drugs story. There will be widespread pontificating on the immorality of modern sport, yet I and thousands of other Olympic athletes would hardly know the difference between an anabolic steroid and a packet of Smarties. I find it most irritating that the drugs story, which for me is the least interesting and relevant aspect of these Games, will dominate the Olympics.

The problem is that for years too many people have considered the drugs issue the least interesting and relevant aspect of the Games and of other major events. When these people awaken to the realities of modern sport, namely that it stinks and needs help, then perhaps some progress can be made.

Who is to blame for the madness? Where is the antidote for this cancer incessantly devouring what was once straightforward competition? Well, in order to combat the cancer we must admit that it exists. The professional cycling body won't admit their sport is dying of cancer. They will admit to a sore toe but not a cancer. Their defence of the system never changes: 'No other sport controls their members with the regularity with which cyclists are controlled.'

So what? If this book is saying anything, it is saying that these controls are inadequate. Passing the buck is not a solution. Sooner or later the can of worms must be opened and the full magnitude of the abuse exposed. The governing body must be prepared to wash its dirty laundry in public if the sport is to hang on to some decency. When every professional race has comprehensive dope controls; when random controls are carried out anywhere and at any time; when penalties for offenders are stiffened to provide a reasonable deterrent: then, and only then, can we relax.

But at the moment we are a million years from change. The men in power want a solution all right, but a painless one. One that won't damage the sport in the eyes of the public and the television companies. There are few morals in business, and cycling has become a business. The television companies have stepped in, cheque book in hand, followed closely by the marketing men and their lucrative sponsorship deals. It's all about money now. Make it on the small screen and you make it big, and the sport of cycling now holds a coveted place. There are no morals left in professional sport and amateur sport ceased to exist a long time ago. Money, money, money: television sport is big business. There are a lot of race organisers lining their pockets and the last thing they want is a dope scandal. It's bad publicity, it tarnishes the glitter – and with bad publicity the sponsors start running.

The grapevine is a dreadfully frustrating source of knowledge. Facts are often distorted, but there is no smoke without fire. I've heard stories of corruption that would make you ill: of race organisers giving the green light to champions to take anything they want; of urine samples that never reach laboratories. The temptation for those on the make is to cover up rather than own up. But by not owning up we will continue to suck in the innocents and spit out the victims.

Thank God we don't see any of this on television. Thank God we don't hear about the nastiness, the dealing, the dirt. The champions deserve our applause. They merit our encouragement. They are not to blame. They need our help. Should I remain silent? No, I can't because it's what *they* want, the people who profit from the rule of silence. They would prefer that we sit back in awe, admiring but not questioning. Well, I'm questioning. It's such a beautiful sport . . .

Would I encourage my child in the pursuit of sporting excellence? No. I don't think I would.

24
ANDRÉ

Rumilly, Sunday, 29 October 1989. A crisp October afternoon. At three, the sharp sunlight has only just lifted the last whiteness of the morning's heavy frost. Soon, light will fade and the whiteness return. The apartment block is difficult to find. I had been here once before, late at night. We had taken his car to go to a cyclo-cross, but I hadn't paid much attention to where he lived. Today, I don't recognise anything. Thought it was posher than this, though. It's a bit rougher looking in the daylight. You sense hostility in the kids' stares. Perhaps they sense it in mine. These are not apartments, more like flats. André's was definitely an apartment. After a long search we find one that fits that description. It has four floors, seven dwellings to a floor. Twenty-seven of the doors have plaques with the occupant's name, then just one door with no plaque. We ring. It opens. André Chappuis is standing at the other side. He smiles his lovely, innocent smile and we shake hands.

He is thirty-four and going a bit light on the crown. We used to slag him about it. There was a cheese ad on television, with monks gathered at a dinner table singing in praise of the cheese, their bald patches glowing. We used to sing it for André, but he never liked it.

He needs new shoes. He is wearing a pair of those given to us by RMO two years ago. The jeans are almost as worn, but the leather jacket is nice – his sister gave it to him. I haven't seen him since we were both given our marching orders from Vallet, twelve months earlier. I had panicked, worried about my future, but was saved by the offer from Stephen. I rode the Tour de France, stopped, and am now a journalist. God, it seems more than a year. André didn't panic, he knew it was coming: 'Que sera, sera.' He was an unemployed cyclist. He still is.

He spent the winter in Africa. He was one of six unemployed pros invited to tour the African continent for a series of criteriums against amateurs. Rumilly wasn't offering much. Why not? He laughs about it now. The amateurs, mostly inexperienced blacks, were not much opposition. Ghana, Togo, Senegal, Benin, Nigeria, there was no end to the countries he visited. The travelling was tiring, but the wily old pros would reach for their medicine bags and a tiny syringe. The secrets of the old job were an instant cure. There was no money to be made, but all expenses were taken care of. When the series ended, five of the wild geese returned to France, but André stayed on. He got friendly with the organiser, himself an ex-pro, and was asked to help organise the next series. He returned to France in the summer to recruit new men for the next campaign, but never appeared at a pro race. There was no point: only the desperate go to Africa, those just laid off and disillusioned. He had their phone numbers.

The flat is almost empty. He has decided there is not much point in paying rent for it when he is never there and is moving out. The phone has been disconnected, the furniture sold and all that's left is a couch and a cabinet containing relics of old glory, cups and medals. He has moved his personal belongings to his parents' derelict house just up the road. He sold his bikes and racing equipment and only kept an old frame and a few bits and pieces for Africa.

He doesn't have to go back. The headquarters of Tefal, the non-stick kitchen appliance company are in Rumilly. If he wants, he can start work and earn £500 a month on the conveyor belt. But he doesn't want to. He's not ready for the factory floor yet. He's not ready for anything at the moment. He stopped being a professional cyclist a year ago, but he hasn't come to terms with it. It's hard for him in Rumilly. Everyone knows him. Along with the rugby team he was once the town's most famous asset. That was in the early 1980s, when he was winning stages in races like Criterium International. Now, after seven years of professionalism, of the Tour de France, of life at the top, he's an ex, a has-been. He has no house, owns no land and isn't married. He doesn't even own a car. He loves cars, loves driving and has gone through nineteen cars since he left school, all good cars, powerful: Porsche, Alfa Romeo and his favourite BMW. The last BMW he had was a 528. He bought it in Marseille and we think it was 'hot' because one day, when he went to have a job done on the engine, the garage told him it wasn't a 528 engine but a 535. Anyone else would have been disgusted, but André was thrilled – more power.

It was when he wrote off the BMW that I started to realise he was cracking. It was the night before the Grand Prix of Wallonie in 1988, our last year together. He started drinking whiskies at the dinner table, just kept knocking them back. The lads were making fun of him, but I tried to make him stop. I knew that inside something was eating him. After dinner, they decided to drive into town to stare at the prostitutes in the shop windows. André took the BMW, with Esnault in the front seat, Rault and Pineau in the back. There was a dual carriageway in front of the hotel, with a traffic light on the junction. The light was red. André didn't stop. He put his foot to the floor and the car screeched across the four lanes, but luckily nothing was coming. The other lads couldn't believe he would do something so irresponsible and screamed at him to stop. He did, but the decision wasn't his. The gates of a level crossing were down a kilometre up the road. The two lads in the back didn't hesitate to jump out, but Esnault, content to play the hard man, stayed. The gates were raised and André put his foot down, but instead of going into town he decided to head out into the countryside. The car was moving much too fast on the small tracks and he ran off the road on a tight right-hander. The BMW mounted a pile of stacked tree trunks and stopped. Esnault was thrown forward and hit his head on the windscreen, but wasn't seriously hurt. André looked at the undercarriage and realised the car was gone. Rault and Pineau arrived on the scene in a different car, and persuaded him to go back to the hotel. Next morning, the Belgian police arrived and started to ask questions. André owned up to having had an accident. The car was towed to a garage, good for only spare parts. Everyone had a great laugh. André laughed too; but inside, I knew, he was screaming.

He's pretty low now but he won't admit it. I suppose that's why he takes refuge in Africa. In a way it's like the old days – he can travel and race. But more than anything else, he can hold on to the dream just that little bit longer. Africa won't last for ever, and he knows it, but the future has never concerned him. Africa is an escape. The day he walks on to the factory floor the dream will end.

It's a terrible pity he never married. Marriage might have given him a sense of responsibility, kept him on the rails. He was terribly fond of a lovely girl who lived just down the road, but he could never make the first move.

We left the sad reality of the empty apartment and drove to Annecy. There was just time for a stroll around the lake before nightfall. He told humorous stories of his travels in Africa and we laughed about the good times we had spent together at RMO. We had a couple of beers and later had dinner in a restaurant. At the end of the meal he asked the waiter for the bill. It was typical of him, always first to put his hand in his pocket, give you his last penny. But Ann and I had invited him out. He was our guest and I insisted on paying. He agreed, but said he'd pay next time.

He came to stay with us for a weekend shortly after. I was

covering a rugby match, so Ann collected him from the railway station. He gave her flowers and a chocolate cake. It was a nice weekend, but I noticed his frequent uneasiness. As if his skin wasn't fitting him properly. He seemed happiest when we went to the village bar. He liked the ambience, playing the 'tierce' (betting on horses), drinking a few beers and smoking. He smokes quite a lot now, Marlboro – 'They sponsored the races in Africa.' In the mornings he'd get up early and slip out to the bar for a read of the paper and some coffee. He'd return to the house with some fresh baguettes and we'd have breakfast together. One thing was troubling me: a former team-mate of ours had told me that André was still dabbling with ampheta-mines for kicks. On the day he was due to go home I invited him out for a beer and asked him about it. He smiled and denied he was still using it. He said he had dumped his stock and was clean. I wasn't totally convinced. I told him about my plans on writing a book and of its content. I told him I was going to 'cracher dans la soupe'. He laughed and said I was right, but I knew there was no way he would ever do it himself. To him, it would be like ratting on your mates and André would never rat on his mates. The fact that they didn't give a shit about him made no difference. I asked him about his expe-riences.

'In my first two years with (Jean) de Gribaldy at Sem I never touched the stuff, perhaps once in my second year at a criterium. Then I signed a contract with Système-U. This was the old Système-U team. I met up with a lot of *chaudières* there and picked up some bad habits. Once, twice, three times, the more I charged, the harder it became to stop. Every time I used it I noted it in my diary and each year I found I was using it more and more.'

André never tested positive in his career. Not once. He rarely took a chance when there was control. The shame was in being caught. It says a thing or two about the number of controls in France each year.

He was supposed to come for another weekend before leaving for the winter in Africa, but he never did. The phone never rang. Perhaps my probes about the drugs issue had made him uncomfortable. I don't really know. I have not seen or heard from him since.

One of my biggest criticisms of *L'Equipe* and of the French cycling press in general is that they never talk to people like André. The absence of adequate controls in France is common knowledge, but rarely highlighted. The papers and magazines know about the problems, but choose instead to fill their column inches with portraits of the stars – of present 'greats', Fignon, LeMond, Kelly, Roche; of 'greats' from the past, Hinault, Merckx, Anquetil. Of greats. When Philippe Brunel from *L'Equipe* came to interview me during last year's tour I told him about Chappuis.

'Go and talk to him, he will give you a great piece.'

He agreed, but the interview was never done. It is as if the André Chappuis's of the world do not exist; and yet under the carpet there are crowds of them. They have great stories to tell but no one will ever hear them.

I don't know if I will ever meet André again. When I'm in France I'll go looking for him, but I'm not sure he will be there. In Ireland, my door will always be open to him, but I know he won't come knocking. In my four years in the peloton, of the hundreds of professional cyclists I've had the pleasure and often displeasure of meeting, he stands alone. He was the most likeable and most decent of them all.

EPILOGUE
THE SOUP TURNS TO BLOOD

One month after the final chapter of *Rough Ride* was delivered to the publishers in 1990, professional cycling was rocked by a spate of sudden and mysterious deaths. Twenty-six-year-old Johannes Draaijer, a fourth-year professional with the PDM team, had just returned home to Nijamerdum after the opening races of the season when he died in his sleep on 27 February. The results of the autopsy sent tremors through the sport. Six months before another Dutch professional had also died in his sleep. Bert Oosterbosch, a former World Champion and Tour de France stage winner, had a heart attack. He was thirty-two.

It was a worrying time for those who earned their living in the *peloton*, especially when the trend continued with the death of the 1989 World Amateur Champion from Poland, Joachim Halupczok. Rumours began to circulate about a new wonder drug called Erythropoietin (EPO) which had just come on to the performance-enhancing market. A naturally produced hormone which stimulates the production of red blood cells (and increases aerobic capacity), there was no factual evidence linking its abuse to any of the deaths. It wasn't until October 1997, when the wall of silence finally cracked, that we were offered the first real clues. The picture that emerged was shocking. In the six years since the death of Johannes Draaijer, the sport had edged its way to the brink of the abyss.

Sandro Donati is secretary of the Italian National Olympic

Committee's scientific commission on doping. A former national athletics coach, he established his reputation as an anti-drugs crusader in the 1980s when he rowed against the tide by opposing the blood 'transfusion' methods propagated by the celebrated Italian sports doctor, Francesco Conconi. In 1993 Donati turned his attention to cycling. For two years he had been hearing stories about the extensive abuse of testosterone, Human Growth Hormone (HGH) and EPO in the *peloton* – abuse that wasn't being reflected in the number of positive controls. Adamant that the sickness must be purged, he decided to investigate. In order to breach the law of silence, he guaranteed complete anonymity to those who agreed to co-operate. Catching the transgressors wasn't Donati's objective: his goal was to highlight the extent of the abuse by exposing the inefficiency of the controls. Twenty-one riders and seven doctors were interviewed. Confessions were also secured from team managers and racers who had recently retired. All the interviews were recorded and each tape was allotted a secret code and seal.

When he had completed his investigation, Donati's dossier told a depressing tale. There was the confession of the top Italian 'Y' and his explanation of how he had narrowly cheated death after a stage of the Tour of Italy. Boosted before the stage by an injection of EPO, he had gone to bed that night and slept peacefully for two hours, unaware that the oxygen-enhanced blood, flowing through his veins, was rapidly thickening to treacle. EPO is transformed into a lethal cocktail, not during a race when the blood is pumped around the body by a 180 beats-per-minute, high-revving, super-fit, heart rate but at night when the revs drop way below the norm. As Y's pulse dropped to a low of twenty-five beats per minute, his blood began to clot and his heart began to stall. Had he not been sharing with a team-mate, there is every chance they would have found him dead in the morning. But Y was lucky. His team-mate heard him struggling for breath and immediately raised the alarm. When the team doctor arrived he immediately administered an injection of Warfarin to thin the blood. Y lived to tell the tale. Others were not so fortunate.

When Donati began to probe into the death of Joachim Halupczok (who raced for an Italian team), he was informed that a *soigneur* with whom he had been in contact, was a well-known trafficker of EPO. And then there was the case of the former World Champion 'X' – rushed, close to death, to the emergency ward of his local hospital, just a few weeks after he had beaten the best in the world. Shocked by the gravity of the situation – 80 per cent of Italian professionals were abusing EPO – Donati submitted his secret dossier to the Italian Olympic Committee in February 1994. 'The abuse has spiralled out of control,' he told them. 'In some of the races, they are now climbing hills at speeds they used to reach on the flat! And why? Because the majority are pumped to the gills with shit like EPO, HGH and testosterone. For the good of sport, it is imperative we act immediately to stamp this out.' But not everyone on the committee was as committed to immediate action as Donati. There was the fall-out to be considered . . . the financial implications . . . the frenzy it would trip in the press. Donati had presented them with a dossier that was too hot to handle. For the next year and a half they allowed it to cool.

The three seasons that followed were the most bizarre in the history of the sport. In pharmacies, sales of Aspirin (a blood-thinning agent) soared. In the classics, losers started winning and then quickly returned to the ranks of obscurity. In the tours, entire teams were being mysteriously wiped with curiously selective bacteria. Professional cycling became a dangerous game in the 1990s. Every race was like an episode of *The X-Files*. Every month brought a new and unexpected twist.

1 In April 1994, two months after the suppression of Donati's report, three riders from the Italian team Gewiss – Moreno Argentin, Giorgio Furlan and Evgeni Berzi – broke clear with eighty kilometres to race in the classic Flèche–

Wallone and finished first, second and third. One of the journalists covering the race was Jean-Michel Rouet from *L'Equipe*. In fifteen years of reporting, he had never seen anything like it. 'I was intrigued by the result,' he explains. 'It just wasn't possible for a classic to be dominated in this way! The next day I went to the Gewiss team hotel to interview Emmanuele Bombini, the *directeur sportif*. Bombini had been called back to Italy on business and I was just about to leave when I noticed three Italian journalists talking to Michele Ferrari, the Gewiss team doctor. My Italian isn't great so I asked my driver to interpret and we had only sat down when the conversation turned to EPO. "I don't give it myself," Ferrari told us, "but if others are doing it, well . . . why not? It's no more dangerous than orange juice." I couldn't believe it! Two days later when Ferrari had been fired by the team and the story was all over the papers, Hem Verbruggan (President of the UCI) gave a press conference on the morning of the Amstel Gold Race. Insistent that there was minimal abuse in the sport, he began reading us statistics to back up his theory. It was total hypocrisy. We were writing about a product that couldn't be detected and he was quoting us statistics from dope control.'

2 Later that summer, on the morning of another major race, the *peloton* had just left the start when syringes were found in a mobile toilet beside the assembly area. After a quick survey by the organisers, the culprits – all from one of the smaller teams – were identified and selected for 'random' dope control when the race had finished. No action was taken. All tested negative.

3 In 1995 the French Federation conducted 1,235 dope tests. Twenty were positive, that is 1.61 per cent.

4 In April 1996, three weeks before the start of the Giro d'Italia, NAS – the anti-drugs unit of the Italian police – was alerted to unusually high sales of EPO in the region of Tuscany. Immediately making the connection, they began to formulate plans for a surprise raid on the race. Noting that the race was

scheduled to start on 18 May with a prologue and two stages in Greece, they decided to make their move three days later on 21 May, when the race returned to Italian soil after a ferry crossing to the southern port of Brindisi. On the morning of 20 May, however, they made one fatal mistake. Unsure when exactly the first ferry was due to arrive, a call was made to the Italian Olympic Committee to check the schedule. Somehow the teams were tipped off and the next morning, when they assembled for the short crossing to Brindisi, twelve unmarked cars were seen to take the northern mainland route back home involving a diversion through Albania, Montenegro and Croatia. Each was driven by a different team official. Each carried a small refrigerator. EPO must be stored at a temperature of between two and eight degrees Celsius.

5   Later the same year, during one of the major Tours, three journalists happened to be staying the night in one of the team hotels. At three a.m., after a night spent on the town, they were about to hit the sack when they noticed a door had been left ajar. Drawn to investigate by the noise, they walked through and found one of the stars of the Italian *peloton* hanging from a door frame doing stretching exercises. The rider immediately dropped to the floor and slammed the door shut. When your blood is thicker than it should be, stretching is another means of avoiding a clot. Only circumstantial evidence, but not the kind of thing you want the press to witness.

6   At a training camp shortly before the Olympic Games in Atlanta, two prominent racers were randomly dope tested by their National Olympic Committee. Both tested positive and were immediately withdrawn from the team. No other sanction was imposed. The UCI was not informed. The IOC (International Olympic Committee) was not informed. The affair was kept 'in the family'.

7   Reflection of a French *directeur sportif* in 1996: 'There was a time when the only question a rider would ask before signing a contract was "How much?" Today, you can be sure

he will ask three: "Who is the team doctor? Who is the team lawyer?" And then, "How much?"'

8   In late June 1996 Philippe Bouvet, the chief cycling correspondent at *L'Equipe* got a call from Roger Legeay, the team manager of the French team Gan, who wanted to explain the reason he hadn't included two of his better riders in his selection for the Tour de France. Philip Gaumont and Laurent Desbiens would not be riding, Legeay announced, because they were both serving six-month suspensions after testing positive (anabolic steroids) when they finished first and second at the Tour of Vendée in April. Bouvet, who hadn't received any official communication about the positive controls, was stunned. But there was more. Legeay also announced that he was firing Patrick Nedelec, the team doctor. Doctor Nedelec, who was also a member of the French Federation's Medical Commission and officiated regularly on the Tour de France, had prescribed the drugs to Gaumont and Desbiens the previous winter.

9   Jacky Durand, a former French national champion, was also netted for steroids in the summer of 1996. Handed a six-month suspension which should have kept him out of competition until 1997, he was racing again as early as September. Again, there was no official communication from the Federation that Durand's suspension had been cut. The first Philippe Bouvet heard of it was when he spotted his name on a start list.

10   The Spanish team, Once, were victims of a mysterious bout of gastro-enteritis during the Tour of Spain in 1996. It seemed most of the team was affected. One who was not was the Swiss, Alex Zulle, who held the race lead. Infected creamed rice was offered as the official explanation for the sickness – Zulle was the only member of the team who hadn't eaten any. Jean-Michel Rouet, who was covering the race for *L'Equipe*, thought the explanation bizarre: 'In many ways it was a re-run of the PDM affair in 1991; other teams who had stayed in the

same hotel as Once and eaten the same meal weren't sick. The symptoms were also bizarre: with gastro-enteritis, you are running to the toilet day and night, but whatever they were doing at night, they never seemed to have the urge during the day and we wrote that it wasn't normal. We didn't say it was EPO or anything else, just that it wasn't normal and were immediately blacklisted by [Laurent] Jalabert [Once's top rider] and [Manolo] Saiz [Once's *directeur sportif*] for the rest of the race.'

On it continued to the end of 1996 like a runaway train. Fear had gripped the *peloton*. Suspicion was everywhere. Cynicism reigned. The more journalists questioned, the more officials covered up. Rouet and Bouvet had had enough. Rumours began to circulate that they had begun an investigation and uncovered information that would shake the sport to its roots. As winter approached, there was an overriding sense that something had to give. On 23 October, it did. In an open letter published in *L'Equipe*, Daniel Baal (President of the French Cycling Federation), Roger Legeay (President of the French Professionals League) and Jean-Marie Leblanc (Director-General of the Tour de France) announced their concern that the battle was being lost in the war against drugs. The letter, which was addressed to the French Minister for Sport, Guy Drut and the President of the UCI, Hein Verbruggan, urged the International Olympic Committee and various state bodies and international federations to 'invest in the scientific research' that would restore the credibility of dope controls. 'If it is confirmed that blood tests are a more effective means of detection, then we must change the legislation immediately. We must stop the development of forbidden practices which put athletes' health at risk and sport under suspicion.' The letter also stressed the need to 'continue the research into the use of corticoids and testosterone, despite the legal problems that have been encountered in this domain and to reinforce the fight against the continued use of anabolic steroids outside the period of competition'.

For the three most powerful men in French cycling to go public on a subject that has always been taboo erased any remaining doubts about the gravity of the situation. The letter was, as Philippe Bouvet observed in the same edition of *L'Equipe*, a '*cri d'alarme*'. 'For sure we didn't need to wait until the autumn of 1996 to discover that the problem of doping exists. Or that the problem exists in other sports than cycling. But it exists a lot in cycling. Proof? No, apart from the one or two who occasionally get caught (and you really do wonder sometimes how that even happens), there is no proof. But let's not kid ourselves that we don't have a problem.'

Once the big guns had spoken, it didn't take long for the wall of silence to crack.

- On 25 October, two days after the publication of the letter, Flavio Alessandri, a former Italian national team doctor, confided to a journalist from *La Gazzetta dello Sport* that he had collaborated, a few years back, in a survey with Sandro Donati from the Italian Olympic Committee about drug abuse in cycling that had never seen the light of day. When the journalist made a follow-up call to Mario Pescante, the President of the Italian Olympic Committee, the story was denied.
- On 26 October Walter Veltroni, a prominent politician, announced that he would investigate the missing dossier immediately.
- On 28 October Pescante announced that he had found the dossier but that it was too 'generalised' to be of any worth in the public domain.
- On 29 October the dossier was handed to an examining magistrate.
- On 30 October the full contents of the dossier were revealed to the public.
- On 8 November, on the eve of the presentation of the route for the 1997 Giro D'Italia, a delegation of Italian

professionals, which included the former World Champions, Gianni Bugno and Maurizio Fondriest, demanded that blood tests be introduced for everyone from the start of 1997.

L'Equipe published their investigation 'Le Terrible Dossier' in January 1997. Spread over four days, it opened with the story behind the suppression of the Donati dossier and then focused on the problem in France. Two doctors were interviewed in the second instalment and two riders in the third. Jean-Michel Rouet explains, 'As soon as we started, it was the usual brick wall: "Ahh, you're going to start stirring the shit again, why are you always picking on us?" We contacted a lot of riders; some still racing, others who had just retired. Presenting them as "X" or "Y" had no value for me. It was important they went on the record. We had a fair idea that Gilles Delion would talk – throughout his career he had refused to get involved with doping and always spoke without bitterness on the subject. And then I spotted something Nicolas Aubier was quoted to have said in one of the Brittany papers and I thought that maybe he would agree too.'

The interview with Nicolas Aubier appeared in *L'Equipe* on 16 January. Pierre Ballester asked the questions. It will probably ring a bell.

Nicolas, you are twenty-five years old, four years as a professional and you've decided to pack it in. Why?
Because of the atmosphere that reigns in the sport. Professional cycling is a fantastic job but one that has become more and more unnatural. Vicious.

Without beating about the bush, you're talking about doping?
Yes, doping. It wasn't possible to continue in this way. With one or two exceptions, you can't be competitive without turning to it.

So how did you tackle the problem?

When I signed my contract at the start of last year, a person on the team, who wasn't one of the medical staff, advised me that it was time I applied myself. Until then, I had spent three years in another team and while I had dabbled a bit here and there, what this guy was proposing was more serious. In order to optimise my physical capabilities, he suggested a cure of EPO. The cure consisted of seven ampoules of Eprex 4000 to be taken by subcutaneous injection over the period of a month. I was also to take plenty of aspirin to keep the blood fluid. I refused. The season started badly. I picked up a dental infection and when I abandoned Paris–Nice, the same person offered me a testosterone tablet and an injection of a product containing amino acids he had secured from Italy, which was supposed to help you recuperate. I didn't want to take it but . . . well, I wasn't going well. I had a gun held to my head so I succumbed like a lot of others. In stage races, the dose was a tablet and an injection each night but because I was really creeping, I accepted two tablets a night. During some of the earlier races I had been taking 'persantine' – a heart vasodilator – with fifty kilometres to go, but when I mentioned this one day to my family doctor he advised strongly against it so I stopped . . . Which kind of relegated me to the subs bench as far as this person was concerned. That's the way it works, you either adhere to the system or they kick you into touch.

And do many of the riders adhere?

Yes. A lot. To be honest, I don't think it's possible to make the top 100 on the ranking list without taking EPO, growth hormone or some of the other stuff . . . well, no, that's no true, Chris Boardman is there. During my first two years, I roomed with him a lot and never saw him take an injection. I still don't know how he managed to be competitive. He had his own doctor in Liverpool and just stuck to what he knew – which is probably one of the reasons he has never been able to attain his ambitions in the Tour de France. But to be honest, the riders are not to blame, it's the system . . .

How do you make that out?
It's simple. As I understand it, it all came from Italy at the end of the 1980s. The Italians were winning everything, dominating the races. They discovered a magic formula, a thing that was undetectable and the French were just making up the numbers. Slowly, we started getting into it. If we were going to compete with them, we needed the same arms.

Take me back to the start and your first experiences.
I had a pretty quick graduation to the professional *peloton*. At the age of nineteen, I went from being a third category amateur to a first category amateur with the Bataillon de Joinville team and signed my first professional contract at the end of 1992. In my first season the only thing I used was oral multivitamins like Supadyne and Tardiferon and no *soigneur* or *directeur sportif* ever suggested I should start to dope. It was happening all right, but it was the rider's decision on whether he went down that road or not. At the end of my second year, I started using banned products for the first time – a medicament that was used for the treatment of allergies and asthma. In three years, I took a fifteen-day cure of corticoids twice. Then, in 1995, I won the Tour of Poitou–Charentes, a five-day stage race. To be honest, I don't know how I won. I took nothing, just a vitamin and caffeine tablet fifty kilometres from the finish. If I had taken two, I still wouldn't have had any problems with the sample at the finish. But that didn't stop me being scared.

So riders know exactly what they are doing?
Of course they do. The team doctor or the guy selling the stuff will never make the approach; the first step is always taken by the rider. The terrible thing is, that the abuse of doping products is so commonplace that the guy who doesn't take

anything is considered abnormal. You should see, for example, the race for ice-cubes in the morning at the hotels . . . it's crazy. The guys taking EPO have to inject every two days and it has to be stored at the right temperature. You only have to stand watching in the corridors and you can figure out who is using it.

And no one says anything?
But why should they? Everyone profits from the system. The riders optimise their performance. The teams are more competitive and as a result more attractive to sponsors. Even you guys in the media . . . the slant is always about winning. Everyone knows exactly what's going on. No one says a word.

So you never took EPO or growth hormone?
No. I'm Cartesian by nature. I like to know how it works and where I'm going. With that (EPO and growth hormone), it's the unknown. I prefer to pack it in.

But how do you acquire this stuff – it can't be bought in France?
From dealers. It might be your team-mate or a *soigneur*, they'll sell it and take a commission. They buy the stuff in Belgium, Holland and Switzerland. These guys also profit from the system, as do the laboratories. You can even order it from the Internet.

Is the subject taboo? Do the riders speak about it among themselves?
Sure they do, but with derision. In the *peloton*, it's paraded as a joke which serves as a front for the riders' fear. In a serious one-to-one, I'm sure that a lot of the riders would admit to being concerned and wondering where it's all leading to.

What do you think of the Italians and their recent demand for blood tests to be introduced?

It makes me laugh. They were the people who introduced it in the first place. And now they want to wipe it out? Well if they do, it's obviously because they've found something more sophisticated already. Having said that, I think the introduction of blood tests is a good thing. Someone told me EPO was detectable in urine, but that you'd need a sample of half a litre! There is no point in dreaming that they are going to find a means to defuse the bomb, but blood tests would still be a dissuasive. The international authorities need to understand that you can't expect to take on a tank with a penknife. Because this is a serious mess we're in. It's one thing taking amphetamines in the criteriums when there's no controls, but EPO and growth hormone is a much more dangerous game. One of the biggest disappointments I will take from my career is the wait-and-see attitude that has been adopted by officials. Why aren't they doing something about it? Why haven't they made every possible effort to eliminate this cancer? It's as if the riders are entirely disposable; wheel them in for the show and then discard them. It's time to put a stop to the massacre.

On the day after the interview was published, the President of the UCI was interviewed about the planned introduction of blood tests for 1997. Hein Verbruggan had some interesting observations to make about the coverage in *L'Equipe*. 'I will probably disappoint you,' he informed Philippe Bouvet, 'but I was not at all impressed, not at all, with the accounts given by riders like Delion and [Graham] Obree. [The Scottish former World Champion told *L'Equipe* on 19 October that he was giving up the sport because he couldn't compete with riders who were using EPO.] What we are dealing with here is guys at the end of their career who can no longer hang on. I found it cowardly, there is no other word.' But Bouvet wasn't having any of it: 'On the contrary Mister President, there are grounds for suggesting that cowardice is to hide behind statistics for years that do not represent reality.'

ROUGH RIDE

Blood tests were introduced in 1997. One small step for (sports) mankind. As we close for press, the scandals and the cover up continue. There is still much to be done.

POSTSCRIPT
IT'S ALL WRITTEN DOWN

The morning was crisp, sunny and perfect. I stepped from my car and followed the voice of the race announcer to the sign-on podium, where the first sight of racers and the smell of embrocation quickened my pulse. It was the first Sunday of October in the village of St Arnoult-en-Yvelines and I had made the trip from Dublin not to report on Paris–Tours, the penultimate classic of the 1997 season, but to find André Chappuis. Eight years had passed since our last meeting. Then he was leaving home to start a new life in Africa. I was leaving France to start a new life at home. Maybe, if things had been different when *Rough Ride* was published, I would have delivered on my promise to keep in touch. But the reaction of Roche, Colotti and Claveyrolat had shattered my understanding of friendship and, much as I wanted to believe that André still regarded me highly, I was afraid to find out.

As I made my way through the gathering crowds, I was surprised that most of the officials in the crisp blue blazers seemed to recognise my face, but then I suppose I recognised most of theirs. There was Eric Caritoux, the former winner of the Tour of Spain and Charly Mottet, an *ancien maillot jaune* of the Tour de France. There was Maurice LeGuilloux, once one of Hinault's most loyal lieutenants and Frank Pineau, a former team-mate. I nodded polite greetings to those who were polite and it struck me that the more things change in this

259

sport, the more they remain the same. We are all brothers in the same family. Those who break the law of silence may be despised, but they are never really excluded. There are black sheep in every family after all.

After half an hour of searching there was still no sign of André. Guy Roger from *L'Equipe* confirmed that he was definitely working on the race but wasn't sure in what capacity. Most of the former professionals had been hired to chauffeur sponsors and corporate guests, but I had dismissed that possibility immediately. Although the driving would have appealed to him, the bullshit that went with it just wouldn't have been his style. Resigned to the probability that Guy had made a mistake, I drove ahead of the race to Tours and watched as the Russian André Tchmil outsprinted Max Sciandri to win.

Half an hour after the victory ceremony, I was making my way back to the car when André emerged with a friend from behind the finishing barriers.

'*Du Dieu!*' (Good God) he exclaimed with a grin as we hugged, 'What are you doing here?'

'I just came over to cover the race,' I lied. 'You look good. How have you been?'

His face was fresher than I expected. His hair, longer than it used to be in his racing days. Lighting up a Marlboro, he explained that they had driven down from Paris on Friday evening to prepare the finishing area for the race arrival. The hours were long but he enjoyed it. The Société du Tour (the organisers of the Tour de France, Paris–Tours and a number of other classics) had been using him a lot of late, but he expected things would get quieter when winter came round. I asked if he wanted a beer, but he was too busy so we arranged to meet for dinner that night

When we sat down later that evening there was so much I wanted to talk to him about his time spent in Africa . . . his marriage and the birth of his son . . . his return to Rumilly . . . his problems finding work . . . what he thought of my book. I knew he must have known what I'd said about him by now, even though *Rough Ride* had never been published in France. But the more the evening went on, the less inclined I was to ask. Three of his colleagues had joined us for dinner and he seemed more comfortable speaking about the present than the past. So I sat back and listened to stories of their adventures on the road, watching as he lit another Marlboro.

'Dede, you shouldn't smoke so much.'

'Paul,' he said, 'the date, the day, it's all written down. There's nothing to be done.'

We looked at each other and smiled.